MW00720552

"I feel happy because it was so easy **to move** to Bupa"

Do you want to move to the world's largest international expatriate health insurance provider and avoid all the headaches? To get the feeling, there's only one number to call.

Simple transfer of corporate cover
Call +44 (0) 1273 208200
or visit www.bupa-intl.com

Your calls will be recorded and may be monitored.
The above example draws from the experiences of a number of our members or staff; it is not intended to represent the details of any specific individuals or their circumstances.

THE QUEEN'S AWARDS
FOR ENTERPRISE:
INTERNATIONAL TRADE
2005

THE CORPORATE GUIDE TO

Expatriate Employment

An employer's guide to deploying and managing internationally mobile staff

Consultant editor: Jonathan Reuvid

**KOGAN
PAGE**

London and Philadelphia

Publisher's note

Every possible effort has been made to ensure that the information contained in this book is accurate at the time of going to press, and the publishers and authors cannot accept responsibility for any errors or omissions, however caused. No responsibility for loss or damage occasioned to any person acting, or refraining from action, as a result of the material in this publication can be accepted by the editor, the publisher or any of the authors.

First published in Great Britain and the United States in 2009 by Kogan Page Limited

120 Pentonville Road   525 South 4th Street, #241
London N1 9JN   Philadelphia PA 19147
United Kingdom   USA
www.koganpage.com

© Kogan Page and individual contributors, 2009

The right of Kogan Page and individual contributors to be identified as the authors of this work has been asserted by them in accordance with the Copyright, Designs and Patents Act 1988.

ISBN 978 0 7494 4991 9

The views expressed in this book are those of the individual authors and may not necessarily reflect the views of Frank Hirth plc.

British Library Cataloguing-in-Publication Data

A CIP record for this book is available from the British Library.

Library of Congress Cataloging-in-Publication Data

Reuvid, Jonathan.
   The corporate guide to expatriate employment : an employer's guide to deploying and managing internationally mobile staff / Jonathan Reuvid.
      p. cm.
   ISBN 978-0-7494-4991-9
  1. International business enterprises--Employees. 2. International business enterprises--Personnel management. 3. Employment in foreign countries. I. Title.
   HF5549.5.E45R48 2008
   658.3--dc22
                            2008040095

Typeset by Saxon Graphics Ltd, Derby
Printed in Great Britain by Cambridge University Press

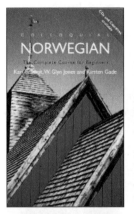

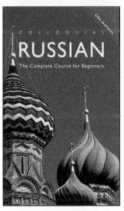

"I love the feeling
that my employees
have a **choice**
of hospital"

Would you want to know that,
no matter where you were in the
world, you would be taken to the best
place for treatment? To get the feeling,
there's only one number to call.

Unrivalled network of hospitals and clinics
Call +44 (0) 1273 208181
or visit www.bupa-intl.com

THE QUEEN'S AWARDS
FOR ENTERPRISE:
INTERNATIONAL TRADE
2005

More than just international health insurance

Many health insurance companies promise you a quick and value added service when you call their health and evacuation line. However, the service you receive depends on the company you choose, their expertise and the companies they work alongside.

At Bupa International we have an in-house medical assistance centre, which handles emergency and health related calls. Our staff includes specialist doctors and nurses and we use the latest technology to find out where in the world there might be epidemics or trouble hot spots. We feel that our speed and customer service during emergencies adds real value to members.

The following case gives both hints about what you need to be careful of when you are travelling abroad and it also shows how quickly an insurance company, with its own in-house medical assistance centre can react.

A member of Bupa went from his native home in Denmark to Texas to attend a work-related workshop. One morning he felt slightly unwell during his walk to the workshop, but he told himself it was because of the temperature, which was 35 °C with a humidity of 80-85%. As soon as he was back indoors, he felt ok again.

After 14 days in Texas, he started jogging in the evening together with some colleagues. Even though it had only been a couple of months since the last time he went running, he felt he was so unfit that he couldn't run for very long. He felt as if his larynx was being squeezed, he couldn't breathe, and his left arm was aching. He chose to run to an indoor fitness centre where it was cooler, but unfortunately, never got that far. Our member passed out. When he regained consciousness after a couple of minutes, he saw his colleagues had stopped a car to call an ambulance and the police.

When the ambulance arrived, the paramedics quickly established that our member's blood pressure was too high and that his heartbeat was irregular. He needed to be taken to the emergency room, so he showed the paramedics his insurance card and that was a green light. After approximately five hours, he was transferred from the emergency room to a room in the cardiology department of the hospital.

In contact with Bupa International medical staff doctors

As soon as possible Bupa International made contact with the member. One of our in-house doctors called and confirmed that he would case manage the member's treatment. He spoke to him in his own language and that alone can be reassuring. With the help and persistency of Bupa International's doctor, our member successfully went through a balloon angioplasty surgery that same day.

Following the operation, Bupa International made contact with the member again to reassure him and to let him know about the surgery results. Bupa International also arranged for his wife to travel to the USA. Due to the surgical intervention, we recommended that the member shouldn't fly home for one week. When he was allowed to fly, we arranged for a flight back home for the member and his wife.

Good advice

This story highlights some key points to consider to stay healthy:

1) Exercise is important. Had our member not provoked the collapse, it would have happened at a later stage, and probably resulted in a fatal heart attack or brain damage and reduced heart function.

2) Be aware of your body's warning signals. High blood pressure, weight on the chest and pain in the arm under strained conditions are all typical symptoms of something being wrong. Our member ignored all those symptoms on the pretext that these might be caused by the heat and humidity.

3) Our member had international medical insurance and had brought the documentation with him. Our emergency centre was able to react quickly, sort out papers and assist throughout the treatment. That made things considerably easier for our member.

Being abroad can bring its health challenges. If you travel a great deal, or live in some less developed parts of the world, it is vital that you have evacuation and repatriation cover so that you can get to the nearest centre of medical excellence to receive the treatment you need. It is also important to find out what you are covered for if you want to return home for treatment.

Whether you use an insurance company with in-house medical assistance cover or not make sure your plan offers you the following:

- 24-hour multilingual emergency service.
- Advice on the selection of hospitals and doctors worldwide.
- Access to the insurer's expert medical consultants for advice.
- Participation in preventive health programmes.
- Access to any recognised hospital and clinic worldwide.

At Bupa International we have over 35 years' expertise in caring for the healthcare needs of expats and their families around the globe. Covering more than 800,000 people in 190 countries, we are the largest expatriate health insurer in the world, with a range of high quality and flexible plans, designed for companies and individuals living and working abroad for six months or more.

Bupa International understands that when you're working abroad you want peace of mind about your health - and a health insurer you can rely on to provide a high quality service and comprehensive coverage. That is why we have developed a worldwide network of over 5,500 participating hospitals and a 24-hour helpline, open 365 days a year, which is manned by a team of experienced advisers who, between them, speak 34 languages.

We are also set apart by the medical expertise we offer our members. Our emergency medical team consists of highly-trained doctors who are experts in high altitude diseases, tropical infections, patient evacuations and home transportations. They are available around the clock to members, ensuring they receive immediate and correct treatment, when the need arises.

Industry Leader

Bupa International has achieved a number of accolades over the last 35 years including winning the Queen's Award for international export achievement in 1999 and for enterprise in 2004. It has also been voted International Health Insurer of the Year by the readers of the UK's leading industry magazine, Health Insurance, seven times between 1999 and 2007.

For more information, please visit www.bupa-intl.com.

By David Grint,
Commercial Director
Bupa International
Tel: +44 207 656 2000.

The sharpest minds
need the finest advice

visit
www.koganpage.com
today

Contents

Healthcare – wherever your employees are in the world

AXA PPP healthcare – Our dedicated team of experts know that it's the personal touch that counts

Wherever your employees are in the world, their health and wellbeing is your main priority.

Our corporate International Health Plan gives employees and their families immediate access to private healthcare and dental care as well as our emergency evacuation or repatriation service at no additional cost.

We also offer the option of cover for treatment of chronic conditions, health screens, and disability compensation.

To find out more contact us on international@axa-ppp.co.uk

PPP HEALTHCARE

Be Life Confident

PPP HEALTHCARE

Choosing your corporate health insurance wisely.

Every successful company acknowledges the importance of its employees. They are its greatest asset, but also it's most valuable resource. Quality medical insurance for people working abroad is particularly important, especially where local medical facilities may be very basic or inaccessible.

From an employer's point of view, providing prompt access to medical care through a private health insurance policy may help reduce sickness absence. Helping your employees to get access to care sooner and back to work without delay also means you look after the health of your business.

Additionally, research* has shown that 46 per cent of employees state that private medical insurance (PMI) is a highly desirable part of an employment package so it's vital to understand what insurer's offer, giving both your employees and your business the most suitable product on the market.

About your provider

It is a good idea to check if you are dealing with the insurer directly, you may be surprised as often the policy may not be supplied by the company named on the documents. It is also prudent to check the financial status of the company and if you are in any doubt ask them to supply references from existing clients. By asking questions such as these about providers you will ensure you know who the company really are, what experience they have in your company sector and who is backing your scheme.

Customer service and support

Employees and scheme administrators need to know that any queries relating to their corporate cover can be dealt with. For example is there access to a telephone based interpretation services and facilities to help find English speaking doctors and dentists locally? What languages are spoken by the advisers answering the calls and what is their experience?

Also, can they speak to medical professionals about their condition should they need further information or just some reassurance.

In some cases, both calls and claims may not be undertaken by the insurer, but by a third party, and you should be certain on this point so as to understand who is supporting your employees.

Catering to your needs

Do you have staff requiring different levels, or areas, of cover on the same scheme and can your provider cater for this? You should also look closely at how you will be invoiced and look to ensure that the processes are easy and flexible. A further consideration is whether you have options on payment frequency.

What does the scheme cover?

Are the benefits bespoke, or provided as standard? What about the needs of staff in more remote or challenging regions, for example is evacuation and repatriation cover provided for all staff and if so is it at an additional premium to you?

What benefits are there available from your chosen provider; the following pointers may be useful when considering your options:

- Can they pre-authorise treatment before it commences so you can be assured of cover and, in some cases, arrange for bills to be settled directly with the hospital, saving you time on administration.

- The level of cover provided under the in-patient benefits. For example will benefit be sufficient to pay for treatment received in the USA?

- The level of cover for day-patient and out-patient treatment: this includes procedures which don't require an overnight stay, diagnostic tests and physiotherapy. Most insurance companies vary the level of out-patient cover depending on what plan you chose.

- Parent accommodation – can parents stay with their child whilst they are receiving hospital treatment?

- Ambulance transportation costs for emergency transport or when medically necessary.

Make sure you appreciate the scope of your cover to avoid costly misunderstandings, no insurance policy is designed to cover all eventualities and all claims will be assessed for eligibility against the terms of our policy.

The final couple of things you may wish to consider is the time saving elements that a specialist international provider can offer your human resources team through:

Account Management

Your Account Manager should be in regular contact with you to ensure that the scheme runs smoothly and efficiently and that you are kept regularly up to date with claims and trends within the scheme. They should volunteer updates on health related issues and advise of specific issues affecting scheme employees. You should be able to plan through the scheme year and be aware of items such as ongoing claims, the renewal cycle and likely projections for renewal. They should be comfortable talking about these issues openly. If you do not have this contact, how are scheme premiums being driven and how are these being justified based upon claims? Are your renewal premiums sent to you without justification or discussion?

Technology and Information

With the majority of overseas staff having access to the internet, online facilities mean that they can access information about their cover at a touch of a button allowing them access to information around the clock.

Our Expertise

With over 35 years experience in the international health insurance market, AXA PPP healthcare is dedicated to looking after the healthcare insurance needs of people who are living and working outside the UK.

We believe that what really makes AXA PPP healthcare different from other healthcare providers is our excellent support and service coupled with our personal touch. These are values that, alongside access to private healthcare, allow AXA PPP healthcare to give peace of mind to employers and employees. Not only are our employees friendly, professional and efficient, they have also made it their business to help and look after your company.

For further information on international health insurance from AXA PPP healthcare please contact us:

By telephone on **+44 1892 508 909** for corporate groups;

By email at **international@axa–ppp.co.uk**

Or visit us at www.axappphealthcare.co.uk

*AXA public policy research May 2006

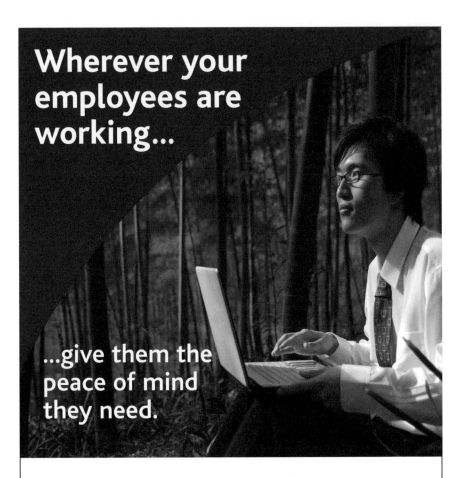

The corporate guide to expatriate employment

What is group healthcare insurance?

If you employ expatriates in your business, you want to make sure they are healthy, happy and able to perform their job effectively. One way to contribute to this is by purchasing healthcare insurance, also called private medical insurance (PMI), for your employees to make sure that the majority of their medical costs are covered should they need medical treatment.

Why invest in group healthcare insurance?

There are many benefits for you as an employer in buying healthcare insurance for your employees, in fact so many that it should really be viewed as an investment rather than an expense.

Firstly, if employees know that they can visit a doctor or get other medical treatment without having to foot the bill, they are more likely to seek the medical attention needed. This in turn reduces sickness absence and increases productivity and therefore contributes to the corporate bottom line.

This is particularly prevalent in the case of expatriate workers, as they may well be outside of their comfort zone and in unfamiliar surroundings, which can have a direct effect on their health. They may be exposed to new health risks, for example different drinking water and food, different levels of cleanliness and different endemic diseases.

Secondly, knowing that their employer cares enough to provide medical insurance can serve to motivate employees and make them feel more loyal towards the company.

Thirdly, a robust healthcare package can attract new employees to the business. In fact, one set of research shows British employees value healthcare more than bonuses!

International PMI

There are a variety of group healthcare plans available on the market, so any investment needs to be carefully considered. For independent advice, you can work with a broker or intermediary (in the UK, they should be registered with the Financial Services Authority (FSA)) who will discuss your needs and research the market for you.

If you have large numbers of expatriate employees, a global workforce or many employees who travel regularly as part of their job, international PMI is designed for you. The plans are tailored to the needs of these audiences, with many unique benefits, such as:

- Emergency evacuation and repatriation – cover for the costs of evacuating a casualty in a medical emergency to the nearest centre where adequate medical treatment can be obtained. For employees based in remote locations, this benefit is a lifeline. The most comprehensive emergency evacuation benefits on the market cover the costs of the insured person's family or a business colleague to accompany them when they are evacuated, the costs of all accommodation and flights back. They will also cover the costs of evacuation and treatment when there is no adequate treatment available in the insured person's location, even if it is not an emergency.

- Compassionate emergency visit - cover for the flights to visit to a critically ill relative, whether they are at home or somewhere else in the world.

- Large geographic areas of cover – meaning that insured employees are not limited to one country when they are seeking medical treatment. This is a particular advantage if employees are based in countries where the medical treatment may not be as extensive or hygienic as it is in the UK, for example.

- Hormone replacement therapy - for women suffering pre- and post-menopausal symptoms, hormone replacement therapy (HRT) can make their lives so much easier.

- Wellness benefit - routine health checks and preventative tests – things like cancer screening (for example cervical smear tests), cardiovascular, neurological, cardiovascular and well-child examinations, vital signs tests (for example blood pressure and cholesterol checks) and vaccinations. This is a particular advantage to reduce the number of employee 'sick days' and increase work productivity by making sure that employees are healthy and treat any medical problems before they become serious.

- Maintenance of chronic conditions - if employees develop conditions such as asthma or epilepsy they may be able to keep the illness under control and avoid acute attacks or worsening of the condition through routine medication or regular checkups. Some plans will cover the cost of this, with generous monetary limits.

- Allergies – expatriate workers in new, unknown surroundings may develop new allergies. As with other chronic conditions, timely medication and treatment can help keep allergies under control and let employees carry on with their life – both in an outside of work.

- HIV/AIDS – insured employees in environments where HIV and/or AIDS are rife, cover for this should certainly be considered. Recent advances in drugs and treatment for HIV, AIDS and related medical conditions mean that sufferers may be able to maintain a higher quality of life for a longer period of time.

- Complementary medicine and physiotherapy - treatment from a specialist, such as a physiotherapist, osteopath, chiropractor, homeopath, acupuncturist or Chinese herbalist can sometimes be seen as a luxury, for example in the case of a minor amateur sporting injury. Cover for this type of treatment can be extremely beneficial, as it encourages planholders to seek treatment and get any issues sorted out at the earliest opportunity. For employers, this can reduce long-term or ongoing absenteeism.

- Security assistance – you may want to offer more than just medical cover for your employees. Some international PMI providers offer extra benefits such as international security assistance in partnership with companies such as red24.

- International helpline – access to a 24 hour, multi-lingual international helpline allows your employees access to their international insurance anytime, anywhere.

In addition to the actual plan benefits within an international PMI plan, there are many other benefits from buying group health insurance for your employees:

- Flexibility in cover – with group health insurance, you can tailor the benefits and monetary limits to the needs of your employees. For example, you can increase the monetary limit for a benefit such as wellness or dental, different levels of cover for different employees or even different geographical areas of cover for different employees.

- Group discounts – like many purchases, the bigger the volume, the better the value for money. Buying international group health insurance for your employees can be very cost effective, with discounts offered for groups of 20 or more employees.

- Easy to buy, claim and renew – with simple, straightforward application forms and no need to complete a form for every single employee, buying a group health insurance can be hassle free. Pre-authorisation and direct payment with hospitals and insurers for in-patient and pay-and-claim for out-patient treatment means that you can use the benefits of the health insurance quickly and easily. Renewing your annual group health insurance could not be easier, all you have to do is agree to the renewal terms and update any changes to employee details.

● Different underwriting terms – many international PMI providers offer different underwriting terms and these need to be considered. Do you want all pre-existing conditions covered for a certain period of time (moratorium) or would you like all medical history disregarded and all conditions, new and old, covered (MHD)?

How to investigate your options

Choosing the right group health insurance cover for your employees is essential and you'll have many questions that are pertinent to your decision making; does the insurance plan cover all reasonable needs and requirements of the employees? Is it within budget? Will the employees use or appreciate the benefits? This is where you need to investigate your options thoroughly.

One option is to research the international private medical insurance market, speak to the providers and ask the vital questions; what benefits can the provider offer, what are the discounts available, what kind of service can they provide you with, can the provider cover all of your employee's needs, what makes the provider stand out from the crowd? Once the providers are aware of your needs as a client, they can provide you will all the information needed to make an informed decision as to which is the best provider for your employees.

Alternatively, you can use a specialist broker whose expertise lie within the international health insurance market. They will be experts in the field and have extensive knowledge about the market, the providers and their products, their service and unique selling points. The broker already has the information and built relationships with many of the providers in the market. They can advise you as to which providers are the better ones to work with, negotiate on your behalf in terms of the benefits offered and the flexibility available on the benefits. A broker can also tell you which providers have the right product and service to meet and exceed your needs and requirements for group international health insurance for your employees.

However you choose to investigate the options available to you and your employees, you can be sure of finding a plan that will support your clients in both sickness and in health.

Contributors' notes

Stephen Asher is a Fellow of the Institute of Business Consulting, a member of the Society of Business Economists and a member of the management committee of XBHR, a multidisciplinary global forum for professional advisers and academics who are experts in cross-border human resource issues. Stephen writes regularly for publications such as *Pay Magazine* and *Payroll Professional*, the official journal of the Institute of Payroll Professionals.

Geoff Davidson is a director of Hessel, an organization specializing in providing expense management services and technical solutions worldwide. Geoff has 14 years' experience in relocation expense management deliverables but rather wishes he had spent more of that time playing golf.

Owen Davies is a senior solicitor in Fragomen's London office. Owen speaks regularly at international conferences on UK and global immigration issues. He has advised the UK and other governments on immigration policy and changes and has presented on immigration law at a number of universities, including Yale, University of California, Berkeley, London Business School, Manchester Business School and Imperial College, University of London.

Donald C Dowling, Jr is International Employment Counsel at the New York City office of the international law firm White & Case LLP. He dedicates his law practice to advising multinational headquarters on employment law compliance in overseas employment operations. This includes expatriate matters (such as structuring secondments and expatriate terminations), as well as global human resources counsel regarding matters such as: global handbooks and codes of conduct; cross-border transmissions of human resources data; and multi-country restructurings and redundancies.

Jonathan Exten-Wright is a partner at international law firm DLA Piper UK LLP. He practises in all areas of employment law on both contentious and non-contentious issues. He has a particular interest in senior executive and international issues and has been named in *Euromoney Guide* among the world's leading labour and employment lawyers and as an expert in the *Insider's Guide to Employment Lawyers*.

Stephen Gill is a freelance consultant who runs his own engineering and business consultancy, Stephen Gill Associates. An experienced business manager and company director with an international and strong engineering background, he has experienced the highs and lows of being an expatriate and interim manager. Busy as he is, he is always looking for his next assignment.

Alex Paterson is the Managing Partner in the London office of Fragomen. She is a member of the Immigration Law Practitioners' Association, the Joint Council for the Welfare of Immigrants and the American Immigration Lawyers' Association. Alex was recruited by Fragomen in 2003, charged with establishing a London office, for which she has management responsibility, and overseeing the UK immigration practice and the London-based EMEA coordination centre. She speaks regularly at international conferences on UK and global immigration issues and represents Fragomen on government panels concerning UK corporate immigration issues and practice.

Philip Pertoldi is Group Managing Director of Abels Moving Services. He has over 30 years' experience of the removals industry at director level. Abels Moving Services is a holder of a royal warrant to the Queen for removals and storage services. Among his many achievements, Philip has established new branches, headed international divisions and led a successful management buyout. He has also served as president of the British Association of Removers (BAR).

Natarajan Sundar is a director of Orgdesign Limited, independent consultants specializing in remuneration, organizational design and performance management. He was formerly head of Performance and Reward, BG Group, and VP Global Reward, Unilever, where he led major global projects. He has had a varied career in finance, general management and HR in India and the UK. He is currently a visiting professor at London Metropolitan Business School, London. Recent projects include global reward strategy, framework for managing people cost, international assignee policy, role clarity and performance management for leading companies in the UK and India.

Paul Thompson is a solicitor at DLA Piper UK LLP. He specializes in international employment issues, investigations and high-value litigation. His recent work includes a leading case in age discrimination and international executive benefits.

Introduction

Sending employees abroad or receiving expatriates on secondment has become increasingly complex for any organization. Even large multinational groups with fully staffed HR, finance and payroll functions find that cross-border tax, social security regimes, and immigration rules and regulations can present formidable challenges in defining expatriate strategy and administering secondment assignments. For them, part of the problem is that none of these functions is, by itself, uniquely qualified to manage expatriate deployment, and some of the more serious issues that most affect employees' well-being can fall between the cracks.

Small wonder then that, for those small and medium-size companies that have extended their business activities internationally, avoiding the pitfalls of the tax and immigration authorities in the countries concerned can become a costly and time-consuming nightmare.

In *The Corporate Guide to Expatriate Employment*, Stephen Asher of Frank Hirth plc, the architect and lead author of the book, and his co-authors offer detailed insight into the complex issues of tax, social security and immigration that surround any deployment of staff internationally.

The chapters of Part 1, 'Developing employment strategy', have generic relevance to all companies, big or small, that are engaged in sending staff abroad on secondment or receiving expatriates from associated organizations.

Part 2, dealing with tax and social security issues, and Part 3, dealing with compensation, benefit and expatriate support, are focused specifically on secondments to and from the UK, although similar issues will arise in transfers from any jurisdiction to another. Likewise, Part 4, authored by Alex Paterson and Owen Davies of Fragomen and Jonathan Exten-Wright and Paul Thompson of DLA Piper, addresses immigration and employment law issues in the context of staff transfers from and to the UK within an organization.

Part 5 has a broader scope, covering some of the commoner practical problems related to relocation. Philip Pertoldi of Abels Moving Services addresses the physical logistics of relocation; Stephen Gill writes, from personal experience, about the critical issues for employees; and Geoff Davidson of Hessel discusses the ongoing administrative issues for the employer.

Part 6 provides a digest of personal taxation and social security regimes in 14 key jurisdictions, representing the locations to which secondments are most common, including, of course, the UK.

I offer personal thanks to all those mentioned above, particularly Stephen Asher, for their contributions to the book in which they share their expertise with readers; my appreciation also to Natarajan Sundar, who has written the chapter on remuneration strategy formulation and design, which has relevance for decision makers in any international organization, and to Alison Ward of IPP for her input to chapters 2.2, 2.3 and 3.4 on compensation, benefits and expatriate support. Finally, we would like to thank Frank Hirth plc for its sponsorship of *The Corporate Guide to Expatriate Employment*, and the advertisers who have made publication possible.

We hope that this book will be an invaluable guide for the managers of any organization engaged in the transfer of employees on secondment internationally. It will also be of interest to all employees who are offered an overseas relocation. Parts One and Three, in particular, will help them to confirm that their employer's policies are in line with best practice; the remainder of the book enables them to check that the administrative support they can expect will be sufficiently robust to avoid the problems of Part 5.

Jonathan Reuvid

Part 1

Developing employment strategy

Frank Hirth

At Frank Hirth we aim to provide our clients access to expert professional advice based on a commitment to technical excellence and integrity. We are able to provide a fully integrated service to individuals and businesses needing assistance in all aspects of US and UK tax compliance. We also provide high quality advice on structuring businesses, employment issues and wealth planning covering UK and US issues.

Our services include:

US Tax Services

- Individual federal and state tax return preparation
- US Estate and Trust planning
- Planning for relocation to/from US/UK
- Tax equalisation and employee tax protection program administration
- Partnership tax return preparation
- 'C' and 'S' Corporation tax return preparation
- Subpart F, Controlled Foreign Corporations and Form 5471 compliance
- Controlled Foreign Partnership and Form 8865 compliance
- FICA and FUTA compliance
- Expatriate payroll outsourcing
- Expatriate compensation policy design and administration
- International payroll tax consulting

UK Tax Services

- Individual tax return preparation
- Corporation tax return preparation
- Residence and Domicile advice
- Employee remuneration advice
- All inward investment tax planning
- NIC planning
- Planning for US and European business operations
- UK Trust tax return preparation
- UK Trust planning
- UK Inheritance tax planning

Accounting Services

- Accounts preparation
- VAT compliance
- PAYE and NIC compliance
- Preparation and running payrolls
- Fully outsourced accounting functions
- Branch accounting
- Management accounting
- Systems review and computerisation of accounts

Frank Hirth plc
1st Floor, 236 Gray's Inn Road
London WC1X 8HL
United Kingdom

T   +44 (0)20 7833 3500
F   +44 (0)20 7833 2550
E   mail@frankhirth.com
W   www.frankhirth.com

Frank Hirth – A Unique Firm

Frank Hirth has been established for over 30 years. Originally founded as a firm of Chartered Accountants in 1975, the firm has grown significantly, developing the practice to the point of being one of the largest and most well respected in the field of international tax. An Accountancy Age survey recently identified Frank Hirth as the 56th largest firm in the UK.

The original Partnership was incorporated into Frank Hirth plc in 2000 and this change has seen the firm go from strength to strength financially, by way of expanding their client base and the range of services provided. An important landmark was reached in 2008 with the opening of a Frank Hirth office in New York (Frank Hirth LLC) that will enable the firm to provide local advice and tax services in the US.

Frank Hirth Know-How

Frank Hirth operates a simple business model based on our unique know-how of helping our clients comply with their international tax obligations, particularly International US tax.

We have accumulated skills and experience which enable us to provide our clients valuable insights into best practice tax and social security formulae, procedures and methods.

Our procedural knowledge helps clients understand what is required of them during re-organisations, mergers and acquisitions, sales of businesses, termination programmes and when they are establishing businesses in the UK.

Often our clients do not appreciate they are required to report a myriad of things and underestimate how much information is needed.

Even in the best regulated environments random audits can still impact the in-house specialist and the employee in an unproductive way. Clients come to us for help with HM Revenue & Customs (HMRC) PAYE enquiries and general investigations into employee compliance.

Over the last several years international tax rules and regulations have become increasingly complex, to the point where it is genuinely difficult for employers and employees to file true and correct returns. At the same time HMRC have increasing power to obtain documents and information, and to inspect business premises. This is backed up by substantial penalties in enquiry negotiations.

We help our clients address any potential non-compliance with reviews of basic procedures that enable some anticipation of Expatriate Employer PAYE reviews and enquiries.

We also advise our clients about the compliance issues that surround international reward and benefit design and in particular ensure low cost and risk free execution.

A large part of our advice centres on helping our clients understand their employer responsibilities and obligations vs. their employee's responsibilities and obligations. This involves identifying when the employer has an obligation to report a transaction or other event, or when it falls on the individual to report.

In all circumstances, we provide support to both the employer and the employee. If the employer is unable or unwilling to help the employee comply, it leaves the employee in a very awkward position. However, there is a competitive advantage in ensuring employees are focused on their business objectives rather than their personal tax compliance.

We work with organisations of many shapes and sizes to achieve:

- Formal employer and employee tax strategies;

- Cross-border tax risk assessments and minimisation techniques;
- Guidelines for operating an effective system of controls and processes;
- Identification of who does what, when and how to ensure the right people with best skills are deployed on international employer and employee tax matters.

Our range of services includes assisting with all forms of employer and employee international tax compliance responsibilities comprising:

- Running payrolls, and operating PAYE schemes for internationally mobile employees;
- Advising employers on PSAs and dispensations ;
- Advising employers on short-term business visitor agreements;
- Advising employers on cross-border social security administration;
- Assisting employers with PAYE end of year returns and agreeing the annual tax payable;
- Advising in respect of Expatriate Employer PAYE reviews and Section 9A enquiries;
- Advising employers on matters affecting their employees' personal tax affairs including the preparation of employee personal tax returns;
- Advising employers on the application for and operation of modified PAYE schemes for tax equalized employees;
- Advising overseas employers and partnerships on setting up and operating in the UK or setting up and operating in the US and other overseas locations.

Other services include:

- Reviewing and designing senior executives' and expatriates' remuneration packages, taking into account benefits, taxation and social security issues;

- Implementing approved and unapproved share schemes and share option schemes, including, where appropriate, the review and modification or replacement of existing schemes;
- Adapting overseas share schemes to the UK environment;
- Using employee trusts in conjunction with approved share schemes, deferred bonus schemes or financing acquisitions;
- Advising on bonus arrangements and in particular the possible introduction of profit related pay into an organisation, including registration of the scheme;
- Designing flexible benefits and compensation schemes, including reviews of car and bonus schemes;
- National Insurance planning, mitigation and avoidance;
- Global pension arrangements;
- Optimizing compensation – balancing salary structure and minimizing benefit administration;
- Flexible benefit plans and internationally mobile employees;
- Outsourcing vs. Insourcing – move to 'strategy, policy and process';
- Strategic management of the global mobility function;
- Challenges in benefit provision for a mobile workforce;
- A successful executive remuneration strategy;
- Advising UK organisations on reward packages in emerging or difficult locations;
- International Reward Strategy.

Contacts

Mark Walters
Director
Frank Hirth
1st Floor, 236 Gray's Inn Road,
London, WC1X 8HL, UK
Email: markw@frankhirth.com
Website: www.frankhirth.com

Kevin Johnson
Director
Frank Hirth LLC
24th Floor, One Penn Plaza,
New York, NY 10119, USA
Email: kevinj@frankhirth.com
Website: www.frankhirth.com

1.1

Developing your cross-border strategy

Stephen Asher, Frank Hirth plc

Despite the investment in human capital strategies – including global talent management theories, benchmarking of best practice and performance management tools – in reality there is no 'one size fits all' solution. Instead managers have to address the operational implications of business needs, international diversity, differences between countries in terms of culture, regulations and administration, and the complexity of the resultant environment.

In addition, the largest multinational enterprises represent only a small percentage of the total number of organizations sending people to work in foreign locations. This is best illustrated by the results of a number of surveys that have consistently shown that a much larger number of companies, including small ones, are now competing in the international marketplace.

Furthermore, whereas large companies have tended to dominate the global business scene, today many small companies operate from greater varieties of business sectors and headquarter locations. Indeed, from available data it can be seen that over 90 per cent of the expatriate populations of international organizations comprise between 1 and 500 individuals. The very largest expatriate populations of over 500 assignees represent less than 10 per cent of the market.

This growth in the small-to-medium-sized end of the expatriate market is also supported by a number of emerging trends. Not least of these is the need to understand the impact of the emergence of mini-multinationals alongside multinationals from emerging countries. In this market, over two-thirds of all assignments are in response to a business demand and not as part of an international career development plan. Often these individuals are working at client premises or temporary project locations with little or no local support.

In response to these complexities, traditional international relocation assignments are giving way to more short-term and localized assignments, as well as cross-border commuting and global team configurations. The challenges of how to address the management of commuters, frequent flyers, localization, project teams and sales teams, with frequent changes of intention, can stretch even the more experienced manager without some ability to anticipate the risks and costs of this emerging landscape.

Any manager responsible for expatriate employees will need to balance such things as the use of technology in tracking, monitoring and storing data, against a backdrop of increasing cyber-crime and the need to understand data protection laws for websites and intranets. Perhaps inevitably, given greater diversity in cross-border working, the complexity of the legal issues surrounding the movement of personnel can be daunting. It is critical to have an understanding of the latest local practices for immigration work authorization, including work permits and visas.

Salary and benefits will continue to be the primary cost relating to international assignments, and in particular the effect on personal tax and social security needs to be considered. Governments and tax authorities are focusing on ways to improve their tax administration in order to address what they see as a significant and growing problem of international non-compliance with national tax requirements.

Not surprisingly in this ever changing climate, being able to respond to real-time business demands in a world of increasing differences is critical, although knowing how to reduce risks or keep costs down remains a key challenge, as is the need to understand how to evaluate the success of or return on an investment in expatriate assignments.

CULTURAL DIFFERENCES

In order to develop an effective cross-border employment strategy, you will need an understanding of the national cultures of the countries in which your organization operates or those locations in which the firm is proposing to set up business.

Before you can evaluate your organization's ability to execute its strategic objectives or, indeed, develop best practices relevant to your organization's circumstances, you will need to be aware of the differences in approach and interpretation in the context of a number of vital subjects at local, regional, national and international levels. The ability to interact with and manage people of different cultures will allow you to recognize different ways of doing things and yet see the practical connections and understand the interconnectedness of your organizational resources. This international perspective will help your resources nurture an international mindset.

THE RISE OF THE MINI-MULTINATIONALS

It is not just the large companies that elect to work globally. As market competition increases, smaller organizations may choose to push their market boundaries beyond their home area, turning them from 'local' businesses to 'international' ones.

Sometimes the decision is based on the need to maintain a position in the market. It could even be essential that they have a physical presence in the country in order to have access to its market, and so the company becomes 'multinational'. As the volume of organizations pursuing expansion into international markets grows, it follows that many more country-based payroll functions around the world will be launched on to the global payroll scene.

The decision as to where to locate an international business is not always made consciously. The head office often remains in the country where the business originally started. There are various reasons why this can occur. Clearly, it is common for industries that are dependent on raw materials to locate where manufacturing costs can be minimized – either by labour value or by proximity to raw materials. On the other hand, industries that can sell a service or provide processed materials will locate for market impact.

Some organizations will be restricted on choice of location because of specific requirements, such as economic stability. However, improvements in transport and a significant lowering of associated costs have led to organizations now considering moves to locations that they would not have previously been able to contemplate, instead making the decision based upon other factors, including the following:

▌ *Communication links.* Telecommunications such as the internet and e-mail have made communication links much quicker and more reliable for businesses. In recent years we have seen telecommunications technology improve with videoconferencing and videophones. All of these improvements increase the speed at which we can communicate and therefore conduct business.

▍ *Transport links.* In many developed countries there have been major improvements to in-country transport infrastructures such as road and rail networks. In addition, the cost and frequency of flights have made a major difference to the speed at which both individuals and materials can be moved – increasing the pace of business activity across borders.

▍ *Skilled workers.* Education has had a major impact on the basic skills of workers. It is no longer the elite in society who are educated to degree level, and the pool of skilled workers from which an employer can choose has grown significantly.

▍ *Wage rates.* The need to maintain low costs has encouraged many businesses to move into countries with lower wage rates.

▍ *Simpler legislation and bureaucracy.* Compliance with strict regulations for employment requires effort and resources for the employer. The stricter the employment, health and safety regulations, then the more costly are the protective steps likely to be to meet those acceptable working conditions. Any reduction in red tape will mean lower costs for the business.

▍ *Government funding and subsidies.* Many governments encourage businesses into their countries with the promise of subsidies and funding in exchange for an increase in employment opportunities. These monetary incentives entice employers to transfer to their localities, but this may create a longer-term problem. For example, what happens when the incentives end? Will the business move away when the incentive is no longer available?

Each of these elements may provide financial benefits to the business, for example saving costs, reducing overheads and minimizing administration. It is also widely accepted that there can be benefits for an organization in owning more than one part of the processing chain, and this can mean being located in more than one country. There are commercial benefits for some organizations to move to international trading, as it can lead to added market capability and availability. Being an employer in a country can allow for trading limits being relaxed, for example import limits would not be in force. European countries can have strict rules related to import limits, but these mainly relate to imports from non-European countries.

In addition, having 'local' involvement may make the employer seem more attractive. This can be promoted as being more patriotic or self-benefiting, supporting the purchase and use of products from a home employer rather than an imported offering.

Many governments will encourage investment from international organizations, believing it can bring significant benefits to a country as a whole. Examples are:

▪ increased employment opportunities;

▪ a raised profile for the country, even bringing in new industries such as tourism;

▪ an improvement in economic stability through financial investment.

However, foreign direct investment is not always found to be beneficial or free of problems; there are some concerns that the existence of overseas provision could lead to a detrimental or difficult situation for the country. Examples include:

▪ Forcing out local and national businesses within a country and creating a dependency for local communities on global employers that, if the employers moved, would destroy whole communities.

▪ The exploitation of host country labour:
  – not appreciating the cultural expectations of the host country;
  – abusing the power of working opportunities for residents;
  – little or no recognition of local agreements or work practices;
  – health and safety.

▪ The undermining of cultural values:
  – disregarding the cultural expectations of the host country, using the promise of work opportunities to persuade locals to accept conditions that would not normally be followed;
  – introducing, by indirect or direct means, challenges to home values, for example on equal rights for women, the hierarchical view of the family and respect to elders, or class structures within a society.

▪ Destruction of the environment through pollution, changes in weather conditions or industrial disasters because of the introduction to new industry from global investment.

EMPLOYEE SECONDMENT

In recent years there has been a significant increase in secondments to work overseas. However, this brings with it a conflict between the high costs associated with secondments overseas and the drive in today's competitive business environment to keep costs down.

It is generally recognized that it is expensive to second employees to work in another country. If we posed this question to a layperson without any preconceptions or specialist knowledge, the person would very likely answer that it was more expensive, based on the core assumption of transporting someone to the other country.

However, in reality the answer to this simple question needs to include an assessment of a much more complex list of reasons for the added cost. There needs to be a careful evaluation of the return on the investment gained by a business from incurring that added cost.

You may have many ideas gathered from your own experiences. A few examples are:

- career development for the individual;

- the need for head office to have a controlling influence locally by having a home representative present;

- dissemination and training of corporate practices by using experienced home representatives;

- short-term projects: development and implementation requiring a short-term contract and using home expertise to simplify role recruitment;

- specialist skills: finding a home-trained individual with specialist skills may be difficult locally, particularly where it relates to in-house home knowledge.

Secondment issues for the employer

Stephen Asher, Frank Hirth plc

Many HR practitioners find that a department manager will take the lead in selecting both the role and the actual person to be seconded. In effect it can become the role of the HR department to minimize the negative impact of the department manager's decisions.

There will be issues related either to the individual being transferred – the correct processes to have the person legally transferred to work in the host country, and the assessment and administration decision to ensure the person being seconded is adequately remunerated and tied in to a contract that will ensure he or she performs the required duties – or how to make the home country staff feel motivated to work with the person being seconded.

The core issues are ensuring that:

▋ the host country can have faith and respect for the person being brought into the country;

▋ the host country employees remain motivated and do not feel under-valued, mistrusted or blocked from role development;

▋ the person being sent has the skill and appreciation of host country requirements to be able to perform to the required standards;

▋ any added benefit from seconding rather than appointing from the host country is worth the cost of secondment.

HR needs to ensure that management recognize the implications of seconding employees overseas. There is an argument that this will be made easier by ensuring that a policy and/or job description exists that includes details of procedures and restrictions. This can highlight and explain potential negative impacts, making the managers aware of the need to assess effectively whether the secondment of an employee is the best approach to dealing with the role involved.

A readiness assessment should be undertaken that includes the impact of increased costs, and consideration of whether a training and development programme for local staff would allow them to be able to learn the skills required for the role effectively at a lower cost.

SUITABILITY OF THE EMPLOYEE

Although a department manager may see development potential or skills in a particular employee that could benefit a part of the organization based in another country, it does not mean secondment may be practical for the employee or the host country.

The personal situation of the employee needs to be considered, for example family commitments and health. It is important to ensure that an employee is not pressured into a secondment, as this could have a negative impact on the original aims of the decision to second.

The individual's suitability to operate in the host country environment is a major factor in the decision on who should be seconded. An employer should take responsibility and be sensitive to exposing its employees to any risk of attack because of the cultural or religious aspects of the host country, for example attitudes to females or religion. For example, a senior female manager being seconded to, for example, Japan or a Muslim country, with supervisory responsibility of male locals, may be subjected to pressures that a male colleague would not experience.

PREPARATION OF AN EMPLOYEE
FOR SECONDMENT

It is important that both the employee and the employer understand all aspects of what will happen during a secondment.

You should begin by identifying areas affecting the employee, such as:

▊ *Remuneration:* what type of payments and benefits should a seconded employee receive? Consideration should be given to medical, travel, accommodation, home leave, holiday and pension values questions. How will the employee be paid? Will it be in home currency, host currency or a mixture of the two currencies? What about exchange rates?

▌ *Long-term benefits:* in terms of pensions – both company and state – will values be maintained?

▌ *Career development:* how does the organization see the employee's career developing from the secondment?

▌ *Job security on return:* will the employee return to his or her old job? Will there be promotion opportunities?

▌ *Family and other commitments at home:* will the family travel with the employee? What about education for children under the age of 16 or 18? If the family does not transfer, what does that do legally to 'state of residence'? What exchange trips between home and host country will be provided for the employee and his or her family?

▌ *Stress of moving:* Will time be given to an employee to sort out personal affairs? Will a pre-travel orientation visit be provided for the individual and/or the family?

▌ *Language:* What language training should be offered? Should it be extended to other family members?

Other issues for the employer will be:

▌ *Personal circumstances of employee:* are there areas that the company can help the employee address?

▌ *High cost of a secondment:* how can the costs of a secondment be assessed? Can they be contained? What contractual terms can be included to ensure the commitment of the secondee to the transfer?

▌ *Cultural integration capabilities of both employee and host country staff:* should cultural training be offered?

▌ *Career development plan:* how will the seconded employee benefit? How can the employer give reassurance at the beginning of a secondment?

Specialist advice required on certain areas of secondment may not be available in-house. It should be acknowledged that in certain areas it may be necessary to resource external specialist expertise to help support the employer and employee through the secondment process, such as legal and tax advice.

IMMIGRATION

Visas

A visa is a document that gives an individual permission to enter a country for a particular reason, for example for work, a business trip or a holiday. It is important to note that the visa itself will not give permission to work where that country sets a requirement to have a specific work permit. Care must be taken over the nature and understanding of the permissions an awarded visa is giving to the traveller.

The need for a visa to enter a particular country is usually dependent upon the rules of the host and home country, the nationality or citizenship of the person who is entering the host country, and the relationship the host country has with the individual's home country.

Particular care is needed when a third country is involved, for example in the case of a citizen of one country who also has nationality of another country and who is then seconded to work in a third country. (For the distinctions between citizenship and nationality, see Chapter 3.8.)

A visa is not always required to enter a country; for example, a national of a country within the European Economic Area (EEA) may not be required to obtain a visa to enter or work in another EEA country, but there are a limited number of exceptions.

The process for applying for and issuing a visa varies between individual countries and may also be dependent upon the type of visa being applied for. For example, a British person travelling to South Africa for a holiday needs to apply for a visa before the start of the journey. A British person travelling to the United States applies for the non-working visa at the point of entry into the United States. A holiday visa to visit Australia is also required in advance.

It is always advisable to check the requirements for a visa as early as possible, as some countries can take several weeks or months to issue them. In addition, each country has its own rules on additional documentation required for a visa. For example, some countries insist on the need for a visa to include a photograph of the individual travelling. For a work visa you may be required to produce official documents to support qualifications or employer sponsorship.

The embassy of the country for which the visa is required is often a good starting place to confirm what will be required. Some countries may not have an embassy presence in all other countries. However, they usually have an agreement with the embassy of another country that will administer advice and guidance to international travellers on their behalf.

Work permits

There are various types of work permit, for example, working, student and training. A work permit will be very specific:

▊ to an individual;

▊ allowing an individual to do a specific job;

▊ to a specific employer;

▊ to that country.

A visa does not give the right to work. Not all situations of working in another country will require a work permit. As with visas, if you are a national of a country within the EEA there is usually no requirement for a work permit to work in countries within the EEA. However, there are exceptions to this that should be checked out first. An example of this is that, although Poland and the Czech Republic are members of the EEA, nationals from these countries still require a work permit in order to have employment in the UK.

Another example of what appears to be an illogical situation for work permits is that of New Zealand and Australia, both of which are members of the Commonwealth. Australians and New Zealanders can work in each other's countries without the need for a work permit or visa. However, holiday visitors who are citizens or nationals of other Commonwealth countries require a visa to enter Australia and yet nothing to enter New Zealand (there are limits on the length of stay).

If a work permit is required, it should always be applied for and issued before travel to the host country.

There will very likely be a need to show that the individual has an employer willing to sponsor the application to allow employment. For example, in the Republic of Ireland (ie not Northern Ireland) there is a requirement for the employer to show why it is necessary to hire a non-resident rather than a local person. Often, specialist knowledge will be claimed, specifically knowledge of the home employer where a global employer is involved.

EVALUATING YOUR ORGANIZATION'S ABILITY TO MANAGE CROSS-BORDER EMPLOYEES

Leading organizations today and tomorrow seek to serve international markets. Increasingly, having an international presence requires transferring key executives from one country or region to another. Managing these transfers may become an important part of the job for the HR specialist, who may be charged with building a policy from scratch or with reviewing an existing programme. In either case, HR specialists must become adept in evaluating their organizations' cross-border operational capabilities.

This is the case wherever an organization may be in the life cycle of internationalization. Where companies want to set up in foreign locations for the first time, have a cross-border project for a significant period of time or expand their existing activities, their ability to manage such changes is often mission critical.

A structured approach

In creating or improving an international mobility policy, you will need to take a step-by-step approach. An example of such an approach involves five steps:

1. clarification of corporate objectives for transferring employees to work cross-border;

2. evaluation of organizational and operational capabilities in relation to managing these transfers;

3. design of the policy;

4. implementation of the policy; and

5. monitoring the effectiveness of the policy.

Frank Hirth

Frank Hirth is a leading international taxation and accounting practice advising on all matters relating to the effects of cross-border taxation on individuals, corporations, partnerships and trusts.

We offer international employer tax compliance services and strategic solutions with an emphasis on evaluating the risks and costs of an organisation's international employment strategy, policy, and its skills and abilities to implement and manage them effectively.

Our core client base is made up of international individuals and businesses with US, UK and European connections. We maintain strong links to a number of firms in a wide range of countries and are therefore able to offer cross-border planning and seamless co-ordinated advice.

The principal focus of these services is to ensure employers and their employees comply with their international tax obligations, and do so in a way they can both understand and afford, without unduly interrupting the business or the employees.

For an initial evaluation of your circumstances, please call Stephen Asher on 020 7833 3500 or email stephena@frankhirth.com

Alternatively for more information regarding the range of services provided by Frank Hirth, please turn to our corporate profile on pages 5 – 8.

Frank Hirth plc
1st Floor, 236 Gray's Inn Road
London WC1X 8HL
United Kingdom

T +44 (0)20 7833 3500
F +44 (0)20 7833 2550
E mail@frankhirth.com
W www.frankhirth.com

Operational challenges

Stephen Asher, Frank Hirth plc

One of the most challenging tasks is to begin with the real untangling of organizational assets. Many international employment projects risk underachievement because either there is no project plan or the plan is not based on a clear picture of the organization's internal and external resources as well as its operational structure.

Evaluations of capability need to be based on a complete understanding of how an organization is linked together. Good ideas can get lost within the spaghetti of the organization and in any attempt to unravel it. This often happens when there is a rush to parachute an employee into a problem location without spending the necessary time at the clarifying and evaluating stages.

This review should provide a clear understanding of connections between and among the various bits of the organization that are involved with the assignment process, including management structure, internal and external resources, and organizational structure.

MANAGEMENT STRUCTURE

The starting point in any evaluation of international capability is to identify how the organization is managed. It is not always obvious who will have this information in a comprehensive format. Management structures do not always reveal every detail of reporting lines and expectations. Nevertheless it is crucial to be able to establish the shape of your organization's HR structure. For example, is the approach to decision making:

- centralized;

- regional; or

- decentralized?

The next step is to build a profile, using a combination of informal conversations, questionnaires, interviews and workshops, to establish the organization's capability in managing the international assignments. The main objective of this type of review is to establish what the organization can do in-house and with its existing external service providers.

Finally, all of this information needs to be encapsulated in an operational plan that has a clear time frame and accounting and budgeting process in place before an assignment kicks off.

IN-HOUSE RESOURCES

Often an organization does not fully consider which categories of in-house people may need to be consulted and therefore does not anticipate any hurdles this may create later on in the project. Often in-house staff are like shadow members of the management of assignees, and their time commitment and knowledge are not fully appreciated. A thorough review will include an analysis of capabilities of all resources, including:

- the HR coordinating manager;

- tax resources (considering both corporate and indirect taxes);

- local HR resources (including payroll personnel);

- technology resources;

- legal resources;

- finance resources;

- communication resources.

These resources may be internal, external or both, depending on the organization's needs. The HR specialist or other professional reviewing capabilities should seek to encourage an understanding of the numbers, dispersion, capability and availability of the in-house network. In particular, account should be taken of any concurrent projects that could overstretch critical in-house resources, causing both the resources and the assignment project to suffer. In some cases, the gap is so great that a need may go totally unmet.

EXTERNAL RESOURCES

An HR specialist may not necessarily be familiar with in-house contacts in overseas locations. Sometimes this type of review is the first time that there has been any significant contact. With this in mind it is not surprising that organizations do not always have, as a bare minimum, a central record of the external advisers used by their local offices, let alone any record of local terms and conditions. However, a clear understanding of these terms is of great importance.

Frequently, organizations do not have one global service provider, allowing for a mixture of external service providers and therefore a variety of local terms and conditions. A reviewer must think very carefully about how to coordinate this, to ensure the appropriate cooperation and to avoid confusion and unnecessary costs arising from managing this process.

External service providers need to know where they do or do not have authority to take action. This should be spelt out in agreements or additions to existing agreements.

In working with external providers, an HR specialist should make sure that the appropriate clearance is in place to communicate and cooperate with the central coordination team. A word of advice: do not expect seamless cooperation in every location. Also, be sure to give unambiguous instructions where necessary about roles and responsibilities, as well as the appropriate reassurance about long-term relationships and intentions. If this is dealt with early on in the international assignment review, it should be relatively easy to manage. If left unaddressed, it can be a major cause of frustration, as it can cause unplanned delay.

ORGANIZATIONAL STRUCTURE

Often it is not easy to establish which individuals will be fully familiar with the detail of corporate entities and corporate tax reporting that can be critical to a complete understanding of the benefit analysis of any planning ideas.

The possibilities are many and will depend to some degree on industry type and the locations of the organization's operations. Here are just a few important areas to consider:

▪ subsidiaries;

▪ joint ventures;

▪ alliances;

▌ recharging;

▌ corporate tax implications.

It is important to consider this area in some detail. It is not unusual for the people dealing with assignee matters to avoid the detail of corporate issues, but the link between the two makes this type of approach a high risk in terms of project success. For example, for each legal entity in any location in which the organization has operations, the following questions need to be asked: What percentage ownership does the organization have? And are there any joint venture arrangements in place that result in a less than 100 per cent effective interest in particular projects?

CORPORATE TAX ISSUES

Personal tax specialists often avoid corporate tax because they do not feel comfortable with the questions that need to be asked. This results in ineffective communication between corporate and personal tax specialists. As a minimum the following questions or points need to be understood:

▌ What is the statutory rate of corporate income tax, including surcharges of state and local taxes generally assimilated to corporate income tax?

▌ By what is the marginal tax rate expected to materially differ in future years?

▌ Does the entity benefit from a tax holiday?

▌ Are expatriate costs deductibles for corporate tax purposes (including surcharges or state and local taxes)?

▌ At the outset, be sure to establish working relationships between in-house corporate and personal tax specialists and involve them in the planning process.

▌ Are there any specific tax or governmental arrangements that mean that, if a dollar of expatriate costs is saved, the saving to the organization is other than one dollar × (100 per cent – the marginal tax rate) × the shareholding or interest?

▌ Does the entity bear the grossed-up costs of the expatriates working for it?

▌ Does the entity hold the employment contracts or are the costs borne via a secondment or service fee arrangements?

ANTICIPATING BARRIERS TO IMPLEMENTATION

The biggest barrier to successful implementation of any project will be achieving the necessary level of buy-in from the broad cross-section of your in-house and external resources, as discussed earlier. The reasons why buy-in can be difficult to achieve may include a mixture of the following:

▌ There is often an antipathy between tax and HR owing to a lack of appreciation of one another's skill sets.

▌ There is natural resistance to change, sometimes because of a sense of ownership of existing systems and working practices.

▌ References to increased efficiency and savings can be perceived as a threat by both internal and external resources.

▌ Potentially you are changing existing assignees' packages. This can lead to suspicion, particularly if there is no buy-in from your internal and external resources that provide support during their assignment. Remember, it is often the assignee who is a key decision maker in a particular location.

▌ There is concern over costs and budgets, without appreciating the benefits. Until clarification is provided, there will be a local management concern over who bears the costs and the impact of this on their budgeting. There will also often be a time lag between costs being incurred and savings being actually achieved.

▌ There is previous experience with failed company initiatives, and cynicism towards involvement in the project, owing to experience with or internal publicity about previous company initiatives that have underachieved.

Evaluation of an international assignment policy to enable key strategic decisions and improvements to be considered can be a difficult task, but it is worth the effort. Upfront investment in time can ensure the success of projects based on a clear understanding of management structure, in-house resources, external service providers and organizational structure. It is also useful to have strong plans and scheduling, and to understand barriers to implementation specific to the organization.

LINKING CORPORATE STRATEGY TO CROSS-BORDER EMPLOYMENT OBJECTIVES

Let's take a closer look at why it is helpful to understand the strategic reasons for transferring employees to work cross-border.

Managing expatriate employees has always been complex and time consuming. However, in today's business environment the costs and risks of employing foreign nationals in the UK are becoming ever more complex. New compliance laws, increased regulation and changes in the patterns of how people are working cross-border demand a fresh examination of how to limit risk of adverse fiscal consequences and how best to minimize unnecessary operational risks.

Up until 1990, employers had very structured expatriate pay programmes planned to last from two to five years. However, expatriate policies are now being driven by a number of factors, including:

▌ Employees may be required in any part of the world, whereas it used to be more common to assign US expatriates to Europe or from Europe to the United States.

▌ Expatriates may be from any country in the world, and expectations related to expatriation will vary widely.

▌ Many international assignments are in less developed parts of the world and in places where there is endemic discrimination; for example, discrimination against women is prevalent in certain countries.

▌ Expatriates are often forced to consider dual-career issues because they have spouses who will have to put a career on hold to move to a new country.

In response to some of these issues, companies are being more flexible in terms of offering short-term assignments of one year or less and, for employees who do want to relocate families, options such as commuting between home and the new work location on weekends. You might also face the situation where a group of employees needs to move from one international assignment to another, and each move may be in response to different corporate strategic objectives.

The corporate strategy of your organization, the implementation of which requires employees working cross-border at any point in time, might include any one or more of the following:

▌ growing new markets;

▌ developing new products and services;

▌ recruiting and retaining the best people;

▌ improving customer satisfaction;

▌ driving operational efficiency.

The organizational objectives in response to these strategic objectives might include:

▌ sending experienced personnel to establish new markets;

▌ training locals from new markets to established markets to gain skills;

▌ creating teams for specific objectives (eg new products, systems or processes development);

▌ transferring and sharing knowledge;

▌ sending experienced personnel to address specific operational problems and needs;

▌ broadening employee experience.

To be able to manage effectively the execution of these organizational targets your operational objectives are likely to address:

▌ limitation of operational risks;

▌ minimization of operational costs;

▌ motivation and retention of employees.

How you develop your strategy for managing cross-border employment in respect of each expatriate employee should be based around four questions:

1. What countries are going to be involved?

2. What resources are available to assist in each country?

3. How will you work with those resources in an effective manner?

4. What external resources will you need in each location?

In addition you will need to consider the mindset of those involved in the process, as a successful approach will demand a skill set that includes:

- the ability to think with an international mindset;

- the talent to act with international leadership behaviours; and

- the qualities to manage a collaborative and cooperative approach to linking people and knowledge across borders.

You will also need to build into your operational planning the impact of a number of differences, including:

- time zones;

- languages;

- currencies; and

- cultural literacy.

An important point to consider when you first begin to formulate your approach to managing expatriate employees is what lessons to learn from other employers that have approached similar situations. Typically this does not amount to a full-blown benchmarking exercise and, if you are working in a small or medium-sized organization, it may not be helpful to simply try to mimic the approach of large multinationals. A bespoke solution will always offer the most efficiency.

The size and shape of your organization will influence the decision-making process you will need to navigate and in turn how you communicate your strategy. For example, your organization may be structured so that the management approach is based on:

- a flat or tall structure;

- a span of control;

- a chain of command;

- a hierarchy;

- a delegation;

- empowerment;

- centralization or decentralization.

Other organizational structures that may help you determine how to structure your operational ability in alignment with your corporate culture might include the following:

▌ by customer;

▌ by function or department;

▌ by project teams;

▌ by product or service line.

As you begin to look at the detail of the potential impact of these structures on how you develop your cross-border employment strategy you will need to consider in the context of your organizational structure:

▌ Who does what in each country?

▌ What are the cross-border reporting lines?

▌ Who are the stakeholders for each aspect of service in each location?

▌ What do you need in terms of the flow of cross-border information and data?

▌ Will your current management information systems help you track and monitor key information and data?

▌ What are the required data-processing or transaction-processing systems?

You will also need to understand how the headquarters and host locations are organized in terms of outsourcing, service company, etc – factors that often make this situation more opaque.

Operational objectives

Stephen Asher, Frank Hirth plc

Pulling together the in-house service unit responsible for the tasks that make up the expatriate employee deployment processes is a little like building a cross-border virtual team.

You will also need to determine roles and responsibilities of people for a number of services that are best outsourced to third-party vendors:

- business need, strategy and purpose;
- identification of candidate(s);
- cost projections and budgeting;
- work authorization, work permits and visas;
- employment contracts and secondment agreements;
- relocation and destination, and repatriation services;
- tax and social security compliance;
- payroll and expense management.

OPERATIONAL DESIGN

Every expatriate management operation has to focus on the needs of both the business and the expatriates. A necessary first step is to understand that the needs of the expatriates and the organization may involve multiple stakeholders with conflicting agendas. You will need to identify these stakeholders and their objectives.

Any operational process you design will need to ensure it has sufficient flexibility to accommodate these differences without allowing a series of exceptions to effectively sabotage your plans. Every operation is likely to be composed of three elements that must fit together:

1. international internal and external human resources;

2. cross-border processes;

3. technology and facilities.

There is no one right way to design an operation to deliver the intended services. Each organization will approach its design differently depending on their mix of people, processes and technology.

Other factors that you will need to consider in order to determine the best approach to your operational objectives include internal factors such as employees with a certain skill set, and intangible factors such as demand for the service, which may fluctuate considerably.

BUILDING A PROCESS

The deployment of each expatriate employee will be subject to an assignment life cycle. You will need to design a process that enables you to identify your operational process by listing its component parts in sequence:

▌ To begin with you will need to identify the sets of tasks or activities required throughout the assignment life cycle.

▌ Then you will need to ensure there is a flow to the process (which may have variations).

▌ Lastly you will need to identify the internal and external resources you will need to carry out the activities.

While in-house human resources perform most of the activities, you should not overlook the fact that the expatriates will carry out some aspects of the process. Finally, everyone who performs any of the activities may need to be aided by technology to help them accomplish the tasks, particularly where large numbers of expatriate employees are involved.

You should be careful to understand your specific expatriate scenario. A process to support a straight-line assignment for a fixed period may be straightforward, but if the assignment is more fluid and subject to a number of last-minute changes you will need to consider how to design a process to accommodate those circumstances.

Flow diagrams

The use of flow diagrams will help you to see quickly who needs to do what and when. A process flow diagram shows activities, flows and storage points where items wait for future transformation. To avoid getting lost in detail, it is best to start with a high-level outline and then break down a process into its component activities as needed.

The key point to understand is whether a task can be performed only after another task is completed. If so, there is a precedence relationship between activities. For example, you cannot operate a No Tax PAYE code without receiving the tax authority agreement that you may do so. At different points in the flow, certain pieces of information will be held in a queue until needed at a later stage while other data are being processed.

Another important element of an operation to understand is the time taken to accomplish each activity. Without activity times, any subsequent analysis of the operation will be very difficult. The ability to track and measure what work is being done in the assignment life cycle is important to enable crucial decisions on resourcing and outsourcing specific activities. This is vital in being able to predict how long it will take to complete the management of a specific assignment, to estimate its cost, to plan future capacity needs and to balance work flows with non-expatriate employee responsibilities.

This analysis is very important for organizations with growing expatriate populations or small but steady numbers of expatriates but limited in-house capability. The more measurements you take, the more confidence you will have in the accuracy of the average activity time. Clearly, if you are dealing with assignments for the first time estimating will be harder.

Some of the variability you will notice in certain process steps may not be totally random. Not all assignments are the same and so there may be variability in aspects of certain moves.

In many activities you may see a distinction between the time taken to set up an operation task and the time taken to perform the task. For example, even a one-person assignment can be a significant time drain. As a general rule, when estimating the assignment life cycle, the set-up time does not vary with the number of expatriates, but overall time varies proportionately with the quality of services delivered. The set-up time apportioned to an individual drops as the expatriate population increases.

ANALYSING AND EVALUATING THE PROCESS

While each organization's need for and management of expatriates will be different, it is helpful nonetheless to understand where expatriates (and third-party vendors) tend to feel aggrieved, for example:

▌ breakdown in the work permit or visa process for the expatriate or family members;

▌ inefficient relocation services;

▌ a slow expense management process;

▌ a limited or non-existent repatriation process.

Understanding this is particularly important where in-house resources are limited and demand is infrequent (so that expertise and experience do not build up quickly) or has specific peaks.

From these observations you might be able to draw tentative conclusions about the efficiency of the expatriate operations, the speed with which the whole process is done, and the quality with which tasks are executed. Your job now is to analyse the operations to find the reasons why these events might happen.

Processes that will inevitably rely on external input, ie third-party vendors, are those where the efficiency, speed and quality of the process to which the expatriate is subjected and not just the end result are all-important.

CAPACITY AND CAPACITY UTILIZATION

The first step in analysing your best approach to expatriate operational management is to identify expatriate capacity, ie the number of expatriates you will be capable of processing in some period of time. It is important, whatever method of estimation is adopted, that it accurately conveys your capacity and the utilization of your internal and external resources. Failure to do this will often lead to individual frustration and stakeholder communication difficulties.

Indeed, the key reasons for outsourcing the whole or parts of the expatriate operational process are a lack of capacity in general and a lack of capacity to respond adequately at peak times or simply on demand to meet short-term business needs.

Bottlenecks

While you will be concerned with the capacity of each internal resource, you also need to be aware of the capacity of external vendors. You will need to identify events that may be considered bottlenecks. Bottlenecks can shift as each internal and external service provider responds to peaks and surges in demand, particularly where these are not planned.

If each internal and external service provider had similar cycle times the overall operation would be well balanced. Balance is important because it determines the amount of idle time for the expatriates. Excessive idle time represents an inefficient use of resources and raises the risk of non-compliant and unhappy expatriates and other stakeholders. As a result, the identification of potential bottlenecks is a critical piece of analysis. The fundamental question you need to ask yourself is: what resource constrains expatriates in meeting their business objectives?

Bottlenecks in the operational process can be a huge obstacle to successful expatriate management. Third-party vendors may be seen as potential bottlenecks. Bottlenecks can be dangerous, for example when parachuting in troubleshooters who need to move in and out of a location at great speed.

Capacity utilization

An operational manager's key objectives are to fulfil demand while containing costs and risks. Thus knowledge of an operation's capacity is critical. You need to examine the way demand for employees to work cross-border occurs to be sure that you have sufficient capacity at key times. Peak demand times are when capacity is most stressed. You will need therefore to have, as far as possible, some awareness of anticipated cross-border projects.

THROUGHPUT TIME

Throughput time includes both the time taken to process specific data requirements and any time the data spend in a queue. When considering the overall assignment life cycle you start the throughput clock when the stakeholder enters the process. The best way to conceptualize throughput time is to visualize following an item of data through every process step in an operation.

An organization's capacity to respond to stakeholder demands for deployment of expatriate employees is determined by: 1) how many expatriates can be processed each month by internal and external resources; and 2) how long it takes to process each expatriate from selection to repatriation.

Throughput time is important. People do not want to wait or be unnecessarily tied up in some part of the process. Therefore throughput time is an important factor in stakeholder satisfaction.

Estimating throughput time is complex. Queuing models are best used to estimate throughput time for small to medium-sized operations, but in very complicated operations simulation models may be the best tools. The variability inherent in intricate operations makes the calculations difficult. Observations may be the best source for this information. If you are new to expatriate employment this is an area you might productively outsource.

QUALITY

Quality may be measured by the percentage of services delivered without errors. Minimizing expatriate costs through remuneration package design or third-party vendor management and so on will backfire if it leads to a deterioration in service quality.

If you are under pressure to reduce costs but improve service delivery, you should consider four perspectives of costs related to quality:

1. actions that can be taken to prevent unnecessary costs;

2. how best to fully evaluate the costs that need to be reduced;

3. how to account for the cost of internal failures;

4. how to account for the cost of external failures.

You will also have to ensure that a focus on quality does not limit your flexibility to manage in specific scenarios such as:

▪ significant increases in demand;

▪ shifts in the demand distribution (geographic or cadre);

▪ changes in the service design, for example the introduction of a flexible plan for expatriates.

Ultimately you will need to manage things in a balanced way. In this respect, an operation can have one or more competitive priorities:

▪ cost;

▪ quality;

- flexibility;

- dependability.

An organization cannot be good at all of these, and it should focus its operational energy on the priorities critical to achieving the strategy of the overall organization for going into international locations.

SAMPLE PROBLEMS

For the following problems, consider a Canadian technology company that has a need to send engineers to work at its UK start-up office for varying lengths of time and often at short notice.

There are three service areas that are outsourced to third-party vendors: immigration, relocation and tax.

1. The UK office has asked for 20 Canadian nationals to be sent within a week. What is the expected capacity requirement for the immigration advisers to meet this time frame?

2. The secondment of the 20 Canadians also calls for relocation and tax services in that order. If these services are dependent on the completion of the immigration work, estimate the potential delay in being able to ensure the employees can be transferred effectively.

3. If the immigration advisers had been notified earlier and had agreed a standardized process with you, what would be their turnaround time? Could you draw a flow chart showing the progression of each third-party vendor?

4. What is the maximum number of Canadian expatriates who can be processed through all service areas in a 40-hour week?

5. How long does it take for each service to complete its work?

6. What is the in-house capacity to manage the service delivery of the third-party vendors?

7. Would service delivery improve if any or all of the third-party vendor services were taken in-house?

8. How would your answers change if the number of Canadians doubled?

9. What criteria would you use to judge the quality of the third-party vendor services?

The following five case studies of varying employment strategies provide examples of the range of complex issues that an employer organization might face.

Case study 1

ABW is a small biotechnology company that was started in the UK but has since developed an international capability, demonstrating that it no longer takes great scale to straddle borders.

ABW has fewer than 100 staff but has a presence in Japan, China, the UK, the United States and New Zealand. The firm has exploited national differences in regulation, cost and expertise to build a mini-multinational corporation.

The firm seeks to maximize the advantages of particular geographical locations and has developed three main national centres. These centres provide it with a Chinese cost structure, Japanese technology and UK research resources. More specifically, a Japanese entity provides access to high-level supercomputers, the UK headquarters conducts research, and a Chinese operation provides access to patients for clinical trials.

Executives of ABW move between each international location for various periods of time, and a few have relocated to support the long-term development of products and services and to drive the efficiency of local operations.

For most of the senior executives, constant internationally mobile communication with and between them is an operational challenge. In order to maintain a high level of communication the executives use videoconferencing facilities extensively, with virtual meetings arranged for mornings in some places and evenings in others. However, with the company spanning all time zones, someone has to be up in the middle of the night. This occasionally includes the involvement of HR resources who manage aspects of the international operations.

Case study 2

High is a UK-based small software company with six employees; Low is a US-headquartered multinational technology company with over 100,000 employees employed throughout its international operations.

High and Low formed an alliance that provided High with guaranteed increased sales and Low with software to bundle in with its hardware with technical support.

From the outset it become clear that Low's sales force needed training to understand High's software. With only six employees, High had to provide Low with documentation in several languages, and it had to find a way to rapidly train Low's international sales force, which amounted to tens of thousands of people in a number of different international locations.

Low agreed to second to High some of its own staff from various locations to help with the translation and production of the relevant documentation and training materials. These resources were then trained by High in the intricacies of its software.

The High secondees were sent back to their home countries, where they arranged local training sessions. Low staff remained available to provide for virtual support and on very rare occasions travelled to some locations where they needed to help clarify detail.

Once the bundled hardware and software had been sold to Low clients it was hoped Low-trained personnel would be able to respond to client problems. However, on a number of occasions the High staff had to travel to Low client premises to ensure customer satisfaction.

Case study 3

Pour is a US-headquartered company and is one of the largest wine and spirits companies in the world. It has 3,400 staff in 60 countries. It has 1,500 staff based outside the United States. Pour operates as a multinational rather than a global company, so the ability of its senior staff to manage international cultural differences is key to its successful operation.

As part of Pour's strategy to recruit and retain the best people to operate in an international culture, it sends its best people on foreign assignments for up to five years with enhanced pay and benefits.

Pour sends people to work in a foreign location only if they are considered to be capable of adding value. In particular, the company uses international assignments to develop staff and increase their flexibility across the business. This ability to move in different cultures and spheres is considered essential to the function of the business.

From the outset the expatriates' return is being anticipated in order to ensure a return on the investment and to ensure Pour retains the best people. Most expatriates return to their home locations to more senior roles where they can apply the benefit of the experience they have gained.

Case study 4

Barrel is a global oil, gas and renewable energy company. Barrel has over 60,000 staff in more than 80 countries. It has 2,700 expatriate employees in 50 countries from 40 different home countries. In addition, a significant number of international resources are contractors.

At Barrel it is the individual business unit that owns the decision on whether or not and whom to send on international assignment. Most of the employees on international assignment are engineers from an individual business unit, with very few financial and administrative staff, who tend to be hired locally.

Barrel has a dual approach to international transfers. It sends experienced personnel to address specific operational problems and needs, particularly where the local alternatives are not available or in short supply. It also sends less experienced people from new markets to established markets to gain or improve their skills and knowledge of the business.

Case study 5

Capital is a hedge fund based in New York. In 2001, it decided to open an office in London to expand its operations into continental Europe and to recruit talent on the local market, as there was some unwillingness to relocate from New York.

It needed someone to set up the UK offices (find premises, arrange for them to be fitted out and coordinate with corporate advisers), implement the US procedures and technology and recruit personnel (traders as well as back-office staff). The company decided to second one of its most senior back-office employees to the UK to undertake this task, initially temporarily.

When premises were found and fitted out, this individual then selected a number of US employees, initially back-office staff, to start up the operations. All these individuals were also seconded to the UK offices on temporary assignments. As the business developed, the senior employee recruited local talent for the trading operations, as well as local back-office staff. A few traders were also seconded to the UK company to provide technical support to the local traders.

Any newly recruited trader was sent to the United States on training for a couple of months at the start of employment. In addition to imparting technical knowledge, it allowed the individual to understand the culture and ethos of the company.

Now that the company has established itself in the UK and local staff are fully trained up, most seconded employees have returned to the United States, with a few having localized as UK employees.

The company has now expanded into Singapore and France.

Expatriate policy evaluation checklist

Donald C Dowling, Jr, White & Case LLP

The following represents a basic selection of the key issues and questions facing those who need to map out a cohesive and effective expatriate policy. While not exhaustive, it will highlight the primary factors facing decision makers, as well as spotlighting those issues that may often be overlooked.

EXPATRIATE PROGRAMME STRUCTURE

▌ Inclusion of stakeholders: make sure you involve all necessary in-house players, such as home and host country line management and home and host country HR personnel, as well as those individuals involved in relocation, travel, finance and tax, benefits and compensation, risk management and insurance, and legal matters.

▌ Decide on the types of expatriate:
  - career expatriate;
  - project-based assignee;
  - expatriate to start up an operation and train a successor;
  - commuter expatriate.

▌ Decide on the types of assignment:
  - long-term;
  - short-term;
  - long business trips;
  - commuter.

▌ Confirm the exclusion of 'cross-border employees' (ie decide on a mechanism for excluding from the expatriate programme any voluntary or requested overseas transferees, locally hired headquarters-country citizens or overseas-company-hired 'trailing spouses', etc).

▌ Decide on the expatriate employer entity:
- home country or headquarters entity;
- host country affiliate;
- dual employers;
- global expat services affiliate

Remember to account for the 'permanent establishment' issue if a home country entity will employ abroad.

▌ Corporate payer entity: which affiliate will cover the base pay? Expat benefits? Bonuses? As to each element of expatriate compensation paid by the home country entity, how will it handle host country withholdings and social contributions?

▌ Decide on intra-company payment and charge-back logistics, such as: intra-company expat reimbursements; the process for intra-company charge-backs; and corporate tax treatment.

▌ Create an intra-company 'secondment' agreement (between home and host country entities: the expat will not be a party) that addresses: reporting; supervision; power to discipline or terminate the assignment; tendering payments and benefits to the expatriate; and intra-company charge-backs and apportionment of liabilities.

▌ Create an expatriate assignment agreement (between employer entities and expatriates personally): dovetail it with expatriates' existing employment agreements or policies (or else expressly 'hibernate' them) and address special issues such as restrictive covenants, alternative dispute resolution procedures, etc, as enforceable across borders.

▌ Confirm a non-discriminatory expatriate selection procedure.

▌ Decide on protocol for when and how to 'localize' expatriates, as well as methods for extinguishing any original employment relationship upon localization or eventual repatriation.

EXPATRIATE DEPENDANTS

▌ Confirm any visas (and apply very early) for dependants, including 'trailing spouses', unmarried partners, children, dependent parents, and household help or servants. (Will dependants' visas be work visas or residency only?)

▌ To what extent will dependants receive expatriate logistical support and benefits? (Account separately for each element addressed below, as to dependants.)

▌ Dependant-specific benefits: placement assistance; education, tuition, arranging schooling; compensation for career interruption; support for special-needs dependants.

▌ Consider contingency issues for family emergencies and divorce or separation.

FOREIGN ASSIGNMENT LOGISTICS

▌ Expat visa and work permit. (Apply very early.)

▌ Will there be any pre-decision trips?

▌ Decide on any issues relating to foreign payroll and benefits delivery logistics: where will they be paid? How will you comply with host and home country reporting, withholding and social contributions obligations? How will you comply with currency, foreign exchange and payroll laws? (For example, in Mexico, employees must be paid every 15 days, and in Belgium the expatriate must be on a Belgian-entity payroll.)

▌ Consider any medical, safety and personal injury claims exposure.

▌ Plan for any other medical issues: medical examinations or clearances; vaccinations; access to medical care and medication abroad (routine and emergency); participation in local government ('socialized') medical systems; expatriate medical insurance; and medical crisis evacuation to the home country.

▌ Do you need to allow for any disabled-access accommodation?

▌ Personal security issues: legal representation abroad; kidnap or emergency response; emergency evacuation.

▌ Is there a strategy for minimizing exposure to overseas-arising personal injury claims? For example, you may need to consider any workers' compensation bar; 'supplementary/voluntary' workers' compensation coverage; the duty of care; the defence strategy for expatriate and dependants' personal injury claims arising outside work hours or off work premises.

▌ Consider any expatriate insurance (beyond medical and workers' compensation): life; disability; evacuation; kidnap; directors and officers.

▌ Confirm any vacation and holiday issues: home versus host country vacation policy (complying with local vacation laws); extra home leave for regular as against 'hardship' assignments.

▌ Consider any cultural training, language training and/or destination counselling (for the expatriate and particularly the family). Would there be a one-off intensive course or ongoing training?

▌ Is there a 'buddy' (company point person or mentor and/or HR liaison) in home and host countries? Have you provided the tools for the expatriate to maintain working links to the home country office?

▌ Will you be responsible for mail forwarding?

▌ Decide on expense management, expense approval and reimbursement procedures.

LEGAL COMPLIANCE

▌ Provide the tools to enable the expatriate staff to comply with destination-specific business legislation.

▌ Decide on a compliance strategy as to mandatorily applicable home country laws (for example, extraterritorial reach of US or home country discrimination laws; US laws applicable to business abroad, such as any Sarbanes–Oxley accounting provisions and the Foreign Corrupt Practices Act; and so on).

▌ Confirm a compliance strategy as to mandatorily applicable host country employment laws (for example, local host country caps on hours and other wage or hour laws; break times; leave; profit sharing; 13th-month pay; termination procedures, notice and severance pay; payroll and currency laws; laws capping the percentage of non-citizens in the workplace, etc).

▌ Account for a choice-of-law provision could backfire (ie minimize the expatriate's power to 'cherry-pick' more favourable rules from two legal regimes).

EXPATRIATE COMPENSATION AND BENEFITS OFFERINGS

▌ Select which one of the three possible expat compensation philosophies applies to your own situation:
  - replicating the home country package;
  - replicating the host country package;
  - replicating packages among company expatriates worldwide.

▌ Decide on a cost containment philosophy (ie 'lean and mean', generous or somewhere in between).

▌ Remember to build in any cost-of-living adjustments ('location differentials').

▌ Ensure that the expatriate compensation package 'fits' with local pay practices; justify any pay differences in advance; confirm compliance with any local laws requiring equal pay among similarly situated employees or laws that prohibit paying foreigners more.

▌ Depending on the destination country, you may need to consider 'hardship allowances' or location differentials.

▌ Confirm any currency exchange issues (when compensation is set in one currency and paid in another).

▌ Home country home disposition: Will you pay a broker fee? Will you support any rental agreements or pay a mortgage?

▌ Decide on issues relating to host country housing: Will you facilitate any search? Reimburse expenses? Will the employee guarantee or sign any lease? Will you provide a loan or set any caps?

▌ In terms of moving expenses, what will be your policy? Will you pay for the packing? Will you specify shipping allowances, or fund new purchases? Will it be a sea or air shipment? What is the cap on quality moved? What about special items such as pets, wine and guns? Will there be any storage of goods? What about electrical conversion? Alternatively, consider providing a flat moving expense.

▌ Confirm a travel policy, and include issues such as class of service or any extra paid trips home (regular versus 'hardship' assignments). Make sure that any policy dovetails with the company business travel policy, and decide on a policy for how to handle requests that payment for trips home be diverted for foreign travel to equal/lower-expense destinations.

▌ Will you offer any settling-in assistance and/or any local facilitation to smooth bureaucratic or cultural barriers?

▌ Will the company provide any personal servants, including body-guards or drivers (as opposed to a local company car, local driving licence facilitation and local motor insurance)?

▌ Will the company provide any club memberships?

▌ Will the company provide equipment such as a mobile phone, BlackBerry or laptop?

▌ Consider a provision for incidental expenses (eg hotel, phone hook-ups, telephone calls home, etc), or offer a lump-sum option?

EXPATRIATE TAX, SOCIAL SECURITY AND PENSION

▌ Confirm the tax policy, and consider issues such as: tax equalization; tax gross-up; tax credits; tax treaties; taxation of expatriate benefits; dual-jurisdiction expatriate tax return preparation (address each by tax year, not by the term of the expatriate assignment).

▌ What about compensation elements beyond base pay (bonuses, savings plans, stock options or equity)? Consider local plans as opposed to continued participation in any home country plans, and remember to account for any related tax treatment.

▌ Are there any social security issues to consider, for example mandatory social security contributions in the host country, the effect of social security totalization or other equalization, or compensation for loss of home country credits?

▌ Confirm any pension continuation issues, such as local pension partic-ipation, pension equalization, host country tax treatment of contribu-tions to home country pension plan, US section 401k plan, etc.

REPATRIATION

▌ Consider the options in relation to job repatriation. For example, will there be:
  - a repatriation job guarantee?
  - an express employer reservation of no right to a repatriated job?
  - the employer's 'best efforts' to place the individual in a repatriated job?

▌ Disposition of host country house and car.

▌ Confirm any procedures regarding return travel (including job- and house-hunting trips, and travel for dependants and/or pets).

▌ Repatriation expense reimbursement: What items will be covered (moving, brokers, rental expenses, extra mortgage payments, temporary living expenses, etc)? What are the reimbursement procedures?

▌ Will you be providing any reintegration tools for the expatriate coming back into the home company? Can you leverage the expat overseas experience? Are you equipped to temper 'reverse culture shock' with preventing 'repatriation failure' and tackle post-repatriation retention challenges?

For each of the above points, distinguish repatriation support for expatriates returning to a home country company job against repatriation support for those whose employment may be being terminated.

APPENDIX TO PART 1

The ideas that have been expressed in Part 1 are summarized in the two flow charts shown in Figures A1 and A2.

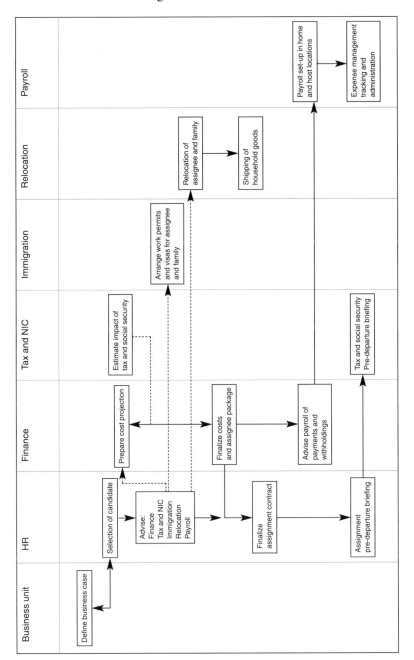

Figure A1 Integration flow chart by department of employer actions in expatriate hiring and pre-departure administration *Source*: Stephen Asher, Frank Hirth plc

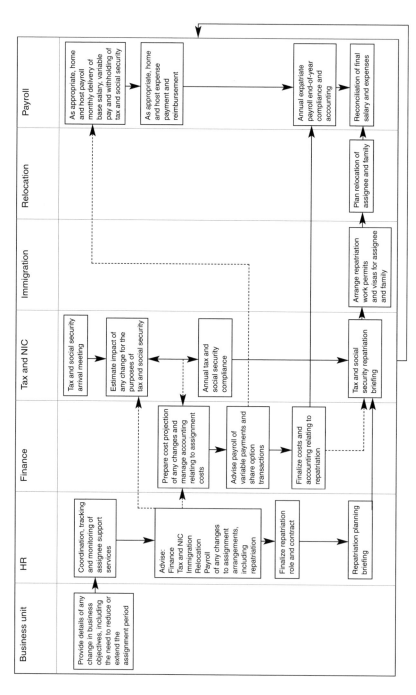

Figure A2 Integration flow chart by department of employer responsibilities in expatriate administration
Source: Stephen Asher, Frank Hirth plc

Part 2

Tax and social security

Tax and social security information requirements

Stephen Asher, Frank Hirth plc

Given that the front line of expatriate remuneration strategy is in the delivery of the correct amounts at the right time, the involvement of the payroll manager at an early stage in tax planning can help to establish good practice from the start by assisting in the design of information and data flow requirements.

Remuneration strategy and tax planning are not only about cost minimization. The effective execution of strategic objectives is also about how employers and employees meet their tax and social security administrative obligations in a cost-effective manner in any given situation. However, these obligations can be different for employees who, on the surface, look as though their circumstances are identical. Any one or any combination of the following factors can affect the employer and employee:

- the tax status of an individual – citizenship, residency and domicile;
- the country in which the organization is incorporated;
- the secondment contract;
- the tax legislation and regulations of the host and home countries.

TAX STATUS OF AN INDIVIDUAL

A key starting point is to appreciate that an employee's tax residency status, even where determined at the start of an assignment, can change during the period of the secondment. Indeed, extending expatriate assignments can have significant consequences if the record of intentions is not managed efficiently. You will need to maintain a record of all the information that may have an impact, for example any documentary evidence to support any change of intentions in terms of length of stay, including e-mail correspondence, notes of meetings, contract addenda and work authorization documentation.

INCORPORATION OF AN ORGANIZATION

The next step to take into consideration is that the country in which an organization is incorporated can affect how the tax authorities of a host country assess seconded employees for tax. For example, employees of a not-for-profit or non-governmental organization who are seconded to certain countries around the world may not have a tax liability.

SECONDMENT TERMS AND CONDITIONS

It is mission critical that you have easy access to the terms and conditions of a secondment, as these will outline the specific detail on:

▌ length of the assignment;

▌ compensation;

▌ benefits and support;

▌ how the expatriate's tax and social security liabilities are to be managed.

TAX LEGISLATION AND REGULATIONS OF THE HOST AND HOME COUNTRIES

You will need to be aware of the information demands beyond direct host country taxation. Inter-country agreements also have a direct impact on the tax administration relating to an employee. Double taxation agreements, detached duty relief, foreign income exclusion and social security conventions may all require specific information to support claims.

An example of how the length of assignment needs to be agreed and fully documented pre-appointment is in the area of detached duty rules. If the secondment is to be for a period of less than two years, accommodation may not be taxable.

OFFICIAL DOCUMENTATION

You will also need to consider the management of official documentation for all related areas such as immigration, tax and social security. Not all countries will require forms to register an employee seconded to work in their country, but it is necessary to check the countries' individual taxation and immigration requirements.

Some examples of where there is a need to retain official documentation include:

- *Immigration – a requirement in the United States.* It is a legal obligation for a US employer to have a copy of the form I9 on its files within three days of an employee starting work for it. This form confirms that an employee has the right to work in the United States.

- *Tax – a requirement in the UK and the United States.* Notification for an employee starting on the payroll, in the UK, is the form P46 and, in the United States, the form W4. The information gathered from these forms helps assess how much tax should be withheld from the employee's earnings. Also required in the UK is the form P86, on arrival in the UK; the equivalent in the United States are the forms 673 and 8833. These forms give the tax authorities information that helps determine the area of legislation that earnings will be taxed under, eg detached duty or foreign earnings exclusion.

- *International social security.* This is an area where there is greater consistency in the approach of the various countries' tax authorities, but there still remain differences depending on the home and host country regulations. There are a number of different circumstances and processes to be applied to the social security of an expatriate employee. Three key processes that could be applied are:
  - certificates of coverage: issued by the US authorities, these certificates allow US citizens or nationals to be maintained in their home country social security schemes;
  - certificates of continuing liability: issued by the UK, these certificates allow certain expatriate employees to be maintained in their home country social security schemes;
  - E101: issued between countries in the EU, this certificate allows European citizens or nationals to be maintained in their home

country social security scheme while seconded to work in another EU country.

▌ The UK has a fourth element known as the '52-week rule'. This rule states that employees seconded to work in another country that does not fall under the certificate of continuing liability and E101 should be maintained in their home country social security scheme for a period of 52 weeks from the start of their secondment to another country.

PENSION

Approval of the host country tax authorities for a foreign pension scheme can avoid a tax liability. In the UK and some other European countries, approval of a foreign pension scheme is a formality for certain types of pension scheme. The decision is primarily based on identifying whether the income, when it is in the form of a pension, has any tax jurisdiction. For example, it is very simple to get UK approval granted for a US pension scheme. Membership of a US pension is only granted to citizens of the United States, and this means that when they retire they must declare the income to the US authorities for tax purposes.

LEGISLATIVE BODIES

Each country will have its own employment and taxation laws and may have different bodies dealing with the different aspects of each area of legislation. For example:

▌ *The United States:*
  - Immigration is administered by the Department of Homeland Security (www.dhs.gov).
  - Labour laws and the minimum wage are administered by the Department of Labor (www.dol.gov).
  - Tax and tax credits are administered by the Internal Revenue Service (www.irs.gov).
  - Social security is administered by the US Social Security Administration (www.ssa.gov).
  - Pension administration is the joint responsibility of the Pension Benefit Guaranty Corporation (www.pbgc.gov/) and the Internal Revenue Services.

▌ *The UK:*
- Immigration is administered by the Home Office (www.homeoffice. gov.uk).
- Employment laws and the minimum wage are the responsibility of the Department for Education and Skills (DfES) (www.dfes.gov.uk/).
- Tax and National Insurance (NI) are the remit of HM Revenue & Customs (HMRC) (www.hmrc.gov.uk).
- Pension administration is the responsibility of the Department for Work and Pensions (DWP) (www.dwp.gov.uk/).

▌ *China:* China has a more complex structure in that an overseas organization cannot be a direct employer of Chinese nationals. The workaround is to employ staff via the organized agency that specializes in this area: the Foreign Enterprise Service Company, known as FESCO.

For countries within Europe, the legislative control of employment matters is taken a step further. Each individual country within Europe has its own legislation for employment and taxation. However, many of the aspects of employment regulations adopt the European recommended standard. For example, the Working Time Directive governs areas of employment law such as hours of work, holidays, terms of employment and treatment of employees. Pay and taxation remain the province of the individual country.

Although a payroll may be localized, there are circumstances where the legislation of another country may need to be considered as part of the process of paying some employees. For example, a company incorporated in the United States that operates a payroll locally in another country, where that company is not incorporated locally, and employs staff as 'local hires' who are US citizens and/or nationals or green card holders, will have a US taxes obligation for those particular employees. These locally hired employees will also have a right to membership of a US pension scheme if the employer operates one for its US employees, although this may not extend to an employer obligation to make payments into the scheme.

Some countries do not have stringent employment legislation. It may be considered that, in order to ensure best business practice and maintain simplified and consistent administration procedures, it is advisable to develop a policy for the employment of staff effective in all countries. This will help ensure consistent cross-border processes.

GOVERNMENT AND LEGISLATIVE REPORTING REQUIREMENTS

There are likely to be reporting requirements in both the home and the host countries. Examples of reporting requirements include the following:

▌ *Payroll related returns.* These can be the usual annual returns within a core reporting requirement. However, in some countries the returns are more frequent: for example, in the United States, payroll-related returns are required quarterly, in March, June, September and December, with annual returns due in January or February.

▌ *Form 1099.* A US requirement, this is reported annually, to advise the authorities of the payments made to certain non-employees.

▌ *National Statistics.* These are a requirement in the UK. There are various types of returns required at different times of the year for different periods of time to the National Statistics Office.

NON-GOVERNMENT REPORTING REQUIREMENTS

There are many examples that fall under this category. The need for reporting requirements will be dependent upon the company and the contractual benefits offered to employees. Examples of the types of benefits that will generate a reporting requirement include:

▌ medical benefit schemes;

▌ insurance schemes, including life assurance, travel insurance, etc; and

▌ pension plans.

ACCOUNTING AND INTERNATIONAL REPORTING

Bureaucracy is one of the greatest burdens for businesses, whether generated internally or externally. Many internal procedures and guidelines will have been created to ensure that an organization meets its external legislative, accounting, governmental and non-governmental reporting requirements.

Internal accounting

Most organizations will try to replicate a standard approach to the principles of accounting, using the same codes for cost allocation. However, there may be specific reporting requirements for the particular country, for example to provide information on legislative information. Where this is not necessary, it is best practice to mirror the same coding structures to allow for easier integration of detail from various host countries in order to consolidate financial detail. Costs need not be moved unless there is a requirement in legislative financial reporting.

Not all employers have a system that allows for the cross-border movement of costs. In these situations a company will operate manual inter-company transfers via invoicing or double-entry recording of financial movements relating to secondments. There may be a need for the payroll function to be involved in the preparation of inter-company journals and transfers for salary-related costs.

It is important when preparing this type of information to consider confidentiality of salary information. Preparation of journals may lead the payroll function to work with finance in order to reconcile control accounts relating to seconded staff.

When managing employees internationally, it is important to consider at the planning stage what the effect may be of time zones between host and home countries.

If the company group accounting system and structure are not fully integrated, there may be differences in the date structure. Questions that should be clarified include identifying clearly the 'accounting' last day of the month: is it the actual last day of the month – for example, 31 December – or is it the last working day?

Particular care must be taken over national holidays. Clashes with a host country national holiday can mean that added stress may be placed on the local workforce compared to that of the home country. There may also be communication issues on such days; for example, banks and postal services may be closed over certain festival periods that are not recognized by the home country.

Managing tax and social security information

Stephen Asher, Frank Hirth plc

When planning to manage tax and social security information for expatriate employees, you will need to consider which details will be required from the various sources of information available to you from both within and outside your organization.

ORGANIZING INFORMATION

To begin with, tax and social security information can be subdivided into the following categories:

▊ regulatory (eg returns for HMRC and the foreign tax authorities);

▊ employer (eg internal reporting for headquarters HR department, finance department, business groups, overseas management, etc);

▊ employee (eg personal tax responsibilities and obligations, investment and pension planning, and private cash flow management).

When exploring how to structure the way you will manage your tax and social security information, you should consider the following issues:

▊ In what format does the information need to be presented?

▊ Who will use the information? What are their information needs?

▍ How do you ensure security, and who will be granted access?

▍ How do you integrate your collection methods with existing systems?

▍ How do you ensure the current content is sufficiently accurate for its purpose?

▍ How do you motivate experts to contribute their knowledge in an effective way?

▍ How do you obtain feedback that ensures you capture informal information?

The collection of compensation and benefit data wholly or in part, from one or more overseas sources, requires a methodology to collect the correct information on a regular basis. Time at the year end will be best served by concentrating on the reconciliation of compensation information rather than data gathering. Other information may be a by-product of transactions related to other parts of the expatriate employment cycle, for example employment contracts, work permits and visas, relocation records, payroll, etc.

When designing your approach, the considerations highlighted in Table 2.2.1 should be borne in mind.

We have begun to identify that the management of internationally mobile employees involves the processing and storage of a great deal of information relating to each individual.

How you choose to manage your taxation and social security information and data flow requirements will be influenced by your organization's general approach to questions relating to privacy, data protection and cyber-crime threats. Most likely you will consider using document and database management tools and will want to link this tracking to requirements of internal and external reporting. Alternatively, you may consider one of the many web-based extranet options that are available.

To support the communication and reporting structures, employers often consider using an extranet facility to coordinate and automate the administrative processes involved. However, these coordination systems should be set up only after detailed analysis of the incumbent systems and processes to ensure that integration with existing HR and other systems is possible.

Access to extranet sites tends to be granted at varying levels, from administrators who are able to view and access all information on a site to the expatriates who are able to view and access only information relevant to them and information in the shared areas.

Table 2.2.1   Sources of information

	Sources of Information
Regulatory:	
Format	Prescribed questionnaires, annual returns and end-of-year documentation, including form P35, 'Employer's Annual Return' for the year, together with forms P60 and P14, 'Employee's End of Year Certificate/Summary', and PAYE settlement agreements (PSAs).
Use	Legislation requires records to be kept that enable corporate and individual taxpayers to make accurate returns. The increasing use by HMRC of enquiries into both employee and employer tax returns means that an even greater emphasis is required on retaining documentation the critical value of which is as evidence to support claims and elections.
Security	Security of personal and corporate information is vital when providing regulatory information.
Accuracy	Information needs to be completely accurate, but it may be difficult to be prescriptive in respect of items open to interpretation of statute and regulatory practice.
Experts	Typically external tax and social security specialists are used to outsource a great deal of the regulatory demands, and their expertise can be invaluable when it is tailored to the context of an organization's specific international circumstances.
Feedback	Feedback from regulatory authorities will be provided by simple approval or investigations and enquiries. Do not be afraid to seek informal feedback when appropriate.
Employer:	
Format	There may be a prescribed content and layout; the requirement is most likely to be for delivery in spreadsheet format.
Use	There should be internal transparency, accountability and due process. In particular, the information created, received and maintained as evidence to support claims and elections made by the employer or employee is critically important in order to be able to manage the potential for HMRC enquiries, which can be intrusive, upsetting and costly where this evidence is not available.
Security	Data protection rules do not prevent you disclosing information where you are legally obliged to do so, for example informing HMRC about payments to workers. You should nevertheless be disclosing no more information than required.
Accuracy	Accuracy will vary but will need to be within prescribed tolerance limits so that information provided for internal reporting is of practical use. Too general an approach to accuracy will render the information too dangerous to use for decision

	making and may have a negative effect on a number of items, including budgets in home and host locations.
Experts	Typically internal and external resources will assist with the provision of data and the preparation of reports. This provides a degree of objectivity that might otherwise be lost.
Feedback	Feedback from internal sources should be sought on a regular basis from regulatory authorities and will be provided by simple approval or investigations and enquiries. Do not be afraid to seek informal feedback when appropriate.
Expatriate:	
Format	Ad hoc requests from expatriates can be minimized by the development of a standardized format that provides a variety of annual personal financial information relating to, for example, pension investment, share option and other incentive payment arrangements, etc.
Use	Employees will require employer information to enable them to complete personal tax compliance requirements of both home and host countries. This may include the provision of third-party support and will mean needing to ensure processes are in place to gather information relating to non-employment-related income and gains. Employees also use this information to help them manage investment decisions and pension planning, including family private cash flow management.
Security	Security of personal information is vital.
Accuracy	Information needs to be completely accurate.
Experts	Internal HR resources are likely to provide most of the personal information and will be responsible for communicating this information to employees.
Feedback	Feedback from employees will be readily available.

The following describes typical features of an extranet site. The flexibility of these sites allows each application to be used in different ways.

▍ *Demographics database.* All information relating to the assignment, tax and social security position of each expatriate is held on a database.

▍ *Project management tool.* The agreed project plan is uploaded to the extranet so that responsibilities and milestones may be viewed and checked off as they are achieved. This allows all those involved in the project to have a real-time global report of work progress.

▍ *Knowledge management tool.* This is used to index and accumulate relevant knowledge and also to disseminate information such as expatriate tax policies across third-party advisers, internal stakeholders or specific individuals.

▌ *Compliance deadline tracking facility.* This is a continually updated area that records the progress of compliance, calculations and refunds.

▌ *Payroll interface.* Compensation information may be sourced directly from in-house or third-party systems and disseminated across a network via the extranet facility.

▌ *Expatriate travel calendars.* Typically, all individuals are provided with their own online calendars. These are a rolling record of dates used to prepare tax returns, and also allow the constant monitoring of residency positions during the year so that any necessary adjustments can be made within the relevant tax year, thus reducing the instance of under- and overpayments of tax and social security.

▌ *Online tax return questionnaires.* Each employee is prompted to complete an online questionnaire at appropriate intervals. Often the questionnaire is pre-populated by third-party advisers with information such as bank account interest.

The benefits that these extranet sites afford can be summarized into three categories:

1. *Automating administration.* There is an enormous amount of administration associated with coordinating the activities of an internationally mobile population, and extranet sites may enable your processes to be fully automated so that compliance is controlled. However, in practice it is unlikely that you will actually be able to automate the whole process.

2. *Centralized information.* An extranet might form a central repository for all information relating to expatriates. The basic idea behind this is that everyone in the expatriate process has access to and uses the same data, resulting in a more efficient programme leading to cost savings. This also allows trends to be identified and complementary planning to be adeptly implemented.

3. *Customization through flexibility.* As each extranet is a stand-alone facility it has the flexibility to adapt to allow it to integrate and work with, rather than impose on, existing systems.

The extent to which you would benefit from an investment in an extranet facility, in terms both of cost and of resources needing to be committed to operating the system, will depend on the numbers of expatriate employees you need to manage, the locations and the complexity of the information that needs to be collected. The following types of information might typically be collected about each individual:

- personal and family details;
- copies of employment contracts;
- immigration, work permit and visa papers;
- copy tax returns;
- forms P85 and P86;
- salary, bonus, benefits, expenses and equity incentive events;
- pension investments;
- travel itineraries;
- e-mail addresses and passwords.

SAFETY AND SECURITY OF INFORMATION

You need to plan carefully how you process this personal information. You will need to ensure that it is used safely and securely.

In this respect you need to be aware of the EU Data Protection Directive, which directs EU member states to pass their own local conforming data privacy laws. The directive regulates data held in respect of personally identifiable individuals via data quality principles and, for example, imposes a duty to purge obsolete data and a requirement to grant data subjects access to data about themselves.

The EU Data Protection Directive also raises an extraterritorial legal issue regarding the regulation of transmissions of personal data about identifiable European data subjects, including employees, to jurisdictions outside the EU.

The main approaches for international employers will need to consider ensuring that their out-of-Europe transmissions of personal data comply with European laws, including the following:

- *'Adequate level of protection' in cross-border transmissions.* Transmissions should only be made to, and therefore access should only be permitted by, countries that the EU Commission has deemed offer an 'adequate level of data law protection'.

▪ *'Necessary' out-of-EU transmissions.* You should ensure you transmit only personal data that it is 'necessary' to transmit abroad so as to comply with data subjects' employment agreements.

▪ *Employee consents.* You need to arrange for a formal programme of collecting 'unambiguous' employee consents to transmit and permit access to personal data out of country.

▪ *Safe harbour.* Where appropriate, you will need to comply with 'safe harbour'; this is a set of principles agreed between the EU Commission and the US Department of Commerce that applies only to personal data transmissions to and access from the United States.

▪ *Model contracts.* Enter model contracts that conform to the EU Commission's models.

▪ *Codes of conduct.* Codes of conduct are detailed in-house codes spelling out, *inter alia*, how a multinational employer transmits HR data across borders. Codes can be especially relevant to personal data transmissions to countries other than the United States.

The UK Data Protection Act applies to information about expatriate employees. Through the data protection principles, it regulates the way information about them can be collected, handled and used. It also gives them rights such as access to the information, and compensation if things go wrong. It applies equally to information held on computer databases and information in well-structured manual records.

The Data Protection Act will generally apply to information you keep about your expatriate employees. The Act does not prevent you from collecting, maintaining and using employment records. However, it helps to strike a balance between the employer's need to keep records and expatriates' rights to respect for their private life.

Employees should be aware what information about them is kept and what it will be used for. Gathering information about an employee covertly is unlikely to be justified.

You don't need to obtain the consent of workers to keep records about them, but you will need to make sure they know how you will use records about them and whether you will disclose the information they contain.

You should ensure that those who have access to expatriate information are aware that data protection rules apply and that personal information must be handled with respect. You should review what records are kept about your employees and make sure you are not keeping information that is irrelevant, excessive or out of date. You should plan to delete information that you have no genuine business need for or legal duty to keep.

You should also build into your processes the opportunity for expatriates to check their own records periodically. This will allow mistakes to be corrected and information to be kept up to date. Keep employment records secure. Keep paper records under lock and key and use password protection for computerized records. Make sure that only staff with proper authorization and the necessary training have access to employment records.

If you collect information about expatriates to administer a pension or insurance scheme, use the information only for the administration of the scheme. Make sure workers know what information the insurance company or other scheme provider will pass back to you as the employer.

The author acknowledges with thanks the contribution of notes and text to this chapter by Alison Ward of the Institute of Payroll Professionals (IPP).

Communication and monitoring of tax and social security information

Stephen Asher, Frank Hirth plc

Communication and monitoring of tax and social security administration are vital to successful execution of cross-border employment objectives. It is critical that everyone affected by the deployment of expatriate employees understands their roles and responsibilities and how they are interconnected. You will need to plan how these features are communicated in terms of your policy and cross-border decision-making process.

LANGUAGE AND WRITTEN COMMUNICATION

Good communication is vital in every walk of life and of course is essential to successful cross-border business interaction. A business moving to a country where the first or second language of the host country is not the same as the international language of the global business, needs to consider what impact this will have in day-to-day transfer of information between countries.

The need to communicate clearly is accepted as essential. This becomes even more important when the medium being used is not the first language for one or more of the people involved. Therefore, when communicating, either in writing or orally, consideration should be given to making it as simple as possible.

Some care is needed over the meaning of words – when translating it is easy to misunderstand the true meaning of some words. English in particular is notorious for having complex meanings, with similar-sounding words meaning totally different things or the same spelling of a word having a different meaning and a different pronunciation.

INTERNATIONAL PAYROLL DELIVERY

One of the key aspects of expatriate tax and social security administration is the method chosen for delivery of compensation and benefits in each country.

There are many factors of tax and social security administration that we take for granted in our own countries. Being familiar with how to talk about the detail of country-based payroll operation in our daily lives means that we do not need to give this special attention; we understand how the process works, so we deal with most issues automatically within our domestic work environment.

However, factors such as political, economic, religious and cultural influences need to be given special attention when working with the communication of delivery of compensation and benefits in other countries or when developing local policies and practices relating to employees. Assumptions should not be made that these factors will operate in the same way as those of the expatriate employee's home country.

Global payroll systems

Legislation relating to payroll is usually complex and country specific, and each location tends to use in-house programming by local staff. The more technically advanced the country, the greater the number of organizations offering payroll software.

As global organizations have been created, there have been numerous claims for many different organizations to introduce payroll systems. This results in there being many systems within countries to deal with the specific requirements of the payroll legislation. The complexity of the legislation of individual countries makes it difficult for software developers to include legislation on a payroll system for more than one country.

In recent years, many more smaller software houses have developed products that cover two or more countries, for example UK-based products often offer a bolt-on module to handle any Irish payroll. Throughout Europe there are many products that deal with other European countries, particularly those that have close borders and a constant traffic of workers living in one country and working in another, for example France–Spain or Switzerland–France–Germany. England may be less advanced than its European counterparts in this area, as it has direct borders with only two other countries – Scotland and Wales.

Although there are products that claim to have a 'global payroll', there is no payroll product on the market that is 100 per cent global. One merely has to consider the number of countries that there are in the world to recognize what an impossibility it would be to make any software capable of off-the-shelf compliance for every possible country combination. Instead, such packages will look to resource for smaller payrolls and countries, and integrate the created payment details with other data as simply as possible.

There is also a trend towards software that has 'multiple functionality', covering all areas of business activity, for example finance, purchasing, distribution, etc. With the advances in the use of the internet, many payroll software companies are making products available online. This is useful to allow a payroll department in one country to have direct online access to payroll software in another country. Also, as the internet does not 'close', the system availability can be 24 hours, seven days a week.

Factors to consider for an international payroll policy

First, one must understand what an international payroll means. After all the reviewing and theory, it really just means making payments in more than one country. In fact if you are paying in England and Scotland, you are already in effect running an international payroll.

The real challenges are how to pay to more than one country when those countries have different legislative requirements and where the situation is made more complex by differences in language, time zone or cultural expectations.

Challenges to setting an international payroll policy

The problem with structuring an international payroll is that neither home nor host company is necessarily a large organization. The other issue is that often the practicalities of how people are going to be paid are at the bottom of the assessment when organizations elect to expand, and consequently the organizations fail to appreciate and therefore communicate the tax and social security implications of their strategy. In fact, for many organizations, the decision as to whether an employee will enter a country to start working is often made long before the consideration of how payment will be made.

Employers go to new countries to expand their market availability, perhaps even to qualify for trading advantages because of low wages or trading tax incentives. Incentives around business regulations usually relate to trading activity alone; the employment legislation regulations are rarely altered from core rules. Understanding what those rules are can be a major headache for employers.

The core administration issues will be language, time zone, culture, and the perception of the role and aims of the business. HR will be focused on the selection of the most effective person for the management role whilst appointing within both business and legislation compliance for both the host and the home country.

Payroll will be focused on paying the employee correctly (the right amount at the right time), complying with both company and statutory regulations, and providing the correct reporting of costs to the necessary financial areas.

Companies rarely set up official policies when they first expand. They do not often recognize that there may be a need, especially in initial cases of expansion. Some believe that, as each country is likely to have its own specific legislative needs, it will also have its own specialist recruitment requirements – that different deals will be needed for each country to get the most appropriate staff. There is an element of fact in the latter but it is only a small part of the process.

If an organization fails to set the parameters of what it is willing to hold as standard offerings there is a serious danger that management will find itself in a complex situation of multiple agreements, paying over the odds for the roles required, and caught up in contracts that are expensive and difficult to remove or change. Multiple approaches to agreements can lead to multiple errors.

In particular, it is known how expensive it is to recruit good staff, and if care is not taken it can be a very costly exercise that wastes company resources and loses business opportunity when the process is not properly controlled.

An international policy can promote proper consideration of all aspects of recruitment: the selection process; the identification of reward (salary and benefits); and, critically, clarity in terms of how the contract can be brought to an end. The need to adhere to a proper procedure should include steps to ensure that statutory compliance is respected and that all company managers are aware of the company requirements.

A sound procedure will promote equitable treatment for employees nationally and globally, meaning that staff can have the opportunity to be flexible without fear of significant changes in their conditions. An international policy is only effective if the senior members of the business agree to support and promote it, so the board must be champions of any such agreement.

The policy must consider the four critical phases in the placement of someone in an international role:

1. *Assessing the need for the role.* Is the job required and who should do it? Will it be an internal or international placement?

2. *Recruitment and appointment.* What is required? How is the individual selected and what type of contract is being offered (fixed or open)?

3. *Reward.* What are the salary, terms or conditions, benefits, overseas allowances, treatment of family, integration values, relocation deals, leave entitlement, etc? Care is needed to assess what family issues may arise, such as schools, home flights, etc. What legal requirements will there be? Will individuals have to process their visa claims or is it a company-sponsored activity?

4. *Termination treatment.* Is this a fixed role? Is the person to be reabsorbed into the home business? What happens if the organization dismisses the person? What if the person resigns?

In addition, consideration of training requirements must be assessed. In this respect motivation and training are required when placing an international appointment. How will local staff feel? What is the long-term expectation for that relationship?

On appointment, payroll will need critical information. This will include when and how much, of course, but there are other issues. Benefits are treated differently depending on the individual country; there may be a requirement to pay in different places, even in different currencies. A decision is needed as to what the exchange rate rules are. Is the company agreeing a net or gross wage, ie what happens with the different exchange rate every month? Does the employee or the employer pick up the fluctuation?

Working in some countries can mean a dual tax liability, ie the employee pays tax in two places, both home and host country. What does the employer expect to happen in such a situation?

In addition, payroll needs to know who is to authorize the payments. Is it to be a fixed sum unless told otherwise, or is payroll to pay each month only as specifically authorized and on whose authority?

What about those benefits? Will they be processed through payroll, local cash box or accounts payable? How will payroll be told about any additional items, such as a company car, meals, or other goods or services paid for?

And what about the finance of the payroll? Is the payroll department going to provide a gross-to-net finance review of costs, or is the company expecting payroll merely to process the net payment, with finance placing a notional reserve for the tax liability?

All of these questions will need to be addressed and the answers communicated to everyone affected by the deployment of expatriate employees.

Outsource, home based or in-source

When an organization decides to trade internationally, it can be looking at having a business of two or 200,000 people. When setting up a small organization, the home payroll has to assess whether it has the capabilities to learn and administer the legislative aspect of a payroll. There are high costs in running specialist payrolls for small numbers, and there is also the complexity of maintaining legislative knowledge.

Where the head office is only monitoring expatriate employees, it can be cost-effective to place the individuals' payroll records in the hands of an outsource support such as a finance advisory house, where it has the resources to monitor legislative requirements. However, where there is a direct involvement with expatriate employees, it remains necessary to have a close appreciation of what is happening to people being sent overseas, as very often there is still a need to report their pay records clearly to avoid home taxation issues.

The larger the work base, however, the greater the chance will be that either a suitable in-house system can be operated – either in the home or in a host country – or a purer form of bureau service will be used. If you choose to seek the support of a payroll bureau that is focused on payroll services alone, your decision should be based on four criteria:

1. *cost:* the benefit of the process that is most cost-effective;

2. *reporting:* ease of provision of cost assessment for overhead appreciation;

3. *compliance:* whether the home or host country can maintain strict security compliance;

4. *security:* where procedures and standards can be maintained most effectively.

Each case is different – it depends on the software in use, staff skills and abilities, company and statutory complexity, and the company mission, whether this is an ongoing or fixed-term ambition. Whatever is agreed, the employer has to recognize that it cannot opt out of its legal responsibilities; outsourcing does not remove the obligation to ensure compliance.

Training is critical whether in-sourced or outsourced and should make use of the most appropriate expertise in the country affected. So, if the company is paying in the United States, for example, you will need to make sure that it is associated with relevant organizations such as the American Payroll Association; if in Canada, it is the Canadian Payroll Association, and so on.

MONITORING TAX AND SOCIAL SECURITY ADMINISTRATION

A key element in the effective monitoring of tax and social security administration is to have a strong idea of the sequence of activities that are required to be undertaken by internal and external resources and, in particular, where you need joint working procedures and combined processes to ensure the successful implementation of policy that affects tax and social security administration.

With regard to how to begin considering which of the various people who might be involved in the expatriate process may have a direct or indirect impact on your tax and social security administration, you could start by considering the key categories for UK tax purposes of foreign nationals working in the UK. As a simple first step, this will enable you to consider the consequences for each category in terms of, for example, the immigration, work permit and visas angles, and the tax and social security consequences. You would then have the beginning of an easy and simple framework (as in Table 2.3.1) that will help you begin to monitor performance.

Table 2.3.1   A simple monitoring framework

Short-Term Business Visitors	Longer-Term Visitors	Long-Stay Residents
Visitors to the UK for 1 to 30 days.	Remain in the UK for at least two years.	UK residents who have been UK residents for more than seven of the past 10 years.
Visitors to the UK for 31 to 60 days.	Intend to stay in the UK for at least three years.	
Visitors to the UK for 61 to 90 days.		
Visitors to the UK for 91 to 183 days.		

A starting point is to identify the roles and responsibilities of people who directly and indirectly influence tax and social security administration. Process mapping enables you clearly and simply to record existing approaches to required actions, examine them and develop improvements by:

▌ eliminating unnecessary tasks;

▌ clarifying roles within the process;

▌ reducing delays and duplication;

▌ reducing the number of staff required.

Process mapping will also enable the execution of a strategically linked process or partnership with any required third-party vendor by:

▌ identifying areas of duplication;

▌ agreeing common processes;

▌ improving communication with third-party vendors;

▌ achieving maximum effectiveness of internal and external operations.

Process mapping involves the use of flow charts to show what services people provide and how they should interact with one another as part of the process. You should be able to see from Table 2.3.2 what people are responsible for and how they fit with others in the system.

Processes are a sequence of actions designed to ensure that the information collected is delivered in the correct format to the appropriate person. For instance, a simple task like completing an arrival document P86 will involve information from various sources, possibly both internal and external. Similarly, the steps required to deal with a personal tax return from the gathering of the required information to the submission of the completed form will involve a process or a series of processes.

Process mapping is an exercise to identify all the steps and decisions in a process in diagrammatic form, which:

▌ describes the flow of information and documents;

▌ displays the various tasks contained within the process;

▌ shows that the tasks transform inputs into outputs;

▌ indicates the decisions that need to be made along the chain;

▌ demonstrates the essential interrelationships and interdependence between the process steps.

Process mapping will help you to identify problem areas such as bottlenecks, capacity issues, delays or waste. You should be able:

▌ to establish what is currently happening or what you need to happen, how predictably and why;

▌ to measure how efficiently the process is working;

▌ to gather information to understand where waste and inefficiency exist and their impact on the service provided to the various stakeholders;

▌ to develop improved processes to reduce or eliminate inefficiency.

When you plan your preparations for process mapping you should involve all of those who work in and around the process. All of the following need to be involved:

▌ internal and external people who do the work;

▌ those who provide information;

▌ the expatriate employees;

▌ the supervisor of the process.

Depending on what services you are able or choose to provide from internal resources, you may need to consider monitoring the involvement of:

▌ business unit leaders;

▌ HR specialists;

▌ the finance team;

▌ tax and social security vendors;

▌ immigration lawyers;

▌ relocation agents;

▌ payroll managers; and

▌ expatriate employees

in the areas where they have responsibility, as identified in Table 2.3.2.

Table 2.3.2 Internal resources to be monitored

Source	Subject to Monitor
Business Unit	Costs and budgeting.
	Time frames.
HR	Salary and benefit changes.
	Expense management.
Finance and Legal	Budgets.
	Cost centres.
	Accounting information.
Immigration Specialists	Work permits and visa expiry dates.
Relocation Agents	Accommodation and removal expenses.
Payroll Managers	Modified PAYE operation.
	End-of-year documents administration.
Expatriate Employees	Arrival and departure information.
	Annual personal tax return preparation.

The author acknowledges with thanks the contribution of notes and text to this chapter by Alison Ward of the Institute of Payroll Professionals (IPP).

Appraisal checklist for international employment strategy and administration

Stephen Asher, Frank Hirth plc

STRATEGY

1. How would you describe the focus of your corporate international strategy?
   - Grow new markets.
   - Develop new products and services.
   - Recruit and retain the best people.
   - Improve customer satisfaction.
   - Drive operational efficiency.

2. What are your organizational objectives in respect of your corporate international employment strategy?
   - Send experienced personnel to establish new markets.
   - Train locals from new markets to establish markets to gain skills.
   - Create teams for specific objectives (eg new products, systems or processes development).
   - Transfer and share knowledge.
   - Send experienced personnel to address specific operational problems and needs.
   - Broaden experience.

3. What are your operational objectives in executing the corporate international employment strategy?
   – Limitation of operational risks.
   – Minimization of operational costs.
   – Motivation and retention of employees.

TAXATION AND SOCIAL SECURITY ADMINISTRATION

1. How do you manage your taxation and social security information and data flow requirements?
   – Track all salary, bonus, benefits, expenses and equity incentive events manually.
   – Use document and database management tools.
   – Link tracking to requirements of internal and external reporting.
   – Taxation and social security information and data flow requirements not managed.

2. How do you communicate and monitor your taxation and social security information?
   – Define roles and responsibilities and share this information with all stakeholders.
   – Map processes to deliver current tax services and use deployment flow charts.
   – Check and test the activities sequence and decision points.
   – Continuously examine current processes and challenge who does what.
   – No communication or monitoring of taxation and social security information.

COMPENSATION, BENEFIT AND EXPATRIATE SUPPORT

1. What compensation and benefit design issues are covered by your international employment policy?
   – Pensions.
   – Bonuses and share options.
   – Practical payroll considerations.
   – UK and offshore payrolls.
   – Pros and cons of outsourced payroll services.

- Termination payments.

2. What expatriate support services do you provide?
   - Banking arrangements.
   - Expatriate insurance.
   - Relocation services.
   - Frequent travel arrangements.
   - Accommodation alternatives for extended stays.
   - Recruitment and offshore employment companies.

COMMUNICATION

1. What best describes your international employment process today?
   - Manual, file driven, exception focused.
   - Stand-alone system, centralized expertise.
   - Stand-alone system, regionally focused policy, exceptions, etc.
   - Partially integrated systems and consistent policy.
   - Consistent and process driven through current, scalable technology.

2. How much time do you spend per week communicating with your expatriate employees and service providers worldwide (eg relaying information and answering logistical questions)?
   - More than I can calculate.
   - About 50 per cent of my time.
   - Between 25 per cent and 50 per cent of my time.
   - Between 10 per cent and 25 per cent of my time.
   - Very little; service providers and expatriates can get the majority of the information through our intranet/website.

3. What level of access do expatriates currently have to their relocation information?
   - HR contact only.
   - HR contact and 24/7 access to the policy.
   - HR contact and access to their own data through the internet.
   - All of the above and direct contact with all service providers.
   - All of the above plus relevant host country information, easy-to-follow to-do lists, and all information accessible 24/7 in one place.

4. How do you initiate/contact a service provider for services?
   - We need to find the correct provider first.
   - We call/e-mail them.
   - We call/e-mail, and fax a form.
   - We use online forms and e-mail information to them.

- We have a work-flow system that automatically notifies our service providers of a new expatriate.

5. How do you communicate policy/benefit changes for expatriates?
    - We update our policy and give it to new expats only.
    - We fax offices with the official change form, and we expect host location managers to communicate changes.
    - We send an e-mail notification to those expats for whom we have addresses.
    - We send an attachment to an e-mail distribution list of all current expatriates.
    - Our policy is updated online and accessible online for all expatriates. We also broadcast changes via a dynamically created distribution list.

REPORTING CAPABILITY AND DATA INTEGRITY

1. How do you survey your expatriate population?
    - We don't do surveys.
    - We use data gathered by our service providers.
    - We use internal staff time.
    - We hire an outside firm to survey.
    - We have a mechanism or web-based tool to continually survey expatriates.

2. What is your current view on benchmarking your policy?
    - We don't have time to benchmark and just hope that all is smooth and current.
    - I believe someone thinks about this every five years or so.
    - An outside firm sends us a report every couple of years.
    - We regularly compare our policy to that of other companies within our industry.
    - We have an electronic means to compare policies.

3. When conducting a survey, what is the response rate from expatriates?
    - We do not invite feedback.
    - If we're lucky, 0–25 per cent.
    - 25–50 per cent.
    - 50–75 per cent.
    - 75–100 per cent.

4. How difficult is it for you to create an accurate worldwide report on your expatriates?
    - It would take blood, sweat and tears to pull something together.
    - I would have to gather the data manually from each country.
    - Not too hard; I contact regional managers to get the data.
    - All of the data to create a report are in our current database, but the data integrity is questionable.
    - Very easy; I can pull any data off an online system that is always current.

5. How difficult is it for you to change a report or develop an ad hoc report?
    - We only have a limited amount of canned reports.
    - We can manipulate information within Access or Excel.
    - Ad hoc reports are possible but would take a lot of time to gather.
    - Reportable data are flexible, so changes are not difficult.
    - We can download any information from our database and sort, organize and present the data almost effortlessly.

TECHNOLOGY

1. How much time do you spend on manual processes (eg re-entering duplicate data, copying fields on to forms, organizing paperwork, tallying expense reports)?
    - Most of my time.
    - At least half of my time.
    - About a quarter of my time.
    - Less than a quarter of my time.
    - Very little; our processes are automated through internal systems.

2. Into how many HR systems are expatriate data manually entered?
    - We don't have a system; information is manually entered as appropriate.
    - At least three databases (HR, home payroll, host payroll, etc).
    - Expatriate database and payroll.
    - HR/expat system only.
    - Our systems are integrated, so, once data have been entered, the information fills other systems.

3. How much IT support is given for HR technology initiatives?
    - None.
    - If we beg and plead and make it top of their project list... maybe.
    - We have an HRIS department and it is generally supportive.

- HRIS has a budget for expatriate technology, but full-time support is limited.
- We have a fully dedicated HRIS or the technology is outsourced.

4. Describe your corporate technology initiatives:
   - We are currently working to get all expatriates connected to e-mail.
   - We use a client server and manual processes.
   - We are rolling out a company-wide intranet.
   - We are continually adding to our company intranet.
   - We are moving all information flow to the web.

5. Who has access to your expatriate data management system?
   - HR only in one location.
   - HR and payroll in one location.
   - HR, payroll and admin worldwide.
   - All of the above and service providers.
   - All of the above and the expatriates and their families.

SERVICE QUALITY

1. What is the ratio of administrators to expatriates within your organization? (Consider home and host country, HR, admin, payroll, IT, travel, relocation, etc.)
   - Don't know.
   - One administrator to 10 expatriates.
   - One administrator to 20 expatriates.
   - One administrator to 50 expatriates.
   - One administrator to 75 expatriates.

2. What type of country-specific data do you provide to your expatriates?
   - They are on their own to research.
   - We provide some books and videotapes.
   - We purchase country-specific data from a vendor.
   - We have online access to country-specific data from a vendor or websites.
   - All of the above plus access to discussion forums, directories and data links for most countries.

3. How does the expatriate know what to do next in preparing for a transfer?
   - The expatriate finds out as things arise.
   - We provide a manual and wait for any questions.
   - Above option plus the service providers assist the employee.
   - Above options plus a checklist of all necessary items.

- We have an online to-do list that sends the employee reminders about every step of the transfer process.

4. How often does your company evaluate your current service providers?
   - We do not evaluate. We wait for complaints and then make changes.
   - Whenever the vendor provides complaints.
   - By management decree.
   - When the contracts need to be renegotiated.
   - Regularly (on an annual basis).

5. What is your vision for expatriate administration?
   - Organized files and better communication.
   - Consolidated processes.
   - Less paperwork, data entry and duplicated information.
   - A single system to handle all of the data, accessible by all who need the data.
   - All of the above.

Part 3

Compensation, benefit and expatriate support

Compensation, benefit and support design

Stephen Asher, Frank Hirth plc

At a time when traditional international relocation assignments are giving way to more short-term and localized assignments, as well as cross-border commuting and international team configurations, salary and benefits are considered to be the number one challenge and cost for employers of internationally mobile employees.

When considering how to design an international compensation and benefit policy there is a balance to be achieved between cost containment, limiting risks and employee satisfaction in each of the different categories of assignment, as the type of assignment will have some bearing on the total remuneration mix of compensation and benefits.

For example, a simple generic comparison of the basis of pay differentiation between categories of visitors to the UK for tax purposes might focus your planning along the lines identified in Table 3.1.1.

Your approach to expatriate compensation in each situation will need to take account of what issues can make the individuals worse off. For example, typical areas for consideration will include:

1. adverse tax regulations and higher effective tax rates;

2. exchange rate conversions, fluctuations and cost-of-living differentials;

3. a shortfall in pension benefit entitlement;

4. the timing of cross-border taxation of equity-based and deferred compensation.

Table 3.1.1 Compensation differentiation between categories of UK visitors

Items	Short-Term Visitors	Long-Term Visitors	Long-Stay Residents
Salary	Home-based pay.	Home-based pay plus fixed allowances.	Localized base pay.
Bonuses	Home related.	Home and host related.	Localized.
Pensions	Normally kept in home pension plan.	Normally kept in home pension plan.	Typically participate in host country pension plan after three to five years.
Stock Options	Home plan.	Home and host plan.	Localized plan.
Financial Reimbursement	Home based.	Currency, cost of living, tax and social security equalization, or protection.	Localization of package including currency; unlikely to be tax equalized or protected. This will typically not involve the buy-out of the cross-border package but will be based on the setting of a local salary benchmarked against the local market.
Housing	Hotel costs.	Leased.	No support.
Transportation	Public transport and taxis.	Company car.	Company car or no allowance or provision.
School Fees	Family unlikely to travel for short periods.	Family more likely to travel.	No support.
Medical Insurance	Home plan.	International plan.	Localized plan.

You will also need to consider the impact of softer issues such as the cost of providing for critical school years, or career spouses and their ability to obtain employment in the host location.

ADVERSE TAX REGULATIONS AND HIGHER EFFECTIVE TAX RATES

Even if you have only one international assignee, an understanding of the interaction between compensation, benefits and taxes is crucial to effective compensation and benefit planning. A documented tax reimbursement policy will aid the effectiveness of your communication and of your overall tax and social security administration. You will need to consider the type of taxation philosophy that is appropriate, such as tax equalization, tax protection and laissez-faire. A clear definition around your tax policy is critical to ensure the overall tax compliance and the design of compensation and benefit packages.

There is a real challenge in being able to explain the policy to employees in such a way that they are not confused or proceed on the basis of a misunderstanding of how the policy applies to their package.

Each country and local taxing jurisdiction has different rules defining when an individual becomes taxable. Some countries use days of presence within their borders during the tax year to determine taxability, while others may look at days of presence in a time period of up to 10 years. Days of presence can be defined differently in different places.

Other countries use income thresholds to determine when an individual becomes taxable. An expatriate who works a few days on foreign soil often exceeds this type of threshold. In addition, the rules may differ between social security and income tax obligations.

To limit the impact of foreign tax liabilities, an employer should be able to confirm not only at what point an individual will be subject to income tax in a specific jurisdiction, but also whether any particular type of visa or other work authorization could lead to a reduced rate of, or exemption from, taxation.

International employers adopt a number of different approaches to tracking and monitoring international business travellers. Some organizations place the onus on employees to keep track of their time and to notify HR only where it appears that they will exceed a predetermined number of days in one country. Other employers prefer to monitor the situation internally by reviewing time reports or analysing accounts payable or travel documents. However, regardless of the method followed, it may be important to set thresholds that relate to the actual filing requirements in a particular country.

There are a number of different ways of structuring how employees work in foreign locations. One of the most important considerations is how to deal with the effect of variable tax rates in different countries on the individual's net pay. Where marginal tax and social security rates are higher (even after relief for double taxation has been claimed), typically employers reimburse employees for the additional amounts incurred. The question then remains of who has the benefit when lower rates are encountered and how you introduce parity between different categories of expatriate employee.

It follows therefore that, where there are no foreign tax issues (eg by virtue of treaty exemption), the need for a formal tax reimbursement policy is minimized. Once you have established if, where and what level of foreign tax liabilities are likely to be incurred, then an appropriate policy for reimbursing the expatriate employee and/or the employer should be considered.

As well as the tax implications of employees working in foreign locations, it is important to understand whether the expatriate should be on a formal assignment to another location or simply engaged in extensive business travel as part of his or her normal employment. This will in turn affect the liability to tax in each country and the availability of double tax treaty relief, as well as the mechanisms for withholding tax and social security.

To be effective a tax reimbursement policy needs to:

▮ be aligned with overall strategy for international employee mobility;

▮ be aligned with how the employees actually conduct their international travel;

▮ make sure that the related compliance matters are managed in a way that ensures the expatriates are able to focus on the business objectives as opposed to whether they will pay additional tax if they spend time in the 'wrong' place or claim reimbursement of expense in the 'best' way;

▮ be appropriate for the employer in terms of its international infrastructure and ability to manage the practicalities of policy requirements;

▮ be sufficiently flexible to accommodate a range of individual circumstances and the corporate need to incentivize employees;

▮ be sufficiently adaptable to meet the changing needs of the organization as it grows internationally;

▮ work within the corporate budget for the post.

Some employers follow an ad hoc approach to tax reimbursement where each individual is treated differently. This may well be appropriate with a small number of assignees, but as the population grows employers often find it helpful to formulate a tax policy.

Once the general policy has been agreed, it is crucial to put it in writing and communicate it to the employees covered. As with any type of personnel policy, it is important to be specific regarding the provisions. For example, a tax equalization policy that simply states 'The employee will incur neither greater nor lesser taxes due to the foreign assignment' is likely to leave many issues open to interpretation and result in misunderstandings that lead to significant policy exceptions.

The following are the common approaches taken to international tax policy:

▌ laissez-faire;

▌ tax protection; and

▌ tax equalization.

Laissez-faire

Effectively, this is where the employer does not operate a tax policy for international assignments and makes it clear that the individual is responsible in full for all the resulting taxes from being on a foreign assignment. The advantages are:

1. It is simple for the employer and requires no work on its part.

2. It is beneficial for the assignee if the host tax rates are lower.

3. It may help promote assimilation of the assignee to the foreign host.

The disadvantages are:

1. There is a risk of non-compliance if the assignee is not responsible or does not have a full understanding of the foreign tax requirements. If the employee gets it wrong or does not manage to maintain an up-to-date tax record, then this may result in enquiries into the employer's tax affairs.

2. It can be expensive for the expatriate if the host country tax rates are higher. This can also be an unpleasant surprise that affects performance and the business objectives for the assignment, and can encourage non-compliance.

3.   There is a high administrative burden for the expatriate.

4.   It can reduce the international mobility of employees.

An important consideration is the effect on the overall international mobility of employees. Individuals need to be sent where the company has the need for them. Where an employer takes a laissez-faire approach, the most attractive locations will be where the host effective tax rates are the lowest, as this will result in a higher income for the expatriate. Conversely, where the host effective tax rates are higher the individual will suffer a reduction in net income. This change in cash flow may influence the decision of whether or not to accept a foreign assignment and may also influence performance, rewarding on the basis of location rather than performance.

Tax protection

Tax protection plans are designed to ensure that an expatriate is not worse off, from a tax point of view, as a result of either foreign business travel or a foreign assignment compared with remaining at home.

The employer uses as a base the gross salary that the expatriate would earn in his or her home country. The employer then computes the tax that the expatriate would have paid on the income, and the after-tax disposable income the employee would have received had he or she stayed home. As a minimum, this amount is then guaranteed to the executive during the assignment.

In addition, the employer may provide extra allowances, such as cost-of-living allowances, to enable the executive to maintain his or her standard of living in the host country, and again these would be computed to guarantee an agreed net amount to the expatriate.

If the actual taxes suffered in the home and host country during the assignment are lower than those that would have been suffered had the employee remained at home (eg owing to lower rates of tax in the host country), the expatriate is allowed to retain the benefit. That is, the employee does not have to reimburse the employer for the difference. This is known as a tax 'windfall'.

If, however, the taxes payable as a result of the assignment are higher than they would have been had the expatriate remained at home, the employer will ensure that the assignee's disposable income is maintained by increasing his or her remuneration or allowances to take account of the higher taxes. This could be achieved either by paying an increased salary during the assignment or by paying an allowance to reimburse excess tax costs once the expatriate's tax liabilities are settled. Under this method, therefore, the expatriate is 'protected' from the effect of higher taxes that arise as a result of the assignment.

The advantage is that the expatriate is allowed the benefit of lower host tax rates, making the assignment attractive to employees.

The disadvantages are:

▌ It can discourage international activity. The executives will be more willing to travel to or locate to countries where they will gain a cash flow advantage.

▌ It can encourage executives to focus on tax savings, not the actual work.

▌ The policy is an expense to the employer. If expatriates are located in high-tax locations, this results in a cost to the employer without gaining any benefit from expatriates who are based in low-tax locations.

Tax equalization

Tax equalization is designed to ensure that an expatriate has neither tax advantage nor disadvantage through being on a foreign assignment. This is known as the 'balance sheet approach'.

As a starting point, expatriates receive the same net income that they would have received had they remained in their home country. An amount representing the income tax that the assignee would have suffered in the home country (termed 'hypothetical tax') is retained by the employer and used to pay, or contribute towards, the tax that is payable in the host country on the expatriate's salary.

In addition, the employer may provide allowances to the expatriate (eg to take account of the higher cost of living in the host country or to enable the assignee to obtain accommodation). Such allowances are also paid to the assignee on a 'net basis', ie the expatriate receives an agreed amount and the employer pays any income tax due once it is agreed with the tax authorities in the host country.

At the appropriate time (ie when income tax payments are required to be made), the employer will compute the gross income that would be required to deliver the net after-tax income that the expatriate has received and hence the income tax that is payable in the host country.

The employer assumes responsibility for all taxes due (home and host countries), and the expatriate's liability is restricted to the 'stay at home' or hypothetical liability. If the taxes payable are less than the hypothetical tax retained by the employer (ie the tax that would have been paid had the expatriate remained at home), the saving will accrue to the employer. If, however, the tax payable in the host country is greater than the tax that would have been payable in the home country (either because of higher tax rates or because of the assignment allowances provided to the assignee), the excess is borne by the employer under this arrangement.

There may be strategies available to help minimize the tax liability of the expatriate employee. If the expatriate is tax equalized then these tax savings will benefit the employer. For this reason, it is desirable for the employer to require its expatriates to participate in tax briefings so that the employee is aware of tax planning opportunities and can play an active role in reducing tax costs.

The advantages are:

▌ Out of the three options this is the most complex. However, it can be a simple policy to administer if the correct systems are in place.

▌ The employer keeps the tax benefit of having expatriates in low-tax countries, which helps to offset the tax costs of having expatriates in high-tax countries. This is unlike tax protection, which is only an expense to the employer.

▌ Expatriate compliance with the foreign country's tax authorities is encouraged through the involvement of professional advisers. Also, any temptation on the part of the executive to under-report income is removed, as this will have no tax consequences for the individual.

▌ The strategies available to help minimize the tax liability of the assignee will benefit the employer.

The disadvantages are:

▌ The expatriates cannot take advantage of lower tax rates.

▌ It does not help the expatriates to become assimilated to a host environment. Rather, by keeping the executive 'whole', it recognizes differences based on nationality.

▌ The 'tax on tax' impact of paying net salary to the employee can be a major expense to an employer.

Careful consideration of the type of income to be covered by any tax policy needs to be undertaken. For example, it is not uncommon for an employee to sell an asset and realize a capital gain while on international assignment. The gain might have been tax-free in the home country but fully taxable in the host location. The policy needs to cover clearly where the responsibility sits for all income, not just employment income.

3.2

Remuneration strategy formulation and design

Natarajan Sundar, Orgdesign Limited

In an increasingly competitive world, each organization has to formulate a unique remuneration strategy aligned with its own business priorities and human resources agenda. The remuneration structure and the fixed-versus-variable pay mix should address its specific challenges, and enable the company to attract and retain required talent in the context of the relevant market and help drive performance. Short-term and long-term incentives should incorporate performance measures that reflect the creation of shareholder value for the company. A case study of Unilever at the end of this chapter illustrates various aspects of remuneration strategy formulation and design.

Remuneration, or the financial returns that people receive from their employers, is among the most important reasons why they work for an organization. For the employers, remuneration is among the biggest costs. The way in which remuneration is determined and paid has a significant bearing on the quality of people it attracts and its performance. Even though remuneration is a major cost, the challenge lies less in controlling it and more in deriving the maximum benefit for the individual and the organization. Therefore, within broad limits of the prevalent norms and practices in the country and the industry, each company has to formulate its own unique remuneration strategy, structure and design. This chapter focuses on the financial rewards, fully mindful that non-financial rewards, such as career, job satisfaction, training and felt-fairness, are at least as important.

REMUNERATION STRATEGY

A good remuneration strategy has three basic policy objectives:

▪ *Attract and retain the quality of people the organization needs and in the required numbers.* To be able to do so, the organization has to be competitive in the market, the 'relevant' market for this purpose being defined in the context of the company's line of business and its strategy.

▪ *Deliver performance.* While what matters ultimately is the performance of the company as a whole, it is the performance of individuals, teams, units and divisions that adds up to corporate performance. Therefore, how performance is defined, measured at various levels and linked with rewards is the second crucial element of remuneration. The company's business strategy and the human resources agenda become important, as it is with these that the remuneration has to be aligned. In turn, this will result in alignment with shareholder interests. The watchword is 'alignment'.

▪ *Enable 'felt-fairness'.* The crucial thing about money is not just how much people are paid but how much in comparison with others, especially those in the same organization. People increasingly accept that differentiation in rewards on the basis of performance is inevitable in the competitive global world, but they want it done in a fair, transparent and objective way. Ensuring a general feeling of 'felt-fairness' requires robust systems, processes and communication, not just in remuneration but in all HR practices.

While external competitiveness, performance link and internal equity are the three key elements of remuneration, all these need to be achieved at minimal cost.

FORMULATING REMUNERATION STRATEGY

Strategy is about being clear on where one wants to be and, broadly, how to get there: formulating a unique winning approach that takes account of the opportunities and risks, core strengths and weaknesses. In today's globally competitive world, organizations need a strategy that deals with their unique context and challenges in human resources including, importantly, remuneration. The remuneration strategy itself should be a differentiating, competitive advantage for the organization.

The industry in which an organization operates has a major impact on the remuneration strategy. There is a wide range of scenarios.

At one extreme are industries that are heavily skill and knowledge based, with relatively little capital, eg IT consultancies. Efficiency and effectiveness of human capital are paramount for their success. One of the world's largest IT consultancy companies ensures that 85 per cent of employee time is billable. These companies have to be very closely market aligned and have strong performance linkages with pay.

At the other extreme are highly capital-intensive industries. While they may need very high skills in technology and science, the numbers required are small and the human resource cost modest in comparison with revenue generation. Oil exploration and gas exploration, especially in the current high-oil-price context, are classic examples. Holding on to top talent is so crucial for such industries that they would not mind paying more than the competition.

Horses for courses

The stage of growth of a company also makes a big difference to remuneration strategy, even between companies within the same industry. At the start-up stage, there is particular need for successful business innovation, and the need is to attract talent of the highest calibre. A total remuneration position at the 75th percentile of the relevant market may be needed. However, the revenue stream in the innovation phase of a company is low. Cash remuneration, ie base salary and bonus, needs to be modest. But stock options have to be well above the market. As innovations pay off and start to be reflected in the share value, the employees also gain a share in the success of the company.

When a company is at a 'mature stage', the need is to control all costs to ensure that they deliver current value. The tendency is to aim at market median position on base pay and higher than median on total pay including incentives, provided that performance is delivered. However, as spectacular share price increases are not expected, the emphasis is on annual bonuses and on stock grants rather than stock options.

REMUNERATION STRUCTURE

'Structure follows strategy' – this is true of remuneration as much as of business. Clearly, it is not possible to achieve all the objectives of a good remuneration policy through one element of pay. It is therefore common to have a mix of pay elements. Some elements of pay are fixed or guaranteed to be paid during the year, for example base salary, pension and benefits

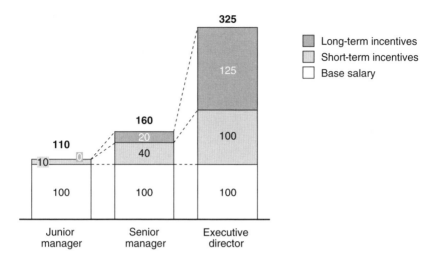

Figure 3.2.1 Remuneration structure across levels

such as health care or a car allowance. Other elements are dependent on, and indeed aimed at incentivizing, performance, both short-term and long-term. The higher that one rises in the organization, the greater the proportion of pay at risk.

Figure 3.2.1 shows the typical mix of pay at different levels in a large FTSE company in the UK. At the level of a junior manager, the bonus is modest and, barring exceptions, there is no long-term incentive. At the other extreme, executive directors qualify for a target annual bonus of 100 per cent of the base salary and a maximum of 125 per cent as the value of shares granted. The actual bonus can be between 0 and 150 per cent of the target bonus. Likewise, the actual performance-linked vesting of long-term incentives can be 0 to 100 per cent of the grant. More than two-thirds of executive directors' 'target' pay is therefore at risk.

REMUNERATION DESIGN

Once there is clarity on the remuneration strategy and structure, one has to decide on appropriate competitive positioning and actual design of incentives to translate them into remuneration plans.

Competitive positioning

Competitive positioning is about deciding whether the remuneration paid by the company should be at, above or below the market rate in relation to the 'markct'. First, one has to answer the question: what is the appropriate market? This depends on what the relevant pool of talent is and who else is competing for them. For most jobs, it is the local or national market, and for many jobs it is also the same industry. However, for some specialist and functional jobs, the competition is beyond the industry. Also, at the most senior levels, regional and international levels of pay become relevant.

Second, there is no such thing as a single 'market rate' for the job. However sophisticated a remuneration survey may be, it makes judgements (albeit informed) on job matches across companies with different organization structures and job profiles and converts the market data into statistical measures such as median, average, 75th percentile, etc. The median is exactly what it says: it could be that no one in the market is actually paid at that rate and merely that half are actually paid higher and the other half lower.

Third, even between two companies with the same total remuneration package, there may be significant differences in the mix. One company could be paying a relatively higher salary and modest bonuses, another a lower base salary but higher long-term incentives, and a third one actually less total remuneration than either but still attracting people because it provides superior non-financial rewards.

Companies therefore need to look at market data not as precise mathematical figures but as a reference point and decide on their own remuneration strategy and pay mix. This is particularly important for small companies. They do not necessarily have to match the big companies in each element of pay, or in total 'financial' remuneration, as they can often offer much better job challenges and working conditions.

Design of a short-term incentive plan

Short-term incentives are designed to include an upside potential, and a downside risk, linked to performance. Three key design issues are:

- What is the performance to be rewarded – the individual's, the company's or both?
- What will be the measure of company performance?
- How will individual performance be assessed?

Performance definition

Ultimately, only the company's overall performance is paramount. However, employee surveys show that paying everyone the same bonus does not help: no one likes 'free riders'. People want rewards to be commensurate with their performance. However, the danger in rewarding only individual performance is that it can hurt group effort. There are two ways of handling this. The traditional option is to have two separate elements of bonus, one for business results and the other for individual performance, and then add the two together to arrive at the total bonus for the individual. An alternative approach that is increasingly preferred is to link the overall bonus amount to business performance and, within the resulting 'budget', to base individuals' differentiation on their contribution.

Organizational performance measures

Each organization will need to choose those performance measures that best reflect its shareholder value creation. For an annual bonus these will usually include a profit measure and an efficiency measure, such as return on capital employed. There could be additional or alternative measures such as cash flow, volume, market share, business development, innovation, health, safety, security and environment.

Assessing individual performance

The standard practice is to agree explicit individual performance targets for the year and make an assessment of performance against these targets. This should not be simply an assessment at the end of the year. Instead, there should be regular performance reviews during the course of the year, with improvement achieved through training and coaching.

Design of long-term incentive plans

In the UK, the performance period for 'vesting' is typically three years, although in the case of stock options employees have a further period of seven years to exercise their options. There are two common types of long-term incentives: stock options and stock grants. A stock option is a right given to an employee to buy the shares of the company at a future date at a predetermined price. A stock grant is like a post-dated cheque: the employee will receive a certain number of shares at a future date. In both cases, there is a requirement that the employee should continue in the employment of the company until vesting, and there are usually performance conditions.

Stock options versus stock grants

Although stock options dominated throughout the 1990s, in recent years their popularity has waned. First, share price growth is not dependent just on company performance but on the industry and overall equity market trends. Second, in a bear market when options go 'under water' there is little 'incentive' value left. Lastly, options have to be expensed and the cost reflected in the profit and loss account of the company: not surprisingly, companies want the best value for money. For all these reasons, incentive plans based on whole shares rather than stock options have become more prevalent recently, especially for the top executives. In the UK, they generally tend to be performance shares, ie a promise to grant stock at a future date, subject to 'satisfactory' corporate performance. Performance shares always have some value, although the performance conditions have to be met. Stock options and stock grants are both relevant, depending on circumstances. Companies therefore tend to use them in a flexible and complementary way, with multiple but relevant performance conditions.

Performance conditions

Performance conditions should be aligned with shareholder interests and such that the employees can influence their achievement. Finding measures that satisfy both these criteria has been the Holy Grail in the last few years. With stock options, especially as they are often granted across levels of employees in an organization, the tendency is to go for simple 'internal' measures such as growth in 'earnings per share' or 'return on investment' to which all employees can relate.

   With stock grants, as they tend to be awarded mostly to the more senior management, the search is for 'external' and more objective performance measures. Total shareholder return (TSR) is considered to be most aligned with shareholder value creation and therefore commonly used. It is the return on investment obtained by holding a company's shares over a period, mainly determined by the change in the market value of shares and dividend flow. As the absolute TSR is heavily influenced by general equity market trends, 'relative' TSR, one that assesses the TSR of the company against a 'comparator group', is commonly used.

Tough choices

Formulating remuneration strategy, deciding on the remuneration structure and designing incentive plans all imply making tough choices. The processes followed are therefore as important as the substance. It is a challenge to come up with a unique, cost-efficient remuneration proposition for any organization within limits discernible in the market. Understanding what the employees really want and value, and engaging the line managers in the

Formulation of Unilever's remuneration strategy and design

Unilever is one of the world's largest consumer products companies, operating in over 100 countries with over 200,000 employees. Several of its brands are household names in home care, foods and ice cream: Dove, Pond's, Vaseline, Persil, Flora, Lipton, PG Tips, Hellmann's, Wall's, and Ben & Jerry's. In recent years, its challenge has been growing in *both* top line and bottom line at the same time. Volume growth alone can be achieved by sacrificing profits. Likewise, it is possible to grow profits in the short run by compromising on marketing and other 'investment' spend. Sustained growth in profits and, in turn, shareholder value can only be produced if there is also growth in volume.

During 2007, Unilever carried out a comprehensive review of its remuneration strategy, as well as the design of its short-term and long-term incentive plans. The overriding objective of its remuneration policy is to ensure that it recruits and retains the best performers and effectively incentivizes them to achieve superior results. It is also the aim to manage the differing elements of total remuneration in a fully integrated manner.

Five strategic principles serve as the platform for Unilever's approach to remuneration for its executive directors and other leadership team members:

■ alignment with shareholders' interests;

■ robust linkage to performance;

■ alignment with strategic priorities;

■ market competitiveness; and

■ ease of understanding and communication.

These five principles provide the foundation for the level and structure of Unilever's remuneration. The different elements of pay are complementary to one another. The remuneration structure shown in Table 3.2.1 pertains to the executive directors and the leadership team across countries, but the principles are valid for managers worldwide.

Table 3.2.1   Unilever remuneration structure

Element of Pay	Payment Vehicle	Value Determination	Plan Objectives
Fixed:			
Base Salary	Cash.	Market median.	Attract and retain high performers.
Pension	Remain in the home fund or equivalent value.		Attract and retain high performers.
Variable:		*As percentage of base salary:*	
Annual Bonus	Cash (75%), shares (25%).	For executive directors (EDs) up to a maximum of 150%.	Economic value added. Top-line growth. Individual key deliverables.
Global Share Incentive Long-Term Plan	Shares.	Grant level for EDs up to 180%. Vesting 0–200% of grant.	Shareholder return at upper half of peer group. Top-line growth. Free cash flow.
Share Matching Plan	Shares.	For EDs 25% of annual bonus paid as three-year deferred shares with a one-for-one match.	Alignment with shareholders' interests through executive shareholding. Retention.

Notes:
– The total remuneration package for executive directors is intended to be competitive in a global market, with a strong emphasis on performance-related pay.
– A significant proportion of EDs' total reward is linked to a number of key measures of group performance to create alignment with strategy, business priorities and shareholder value.
– The remuneration committee of the company sets both short-term and long-term performance targets. In so doing, it is guided by what would be required to deliver top-third shareholder value.
– Internal and external comparisons are made with the reward arrangements for other senior executives within Unilever to support consistent application of Unilever's executive reward policies.
(*Source:* Unilever report and accounts, 2007)

Compensation and benefit problem areas

Stephen Asher, Frank Hirth plc

EXCHANGE RATE CONVERSIONS AND FLUCTUATIONS AND COST-OF-LIVING DIFFERENTIALS

An employee can be paid solely in host country currency, in home country currency or in a percentage of each. Newly internationalizing employers may find consideration of how to manage the impact of exchange rate conversions and fluctuations the most difficult element of total remuneration they have to plan.

Very few expatriates will want to be paid 100 per cent in the host country currency, as they will most likely retain obligations in their home country that require payment in home currency, such as pension plan contributions, mortgages and school fees. Some employers provide guaranteed exchange rates or exchange rate protection policies that apply to a specific percentage of the assignment salary, thereby increasing or decreasing the tax liability.

Take for example a US citizen assigned from New York to London. He is paid in a salary based on US dollars but actually paid in both US dollars and sterling. The considerations relating to exchange rate conversions that need to be taken into account are: Will the equivalent sterling salary be sufficient for the individual to feed and clothe himself and his family in the same way they did in New York? And how will this affect his accommodation arrangements? Will he be able to afford a similar place in London on his sterling salary compared to New York?

If the differential is substantial, the business could consider adding a cost-of-living allowance or goods and service allowance to the assignment package. A number of independent agencies survey and compare the cost of food, utilities, accommodation and so on in different locations and provide an index to assist in determining the amount to be paid.

Taking the same example, a decision will also be needed on what exchange rate to apply when converting US dollars to sterling, for example internal monthly average rate, rate on the date of payroll processing or fixed exchange rate updated on the first day of each quarter.

There are a number of variations, and you will need to understand the circumstances of each employee to decide what is the most practical and easily understood solution. You will need to ensure that the exchange rates you apply are accepted by the tax authorities.

You will also need to address other considerations relating to exchange rate fluctuations. For example, in the two years to mid-2008, the US dollar severely weakened against sterling. This had a serious knock-on effect on the purchasing power of many expatriates working in London on US-dollar-based salaries.

There are a number of ways companies can protect their assignees against exchange rate fluctuations, for example:

▎ Fix the base salary in sterling at the start of the assignment and pay in sterling (the employee may want reassurances that this sterling salary is in line with UK market rates).

▎ Agree an exchange rate floor and/or ceiling, for example 1.80 to 1.95 or, say, the average rate for the three months leading up to the assignment. These exchange rates are indicative of the current climate and you will need to take account of the prevailing economic circumstances when you evaluate this approach.

▎ Ensure that the cost-of-living allowance or goods and service differential is updated regularly in line with exchange rate changes, eg monthly or quarterly.

SHORTFALL IN PENSION BENEFIT ENTITLEMENT

The easiest way to understand how cross-border employment can create a shortfall in expatriate long-term benefit entitlement is to consider expatriate pension arrangements.

When you review the impact of an expatriate compensation and benefits policy on expatriate pensions you will first need to determine whether an individual participates in, or can continue to participate in, one of the following retirement arrangements: a guaranteed home country retirement benefits plan; or a host country retirement programme for service in each country.

Typically, expatriate contracts guarantee their home country compensation and benefits. Therefore, there is no interruption in their retirement benefit accumulation. However, a particular problem arises when employees who had been working abroad on expatriate assignments go on to transfer to other countries, working in multiple countries over the course of their career.

In these situations, the typical solution has been for employees to begin participating in the retirement programme of each of the foreign entities in which they work. Therefore, expatriate employees may eventually participate in the retirement programmes of two, three or even more countries. As a result of this potential fragmentation of retirement arrangements, expatriates may face a shortfall in their retirement benefits.

The highly paid executive who was asked to accept a temporary assignment in another country is one example. Typically, such executives are guaranteed home country benefits and are on a formal expatriate package. For them, there is no shortfall at retirement, as there is no interruption in benefits earned during their career.

However, consider, by comparison, employees who have worked in multiple countries. These employees are on local benefits, payroll and employment agreements in each country and, because of that, can experience a shortfall at retirement. When you are considering your approach to compensation and benefit packages you will need to decide on your strategy to minimize these shortfalls.

One of the key challenges arises from the fact that service and earnings are recognized only in respect of the time the employee was working in that country. Even though these individuals may remain continuously employed by the home country legal entity, shortfalls can arise from the service-related vesting rules. Also, shortfalls may arise in respect of defined-benefit plans that provide benefits that are related to final average earnings.

The situation is complicated further when expatriate employees stay in their home country plan but are paid according to local host country salary scales. In these cases the employee's benefit accruals are sensitive to fluctuations in currency exchange rates.

As an alternative, providing for employees to participate in local plans may be a tax-effective approach that can be beneficial for employees planning on retiring to that host country, because they accrue benefits useful to them in the future. Indeed, keeping expatriates in their home country plan when they are on international assignment can cause legal and tax problems. There is no easy answer, owing to the complexity of legal and tax considerations in each country.

There may also be disadvantages for defined-contribution plans in terms of tax deductibility of contributions and whether the employer contributions are taxable to the employee. For expatriates who are US citizens you will need to understand that they may have a unique perspective that you need to accommodate. The only type of deferred compensation plan, defined benefit or defined contribution, in which a US taxpayer may participate without adverse tax consequences is one that complies with the qualified rules of the Internal Revenue Service (IRS). Participation in any funded plan that does not comply with IRS rules can result in the employee being subject to tax on imputed income arising from contributions to or benefits accruing under the plan.

In evaluating the most appropriate strategy for managing potential pension shortfalls you should be aware that transfers between overseas schemes can also be an issue.

The UK approach to tax planning in respect of pension plan participation for UK expatriates working in other countries and foreign nationals working in the UK has been simplified in recent years. Since 6 April 2006 (otherwise known as A-Day), anyone can participate in a UK-registered pension plan, regardless of whether their employment contract is with the home country or host country operations. However, they must have 'net relevant earnings', ie earnings that are not treaty exempt. Also, an employee cannot participate in two schemes on the same amount of pensionable earnings.

In addition, tax-effective benefits provided under all UK plans are limited to a lifetime allowance. Benefits earned while working outside the UK will in effect not count towards the lifetime allowance, as periods of overseas service attract an enhancement factor that increases an individual's lifetime allowance. This gives an expatriate the potential to earn higher tax-effective benefits than a UK-based employee.

However, an important point to build into your thinking is that UK employer contributions are not allowable for tax if the plan is not recognized as an 'overseas pension scheme' for the purpose of migrant member relief. For UK employers to get tax relief on contributions to overseas plans that they make for their expatriate employees, they have to register those plans with HMRC. Registered plans are then expected to meet the UK's requirements on benefit design, including those that limit how and when benefits can be paid.

Some shortfalls may also arise from the impact of social security. Under some pension plans an employee's state pension entitlements are built into the total pension entitlement. However, the degree of pension generosity varies greatly between countries. In those situations where an employee has participated in different country pension schemes and non-reciprocal social security systems, part of any employee's pension entitlement may rely on less generous social security benefits. For these reasons it is often preferable to try to maintain an employee in his or her home social security plan.

TIMING OF CROSS-BORDER TAXATION OF EQUITY-BASED AND DEFERRED COMPENSATION

For expatriate employees and employers, equity-based and deferred compensation arrangements can cause a great deal of confusion. This confusion is often the result of different countries having inconsistent interpretations of what triggers a taxation charge, together with a mismatch of the timing of the taxation arising from those triggers.

A place to start is to define a reward for completing or undertaking a specific assignment that may be seen as compensation for the inconvenience of a particular location or assignment in terms of its impact on the employee's domestic life or career planning. Often these schemes involve payment after an employee has left the country to which he or she was assigned.

Other reward schemes are part of a longer-term incentive and performance-related compensation plan that might not be related solely to a specific assignment but is paid out during a foreign assignment.

When looking at this issue from the perspective of share option arrangements it is helpful to consider the distinction highlighted by the OECD between US- and European-style arrangements. US-style option plans are granted with a future period of service required of the employee in order to qualify for exercise. By contrast, a European-style plan is seen to be in respect of past service.

It is helpful to start by considering the following: What does your organization mean by equity-based compensation and deferred compensation? Will any gains be covered in the expatriate policy or will taxes due have to be met by the employee?

Equity-based remuneration could comprise any of the following:

- employee share option plans;
- employee share ownership plans;

▌ sharc grant plans;

▌ share purchase plans;

▌ phantom stock plans;

▌ share appreciation rights;

▌ employee options granted by non-corporate employers;

▌ US section 423 plans.

Deferred compensation could involve:

▌ individual performance-related bonus schemes;

▌ assignment completion bonus schemes;

▌ business unit financial performance bonus schemes.

Once you have identified the type of compensation that is relevant you need to consider what information you need to collate:

▌ Category of expatriate – short-term visitors, long-term visitors, long-stay residents, other?

▌ One-off or perpetual expatriates?

▌ To what employment does the bonus relate?

▌ To what period of employment does the bonus relate?

▌ Where has the employee been, or where will the employee be, resident throughout this time?

▌ What type of equity-based plan is it?

▌ Approved or unapproved in home and host countries – where?

▌ When was the option granted, or when will it be granted?

▌ When does the option irrevocably vest?

▌ When will the option be exercised or otherwise disposed of?

▌ When will there no longer be any restrictions on the sale of the shares acquired under the options?

▌ When will the shares under the options be sold?

▌ How will you identify different country rules for taxing these events? Will you need internal or external assistance?

▌ Is the gain assessable to tax via the payroll? If you use an outsourced payroll provider, is it able to deal with this?

▌ Is the gain liable to employee and employer social security contributions? If so, have you built this into your tax reimbursement policy?

THINK LIST FOR DEVELOPING AN INTERNATIONAL COMPENSATION AND BENEFIT POLICY

1. How do you know which assignees require an international compensation and benefit policy?

2. How will you ensure your international compensation and benefit packages are competitive for your industry sector?

3. How will you decide in which currency to pay compensation?

4. How will you understand the impact of local prices on spendable income?

5. How will you ensure there are no benefit shortfalls in expatriate pension plans?

6. How will you ensure you reimburse only actual travel and subsistence costs?

7. How will you set limits on housing costs?

8. How will you manage the taxation process to ensure you collect all hypothetical taxes owed to the firm?

9. How will you ensure expatriates are charged for private use of company cars?

10. How will you ensure expatriate families are provided with orientation and settling-in services?

11. How will you ensure effective cross-border payroll management?

12. How will you ensure your assignees understand how their compensation and benefits package works?

13. How will you ensure there are no significant policy exceptions?

14. How will you ensure you get value for money from any third-party vendors?

15. How will you ensure your firm has agreed expense management and accounting procedures for expatriate costs and taxes?

The author acknowledges with thanks the contribution of notes and text to this chapter by Alison Ward of the Institute of Payroll Professionals (IPP).

Background information for compensation and benefit management

Stephen Asher, Frank Hirth plc

This chapter outlines the meaning of some key terms in expatriate employment.

ABROAD

'Abroad' (or 'overseas') means anywhere outside the home market.

AVERAGE NUMBER OF DAYS IN THE UK

The average number of days is used in determining a person's residence or ordinary residence status in the UK under extra-statutory concession A11. The calculation differs slightly according to whether the person is leaving or coming to the UK.

Absence from the UK

The average number of days is calculated over the period of absence from the UK up to a maximum of four years. In essence, the average is calculated by multiplying the total of the days visiting the UK by 365 and dividing the result by the total period since leaving the UK. Note that: any days spent in the UK because of exceptional circumstances beyond the person's control, such as illness (whether of the person or of a member of his or her immediate family), are not normally counted for this purpose; and days spent in the UK in the tax year before the date of the original departure are excluded.

Visiting the UK

The annual average number of days is calculated by multiplying the total of the days visiting the UK by 365 and dividing the result by the number of days in the relevant tax years. Note that: the number of days in the relevant tax years is either 365 or 366; and any days spent in the UK because of exceptional circumstances beyond the person's control, such as illness (whether of the person or of a member of his or her immediate family), are not normally counted for this purpose.

An individual who is currently not resident in the UK will always be treated as resident in the UK if he or she spends 183 days or more in the UK in a tax year. If the person visits the UK on a regular basis and spends, on average, 91 days or more in the UK in a tax year (taken over a period of four years), he or she will be treated as resident in the UK.

If a person knows that he or she is going to visit regularly and that the time spent in the UK in that and the next three tax years will average 91 days or more in the UK, the person will be resident from the beginning of the tax year in which he or she makes the first visit.

From April 2008, when deciding if an individual is resident in the UK for tax purposes, days will count if an individual is in the UK at midnight for residence test purposes.

There is now an additional exemption for passengers who are in transit between two places outside the UK. The exemption accommodates individuals who have to change airports or terminals when transiting through the UK. It also allows individuals to switch between modes of transport, so they could fly in but leave by ferry or train, for example. Days spent in transit, which could involve being in the UK at midnight, will not be counted as days of presence in the UK for residence test purposes so long as during transit the individual does not engage in activities that are to a substantial extent unrelated to his or her passage through the UK.

DOMICILE

Although there is no definition of domicile in UK income tax or National Insurance law, it has a relevance to the taxation of foreign emoluments.

In UK law there are three types of domicile:

1. A person's domicile of origin is determined at the time of birth and is the domicile of either the father or the mother.

2. If a person abandons his or her domicile of choice or dependency and does not take action to acquire a new domicile of choice, his or her domicile reverts to the domicile of origin. Under UK law it is very difficult for a person to alter his or her domicile by choice. To do so requires evidence that the person has completely abandoned his or her previous domicile.

3. A child's domicile is dependent on the domicile of his or her father or mother, and applies until legally he or she can change his or her domicile by choice. Women may have the domicile of their husband or of their own choice.

A person can have only one place of domicile at any one time. If a person changes his or her domicile during a year, for tax purposes it takes effect from the start of the following tax year.

A person's domicile may be a country, state, province or city, depending on the pertaining laws. In the UK a person is domiciled in England, Wales, Northern Ireland or Scotland and not in the UK.

The person's domicile is normally the place (eg the country) where he or she has his or her permanent home.

DOUBLE TAXATION

Double taxation occurs when income is liable to be taxed both by the taxpayer's country of residence and in another country where the income arises.

FOREIGN EMOLUMENTS

In this context, 'foreign emoluments' means the earnings of someone who is not domiciled in the UK and whose employer is resident outside (and not resident in) the UK (nor resident in the Republic of Ireland).

FULL TIME

In income tax law there is no precise definition of when employment overseas is classed as full time. However, where the employment involves a standard pattern of hours, HMRC regards it as full time if the hours worked each week clearly compare with those in a typical UK working week. If the person's job has no formal structure or no fixed number of working days, HMRC looks at the nature of the job, local conditions and practices in the particular occupation to decide if it is full time.

If the person has several part-time jobs overseas at the same time, HMRC may be able to treat this as full-time employment, for example where the person has several appointments with the same employer or group of companies or there is simultaneous employment and self-employment overseas. However, if the person has a main employment abroad and some unconnected occupation in the UK at the same time, HMRC will consider whether the extent of the UK activities is consistent with the overseas employment being full time.

LONGER-TERM VISITOR

A longer-term visitor is a person who visits the UK intending to remain indefinitely or for an extended period, perhaps stretching over several tax years. (See 'Short-term visitor' below.)

OFFSHORE

In the context of the exploration and exploitation of UK oil or gas, 'offshore' means the territorial sea of the UK and the UK continental shelf outside the territorial sea.

ORDINARY RESIDENCE
AND ORDINARILY RESIDENT

The terms 'ordinarily resident' and 'ordinary residence' are not defined in either income tax or National Insurance law. Generally, however, a person is ordinarily resident (and resident) in the UK if he or she usually lives in the UK and goes abroad only for short periods, for example for holidays or on business trips. (See also 'Residence and resident' below.)

Income tax

For income tax purposes a person's ordinary residence status is determined by the facts and also by his or her long-term intentions. Ordinary residence implies permanence established over several years and is therefore different to residence.

Factors taken into account when determining whether a person is ordinarily resident in the UK include: the amount of time in each tax year that he or she spends in the UK; and his or her intentions regarding the length of stay in the UK (on arrival and subsequently).

Other factors may be relevant, such as the availability of accommodation, including the ownership or the leasing of property on a long-term basis.

Usually a person is either ordinarily resident or not ordinarily resident for a whole tax year. However, by concession a person may be treated as ordinarily resident for a part of a year, such as for the years of arrival or departure.

National Insurance

A person's ordinary residency status is a question of fact. When evaluating a person's ordinary residency (or residency) status, the factors used for social security contributions purposes are different to those used for income tax purposes. The factors derive from decisions in social security contributions cases. A person is ordinarily resident in a particular country if he or she normally lives there (other than for temporary or occasional absences) and has a settled and regular mode of life there. Note that: for social security purposes, a person may be ordinarily resident in two (or more) places at the same time; and whether a person who goes abroad remains ordinarily resident in the UK depends on individual circumstances.

REMAIN

A person remains in the UK if he or she is in the UK on a continuing basis and any departures are for holidays or short business trips.

REMITTANCE BASIS

Here, 'remittance basis' refers to overseas income remitted to the UK, whether paid in, transmitted to or brought to the UK in any way.

The 2008 Finance Act contains significant changes to the remittance basis of taxation. From 6 April 2008, individuals who are either not domiciled or not ordinarily resident in the UK, and claim to be taxed on the remittance basis, will be subject to an extra charge of £30,000. The claim is to be made via the individuals' annual personal tax returns where possible or otherwise by notice to HMRC in writing.

There is also to be a fundamental change to how individuals access the remittance basis, regardless of whether they are subject to the £30,000 charge. When an individual claims the remittance basis, he or she will not be entitled to claim the tax-free personal allowance, the married couple's allowance or the blind person's allowance, and he or she will also not be entitled to claim the annual capital gains tax exemption.

There is an overriding limit: where an individual has unremitted income and gains under £2,000 then these new rules will not apply.

It is important for employers to appreciate that where they have employees who enjoy the benefit of a tax equalization policy these arrangements may become more expensive as a result of lost personal allowances.

RESIDENCE AND RESIDENT

The terms 'residence' and 'resident' are not defined in either income tax or National Insurance law. Generally, however, a person is resident (and ordinarily resident) in the UK if he or she usually lives in the UK and only goes abroad for short periods, eg for holidays or on business trips. (See 'Ordinary residence and ordinarily resident' above.)

Income tax

A person's residence status for income tax purposes depends on the facts but differs from his or her ordinary residence status, as it applies to a whole tax year. For tax purposes a person becomes UK resident in any of several ways.

The income tax legislation provides, however, a definition of a person temporarily UK resident as someone who is in the UK for some temporary purpose only and does not intend to establish his or her personal residence in the UK. If such a person spends less than six months in the UK he or she is non-resident. If he or she spends at least six months in the UK he or she is resident.

National Insurance

A person's residency status is a question of fact. When evaluating a person's residency (or ordinary residency) status, the factors used for social security contributions purposes are different to those used for income tax purposes. The factors derive from decisions in social security contributions cases, and include, for example:

▊ the actual physical presence of the individual in Great Britain or Northern Ireland;

▊ whether the individual has an abode in Great Britain or Northern Ireland;

▊ the regularity and frequency of the individual's visits to the UK, and the extent of ties (eg family) to the UK.

Note that, for social security purposes, a person may be resident in more than one country at any one time.

SHORT-TERM VISITOR

A short-term visitor is a person who visits the UK for only limited periods in one or more tax years, without any intention to remain for an extended period. (See 'Longer-term visitor' above.)

SPLIT YEAR TREATMENT

Although, strictly, a person is taxed as a UK resident for the whole of a tax year, if he or she is resident in the UK for any part of it an extra-statutory concession (A11) is available if the person leaves or comes to the UK part-way through a tax year. Where the concession applies, the person's tax liability (on income that is affected by tax residence) is calculated on the basis of the period of his or her actual residence in the UK during the year. This effectively splits the tax year into resident and not-resident periods, so that, where a person has been:

▊ not ordinarily resident in the UK and has come to live in the UK permanently or to stay for at least two years, he or she is taxed as a resident only from the date of his or her arrival; or

▊ resident in the UK (other than resident only as a short-term visitor) and leaves to live abroad permanently or for a period of at least three years, and on his or her departure is not ordinarily resident in the UK, he or she is taxed as a resident only up to and including the date of departure; or

▌ resident in the UK (other than resident only as a short-term visitor) and leaves to take up full-time employment abroad, and meets certain conditions, he or she is taxed as a resident only up to and including the date of departure (and from the date when he or she returns to the UK).

Split year treatment does not apply if the person comes to the UK as a short-term visitor, or if he or she comes for only limited periods with no intention to live in the UK permanently or to stay for at least two years.

However, there has been some confusion following the 2008 Finance Act as to whether or not this concession should also apply to employment-related securities such as employee share and option plans.

For the time being HMRC will accept that the split year treatment applies to employment-related securities in the year of arrival and departure in most circumstances, other than where securities have been acquired for less than market value.

It is important to note that this extra-statutory concession is at some point likely to be replaced by legislation. In light of the changes contained in the 2008 Finance Act, HMRC is undertaking a review of extra-statutory concessions. In addition, the government has also announced it is considering the possibility of a statutory residence test.

TAX EQUALIZATION

The expression 'tax equalization' often refers to an arrangement between an employer and a foreign national employee who comes to the UK to work. Such arrangements are common in multinational groups with highly mobile employees.

Under the terms of a typical tax equalization policy, the employee is entitled to specified net cash earnings and non-cash benefits. The employer undertakes to meet the UK income tax liability arising from cash earnings and non-cash benefits and to provide a professional adviser to deal with the individual's UK tax affairs.

KEY FORMS

The following are some of the key forms relevant to international employees. Some of these can be viewed online at the HMRC website.

Income tax

▌ DOM1 – Income and chargeable gains: domicile.

▌ P85 – Leaving the UK.

▌ P85(S) – Leaving the UK on completion of an assignment.

▌ P86 – Arrival in the UK.

National Insurance

▌ CA3821 – Employer's questionnaire when their employees are being sent to work in a European Economic Area/Reciprocal Agreement country.

▌ CA3822 – Application for a certificate of continuing UK liability when employees are going to work abroad.

▌ CA8421 – Application for form E101 when an employee is employed in two or more countries of the EEA.

▌ E101 – This certificate is issued by a member state of the EEA confirming that social security contributions for the specified national continue to be payable in that country rather than the country in which the person is working. The certificate usually specifies a 12-month period, but a period of up to five years may be possible depending on circumstances.

▌ E102 – This form is completed by employers to apply for an extension (usually 12 months) of the period covered by certificate E101 for the employee in question. The employer can apply for this extension only where, owing to unforeseen circumstances, the period of employment abroad lasts longer than the anticipated period and beyond 12 months. The employer must apply for the extension before the end of the original period covered by certificate E101.

USEFUL GUIDES

▌ HMRC's *Employer Further Guide to PAYE and NICs*.

▌ *Digest of Double Taxation Treaties* (http://www.hmrc.gov.uk/cnr/dtdigest.pdf).

▌ Health advice for travellers (http://www.dh.gov.uk/en/Policyandguidance/Healthadvicefortravellers/index.htm).

▌ IR20 – *Residents and Non-Residents: Liability to tax in the UK* (http://www.hmrc.gov.uk/pdfs/ir20.htm).

▌ SA29 – *Your Social Security Insurance, Benefits and Healthcare Rights in the European Economic Area* (http://www.dwp.gov.uk/international/sa29/).

▌ SA33 – *Social Security Agreement between the United Kingdom and the United States of America* (http://www.dwp.gov.uk/lifeevent/benefits/recip_health_pdfs/2005/sa33-oct05.pdf).

There are other 'SA' series guides in respect of those countries outside the EEA with which the UK has a social security agreement (http://www.dwp.gov.uk/advisers/cat1/all-products.asp#s).

Helpful leaflets about social security in the UK can be viewed at: http://www.dwp.gov.uk/international/sa29/leaflets.asp.

Contact details

For more information about National Insurance contributions and related health care: HM Revenue & Customs, Centre for Non Residents, Room BP1301, Benton Park View, Newcastle-upon-Tyne NE98 1ZZ (tel: 0845 915 4811; fax: 0845 915 7800). If phoning or sending a fax from outside the UK, dial the international code, then: tel: 44 191 203 7010; fax: 44 191 225 0067.

For details of UK income tax while a person is abroad: HM Revenue & Customs, Centre for Non Residents, St John's House, Merton Road, Bootle, Merseyside L69 9BB (tel: 0845 070040). If phoning from outside the UK, dial the international code, then: tel: 44 151 210 2222.

For information about US international policy: Office of International Policy, Division of International Program Policy and Agreement, Room 1104, West High Rise, 6401 Security Boulevard, Baltimore, MD 21235 (website: www.socialsecurity.gov/coc).

The author acknowledges with thanks the contribution of notes and text to this chapter by Alison Ward of the Institute of Payroll Professionals (IPP).

3.5

Outline of PAYE and secondments to the UK

Stephen Asher, Frank Hirth plc

UK organizations often do not realize that they have PAYE and NIC responsibilities for employees sent to the UK by overseas concerns, especially if the overseas entities are actually paying the seconded employees. Employers (including the overseas employer and the UK employer where there is one) often fail to operate PAYE in respect of such employees seconded to the UK.

Multinational businesses frequently send employees to members of the group in other parts of the world. Each company in a group is a separate legal entity, and PAYE applies to a group company in the UK exactly as it does for any other independent UK concern. Whilst the HMRC office dealing with the UK group member may not know about the overseas connection, the group member will.

It is the duty of the UK concern to undertake responsibility for operating PAYE on employees seconded to it. PAYE should be operated by the UK concern on all payments to seconded employees, regardless of whether they are paid by the UK concern, the overseas concern or partly by both. The *Employer Further Guide to PAYE and NICs* (CWG2) sets out the responsibilities of the UK concern in relation to seconded employees.

Although, strictly, PAYE has to be operated in respect of all employees working in the UK, a relaxation of the PAYE requirements may be permitted by HMRC depending on the facts. Note that it is HMRC that decides whether the relaxation is appropriate and not the employer.

TAX PRESENCE IN THE UK

One of the deciding factors on the operation of PAYE is whether the employer that makes the payment on account of wages or salary has a 'tax presence' in the UK. The decision in the *Oceanic* case makes it clear that there is a territorial limitation to PAYE that restricts it to cases where the employer has a 'tax presence' in the UK. For PAYE compliance purposes, it does not matter whether any corporation tax liability actually arises on the UK presence of the employer. It is sufficient that a tax presence exists.

Although HMRC would regard a branch or agency in the UK, or a UK representative office, as establishing a tax presence, HMRC would not regard an overseas employer as having a tax presence in the UK simply because there are employees in the UK. For example, an overseas concern may employ sales staff in the UK who simply travel around from their private residences to seek orders. HMRC would not say that there was an employer tax presence at the private address. Further, HMRC take the view that the overseas employer's use of professional services in the UK, for example banking or legal services, would not thereby give rise to a tax presence in the UK.

For there to be a tax presence there will need to be something in the UK similar to a branch or agency, or office or establishment, where the overseas company can be routinely contacted about doing business. Essentially a UK address is needed where HMRC can send PAYE literature and, if necessary, enforce compliance.

Where there is a tax presence, HMRC will look to that presence for PAYE, even if payments to employees in the UK are not made from the UK. So, for example, the UK employees of a UK branch or agency may be paid by a part of the organization outside the UK. Nonetheless, HMRC would still require the branch to operate PAYE.

WHERE AN OVERSEAS EMPLOYER PAYS THE EMPLOYEE

Where the overseas employer pays the seconded employee, a charge by the overseas employer may arise before, during or after the period of secondment. It may be greater than the employee's emoluments but, whatever the circumstances, it does not affect in any way the operation of PAYE. The UK concern must find out the total amount of the employee's emoluments and remit to HMRC any UK liability to tax and National

Insurance contributions on the total emoluments. It is up to the UK concern to make arrangements to deduct this out of the sum to be paid to the overseas employer.

If the overseas employer makes no management charge, the UK concern must still pay the tax and National Insurance contributions due to HMRC on the total emoluments and, where the overseas concern is actually making payments to the seconded employees, the UK concern should arrange for the overseas employer to remit enough money to meet UK PAYE and National Insurance contributions on the payments it makes.

DOUBLE TAXATION

Double taxation relief

Where an overseas employer pays the new arrival's UK earnings, double taxation relief might be due. If so, HMRC may be able to issue an NT code to the UK employer. But, for this to happen, the employee must make a claim for double taxation relief and prove this claim.

If an NT code is issued to cover UK earnings, HMRC should send a separate instruction about the date from which the code operates, and tell the employer to refund any tax already deducted.

Relaxation of PAYE

Where their length of stay will not exceed 183 days, short-term business visitors to the UK might make claims under the dependent personal services article (Article 15 or the equivalent). If such a claim is likely to be competent under a double taxation convention (DTC), PAYE relaxations are possible where certain conditions are met. The arrangements currently available enable HMRC:

- with minimal paperwork, to take out of PAYE any DTC-protected business visitors who spend no more than 60 days in the UK during a tax year;

- with certain information, to take out of PAYE any DTC-protected business visitors who spend no more than 90 days in the UK during a tax year;

- with further information, to take out of PAYE any DTC-protected business visitors who spend no more than 183 days in the UK during a tax year.

Therefore an employer wishing to reduce the administrative impact of the full operation of PAYE by advancing claims under the dependent personal service article of a DTC must be prepared to supply, or cause to be supplied, sufficient information to enable HMRC to ensure domestic obligations and treaty terms are met.

Whilst some conditions may seem particularly onerous and ungenerous, they are intended to do no more than establish, as far as is possible, that the UK does not have overall taxing rights and that DTC partner countries are aware of the employment income concerned. For these reasons the factors must be an integral part of any relaxations if they are to be acceptable.

HMRC accepts that, to a degree, employers will be able to supply certain information only on a 'best of my belief' basis, but it is to their obvious advantage to ensure accuracy.

These arrangements represent a valuable saving for employers and HMRC alike. Certainly for visitors up to 60 days in the UK, substantial savings arise where an employer confirms that:

▮ the individual spends less than 60 days in a tax year in the UK; and
  – that period does not form part of a more substantial period when the individual was present in the UK; and
  – the individual does not have a formal contract of employment with a UK company.

▮ where liability is subsequently found to arise, the employer agrees to pay all tax grossed up unless arrangements are made by the employer to recover the tax from the employee.

Then, for intermittent visitors, for up to 30 days, no statements will be required from either employer or employee. Where, however, the visit is for a period of 30 days or more, some information will be required. Forms P85, P85(S) and P86 do not have to be completed in respect of those employees who are within the scope of the relaxation.

Effects of the relaxation

▮ *Visitors to the UK (1 to 30 days).* No requirements for either employer or employee to fulfil.

▮ *Visitors to the UK (31 to 60 days).* For an employee who spends no more than 60 days in the UK during the tax year, PAYE can be disregarded provided that it is confirmed that:
  – there is no formal contract of employment;
  – the 60 days do not form part of a more substantial period.

▌ *Visitors to the UK (61 to 90 days).* For an employee in the UK for not more than 90 days in the tax year, PAYE can be disregarded provided that the employer supplies the information below by 31 May following the end of the tax year:
– the full name of the employee;
– the last-known UK and overseas addresses of the employee;
– future duties to be undertaken;
– date commenced;
– date ceased;
– to which country a tax return covering worldwide income is submitted.

▌ The employer must also confirm that:
– the UK company does not ultimately bear the cost of the employee's remuneration and does not function as the employee's employer during the UK assignment;
– in the last four tax years visits to the UK were less than 364 days in total and less than 183 days in any tax year.

▌ *Visitors to the UK (91 to 183 days).* For an employee in the UK for a period of 91 days but not exceeding 183 days in the tax year, PAYE can be disregarded provided that all of the information requested for visitors up to 90 days is provided and in addition:
– In the case of non-US citizens and green card holders, the employee provides a statement from the overseas revenue authority confirming residence in the other state for tax purposes during the period in the UK. This statement should be passed to HMRC by 31 May following the end of the relevant overseas tax year. This arrangement is only provisional until the relevant certificate is received.
– In the case of US citizens it will only be necessary for the employee to provide evidence of continuing residence in the United States.
– A statement is received from the employee by 31 May following the end of the UK tax year giving the following information: nationality; the grounds for claiming this nationality; place of birth; the country in which he or she lives; the date of arrival in the UK; an indication of whether he or she has visited the UK in the five years prior to the most recent date of arrival and, if so, in that time whether he or she spent more than 183 days in the UK in any UK tax year or more than 364 days in the UK in total.

The arrangements

The following arrangements must operate for the PAYE relaxation to be granted:

1. In all cases involving short-term assignment of employees to the UK, the employer will put in place some form of internal reporting system to keep as accurate as possible a record of employees visiting the UK on business. It is expected that this system will have the following minimum requirements:
    -   Staff of all grades will periodically report days spent in the UK on business to the central point controlling this arrangement.
    -   Staff should not spend more than 30 days intermittently in the UK in any 12-month period without reporting to that central point.

2. All records to be kept under this arrangement are within Regulation 97 of the Income Tax (Pay As You Earn) Regulations 2003 and so must be retained and produced for inspection.

3. Where liability is subsequently found to arise on payments of PAYE income made to an employee, the employer will be expected to pay the tax that ought to have been deducted from or otherwise paid in respect of each payment. Late payment of PAYE tax will attract interest in the usual way.

4. Should it become apparent that PAYE is not being applied in the case of employees who do not satisfy the relevant criteria, HMRC reserves the right to insist that PAYE be operated strictly for all employees from day one.

5. Any employee who cannot fulfil the conditions set out above should have PAYE operated from day one.

Outline of PAYE and secondments from the UK

Stephen Asher, Frank Hirth plc

In making a decision about what action to take for an employee who leaves the UK to work abroad, HMRC will require the employee to complete form P85 or P85(S) as appropriate.

Employees of a UK employer may be seconded abroad in circumstances where they continue to be liable to UK tax after departure, so that it is not appropriate to issue an NT code. In such cases the employer should continue to deduct tax under PAYE and, regardless of the tax position, there may be continuing NICs obligations.

WHEN AN OVERSEAS REVENUE AUTHORITY REQUIRES DEDUCTION OF FOREIGN TAX

If a UK employer has UK employees working abroad for all or part of the time, an overseas revenue authority may ask the employer to deduct foreign tax from the employees' wages. The HMRC *Employer Further Guide to PAYE and NICs* (CWG2) advises employers to:

▐ explain to the overseas revenue authorities that they have a continuing responsibility for making UK tax deductions from the employees' wages;

▐ find out exactly why the overseas revenue authority wants the deductions made; and then

▐ seek advice from their local HMRC office.

Where HMRC is then satisfied that the overseas tax is correctly due, the employer can be authorized to operate net of foreign tax credit relief (see the next section).

Liability depends on how long the period of overseas work is to which a double taxation agreement applies:

▌ *Less than six months.* Normally an employee is not liable to overseas tax on earnings already liable in the UK.

▌ *More than six months but less than one year.* Normally an employee is immediately liable to overseas tax, but with double taxation relief from UK tax on earnings overseas. HMRC can authorize the employer to operate net of foreign tax credit relief.

▌ *More than one year.* Usually only overseas tax is payable. HMRC will tell the employer to operate code NT.

Where foreign tax does not have to be deducted by the employer on payments to employees who are taxed through PAYE, but an employee is obliged to pay foreign tax direct to an overseas revenue authority on those earnings, advance double taxation relief can be given through the PAYE code.

NET OF FOREIGN TAX CREDIT RELIEF

The net of foreign tax credit relief relaxation only applies where an employer is required to deduct foreign tax in addition to UK income tax under PAYE from payments being made to employees sent to work abroad. Its aim is to give provisional relief for double taxation to employees who must pay both UK tax and foreign tax from the same payments of earnings.

The relaxation only applies to UK PAYE that should be deducted from an employee's pay under his or her UK code using UK tax tables. The employer must still fulfil other PAYE requirements and all of those relating to National Insurance. There can be no question of abandoning PAYE and NIC altogether for the duration of the overseas contract.

The arrangement should not be used for any other contract or situation where the employer or the agent thinks it should be without prior consultation with HMRC. It is not available if an overseas deduction is borne by the employer.

Employer's responsibilities under this arrangement

Where HMRC agrees the use of the arrangement, HMRC will write to the employer and:

1. request the name and National Insurance number (NINO) of each employee included in the arrangement;

2. ask the employer to provide regular updates of changes in the employees included (the frequency of these updates must be agreed between HMRC and the employer);

3. advise the employer that:
   - for those employees on overseas work in the specified country, PAYE and NIC due should be calculated in the normal way;
   - credit by this method can be given only for foreign tax actually payable on and deducted from the employee's wages and paid to the overseas authority;
   - credit is given by reducing the amount of UK PAYE deducted from wages by the amount of foreign tax deducted from gross wages in the same UK tax year;
   - foreign tax will normally be set off against UK PAYE due in the same pay period before the employer pays the PAYE to the Accounts Office (however, credit can be given retrospectively in the same year where pay was double-taxed);
   - the credit available under this agreement is restricted to the amount of UK PAYE deductible from the employee's wages (NI deductions and contributions are not affected in any way);
   - any net UK PAYE tax remaining due is to be entered at column 7 of the deductions working sheet, and this money should be paid to the Accounts Office in the normal way with all the NI contributions due;
   - any UK PAYE refunds due during the year because of a change of code number must be restricted to the net UK PAYE deducted from the employee during the year;
   - the employer and the employee must undertake to provide details of foreign tax that has been refunded.

For employees who cease to operate overseas but continue in the same employment in the UK or another location, the employer must submit details of pay and UK tax deducted up to the date of redeployment, together with a report of foreign tax credited, and operate the employees' existing codes on the Week 1 or Month 1 basis.

If an employee who has been given credit under this system leaves the employment or dies, the employer must submit a form P45 completed as if the code has been operated on the Week 1 or Month 1 basis, showing the net UK tax deducted, and a report of the overseas tax deducted for which credit has been given against UK PAYE due.

The action that an employer operating this arrangement takes at the end of the UK tax year will depend on the method used to submit the annual return.

On paper the employer submitting the return must:

▌ complete forms P35 and P14 to show net UK PAYE deducted for the year;

▌ make an additional entry in red ink on the bottom of the employee's P14 to record the amount of foreign tax deducted and remitted to the overseas authority that was set off against UK PAYE deductions;

▌ provide evidence of payment of the foreign tax.

Electronically the employer submitting the return must:

▌ show the net UK tax deducted for the year on forms P35 and P14; and at the same time

▌ send to HMRC a statement showing the name and NINO of each employee included in the arrangement and the amount of foreign tax deducted and remitted to the overseas authority that was set off against that employee's UK PAYE deductions due;

▌ provide evidence of payment of foreign tax.

Outline of income tax framework

Stephen Asher, Frank Hirth plc

INCOME TAX TREATMENT

Where a person is resident in the UK, income tax is normally charged on all his or her earned income, wherever it arises. The person may, however, be entitled to a reduction in the income tax he or she has to pay if he or she receives overseas earnings and spends long periods abroad or receives an overseas pension.

In certain cases where the person is resident but not ordinarily resident in the UK, or is resident but not domiciled in the UK, overseas income is dealt with on the remittance basis. The residence and domicile of the person are important issues in the determination of income tax liability.

Where a person is not resident in the UK, he or she is generally taxed on any UK pensions or on earnings from employment, the duties of which are carried on in the UK. Where the duties are carried on partly in the UK and partly abroad, an allocation, based on days worked in the UK and days worked abroad, will normally be made to ascertain the amount of earnings for duties carried on in the UK that are liable for UK tax. Earnings from an employment carried on wholly abroad are not taxed.

In some cases the person may make a claim, under a double taxation agreement, for exemption from UK income tax on his or her UK pension, or on earnings arising in the UK.

Where necessary, HMRC may ask a person to complete form DOM1 in order to consider his or her domicile if it is immediately relevant in deciding his or her liability to UK income tax (and capital gains tax).

TAX EQUALIZATION AND MODIFIED PAYE

Employers can apply to HMRC for agreement to operate a modified PAYE arrangement on the earnings of tax-equalized employees coming from abroad to work in the UK. The modified arrangement does not apply to employees who are resident, ordinarily resident and domiciled in the UK, or equalized on only part of their earnings.

For an employee to be included, the employer must equalize liability to UK income tax on all general earnings subject to the rules applying to employees resident, ordinarily resident or domiciled outside the UK. Broadly, this includes all cash earnings from the employment and all non-cash benefits treated as earnings. However, there is no requirement for the employer to equalize liability on specific employment income, ie amounts that count as employment income such as termination payments and gains on the exercise of share options.

Employers must apply PAYE in accordance with the relevant statutory provisions and regulations to any non-equalized employment income of an employee covered by the arrangement.

TAXATION OF EARNINGS FOR PERSONS COMING TO OR LEAVING THE UK PART-WAY THROUGH THE TAX YEAR

Where a person comes to the UK during a tax year and is treated as resident from the date of his or her arrival, extra-statutory concession A11 provides that he or she will not pay tax on earnings for the part of the year before he or she arrives in the UK, where these are from an employment carried on wholly abroad. Similarly, if a person leaves the UK during a tax year and is treated as resident in the UK up to and including the date of departure, income tax is not charged on earned income for the part of the year after the person leaves the UK, where this is from an employment carried on wholly abroad.

Where a person is paid for a period of leave spent in the UK following work abroad, HMRC treats the 'terminal leave pay' as arising during the period to which it relates even if entitlement to it was built up over a period of overseas employment.

PLACE WHERE DUTIES ARE PERFORMED

The place where a person's duties are performed is a key factor in deciding the tax treatment of his or her earnings. If his or her work is usually done abroad but some duties are performed in the UK, the UK duties are treated as though they had been performed abroad as long as they are merely incidental to the person's overseas duties.

In the case of a seafarer or a member of an aircraft crew, his or her duties are normally treated as performed in the UK if: the voyage or flight does not extend to a place outside the UK; or he or she is resident in the UK and either the voyage or flight begins or ends in the UK or he or she embarked on part of a voyage or flight that begins or ends in the UK.

Whether or not duties performed in the UK are incidental to a person's overseas duties depends on all the circumstances. If the work done in the UK is of the same kind as, or of similar importance to, the work done abroad it will not be merely incidental unless it can be shown to be ancillary or subordinate to that work. It is normally the nature of the duties performed in the UK rather than the amount of time spent on them that is important but, if the total time spent working in the UK is more than 91 days in a year, the work will not be treated as incidental.

The following are not normally regarded as incidental: attendance at directors' meetings in the UK by a director of the company who normally works abroad; and visits to the UK either as a member of the crew of a ship or aircraft or in the course of work by a courier.

Where the work done in the UK has no importance in itself, but simply enables the person to do his or her normal work abroad, it may be treated as incidental. The following are examples of duties regarded as incidental:

▮ visits to the UK by an overseas representative of a UK employer to report to the employer or receive fresh instructions;

▮ training in the UK by an overseas employee, as long as:
  - the total time spent in the UK for training is not more than 91 days in a year; and
  - no productive work is done in the UK in that time.

TAXATION OF EARNINGS FROM SOURCES ABROAD

Where a person is resident in the UK, income tax is charged on all the earnings he or she receives from sources abroad.

Earned (salaried) income

A person's earnings from overseas employment are taxed on the remittance basis (see below) if the person is: resident, but not ordinarily resident, in the UK; or resident and ordinarily resident, but not domiciled, in the UK, but only in the case of foreign emoluments where the duties of the employment are performed wholly outside the UK.

Other earned income

In the case of other types of earned income – such as overseas pensions and income from an overseas trade, profession or vocation – income tax is charged on all the income the person receives from overseas sources if he or she is resident in the UK. However, he or she may be entitled to a 10 per cent deduction from the amount chargeable in the case of overseas pensions.

A person's other earned income from overseas sources is taxed on the remittance basis if the person is:

▌ resident, but not domiciled, in the UK; or

▌ resident, but not ordinarily resident, in the UK and is either:
  – a Commonwealth citizen (which includes a British citizen); or
  – a citizen of the Republic of Ireland.

Note, however, that the remittance basis does not apply to other types of earned income arising in the Republic of Ireland.

Remittance basis

Where the remittance basis applies, a person is liable to UK tax on the amount of his or her overseas income that is remitted to the UK. Where a person is taxed on the remittance basis, he or she cannot claim either the 100 per cent deduction for foreign earnings or the 10 per cent deduction for overseas pensions.

TAXATION OF EXPENSES

The following are additional rules to those that are applicable in respect of expenses incurred in travelling in the performance of the duties of the employment.

Employees carrying out duties overseas

Where an employee is resident and ordinarily resident in the UK, he or she may be entitled to tax relief for the costs of:

▌ board and lodging overseas;

▌ journeys to and from anywhere in the UK while working overseas;

▌ travel to take up the job overseas and to return to the UK when the job ends;

▌ two journeys (out and return) of his or her spouse and children to and from the UK to visit or accompany him or her;

▌ travel between jobs where he or she has more than one job.

Employees from overseas working in the UK

An employee from overseas may be entitled to tax relief for: all journeys he or she undertakes between the place where he or she lives and his or her place of work in the UK; and two journeys (out and return) of his or her spouse and children to and from the UK to visit or accompany him or her.

To determine whether the employee qualifies for the tax relief it is necessary to establish whether he or she was: in the UK for any reason at any time in the two years prior to the date when he or she came to the UK to work; and resident in the UK in either of the two tax years prior to that tax year in which he or she came to work in the UK.

TAXATION RELIEF AND ALLOWANCES

A person resident in the UK is entitled to certain allowances and relief, based on his or her personal circumstances. Further, to avoid double taxation the UK has negotiated double taxation agreements with many countries. The precise conditions of exemption or relief vary from agreement to agreement.

Where a person is resident in the UK and has overseas income (or gains) that are taxable in both the UK and the country of origin, he or she may qualify for relief against UK tax for all or part of the overseas tax he or she has paid.

Even if there is no double taxation agreement between the UK and the other country concerned, the person may still be entitled to relief under special provisions in the UK's tax legislation. Special rules, for example, apply to certain types of employees or workers.

Allowances

A person who is not resident in the UK may claim tax allowances if he or she is any of the following:

- a Commonwealth citizen (this includes a British citizen); or

- a citizen of a state within the European Economic Area (EEA); or

- a present or former employee of the British Crown (including a civil servant, member of the armed forces, etc); or

- a UK missionary society employee; or

- a civil servant in a territory under the protection of the British Crown; or

- a resident of the Isle of Man or the Channel Islands; or

- a former resident of the UK and lives abroad for the sake of his or her own health or the health of a member of his or her family who lives with him or her; or

- a widow or widower of an employee of the British Crown; or

- a national and/or resident of a country with which the UK has a double taxation agreement that allows such a claim.

A person who either becomes or ceases to be resident in the UK during a tax year is able to claim full allowances and reliefs for the year of arrival or departure.

Double taxation agreements

The precise conditions of exemption or relief under a double taxation agreement (DTA) vary from agreement to agreement. If a person is resident both in the UK and in a country with which the UK has a DTA, there may be special provisions in the agreement for treating the person as a resident of only one of the countries for the purposes of the agreement. Furthermore, a DTA may also make special provision for certain types of employees or workers, for example teachers and researchers.

Where a person is a resident of a country with which the UK has a DTA, he or she may be able to claim exemption or partial relief from UK tax on certain types of income from UK sources. Under a DTA he or she will normally receive some relief from UK tax on the following sources of income:

▌ pensions and some annuities (other than UK government pensions);

▌ royalties;

▌ interest.

Some agreements state that the person must be subject to tax in the other country on the income in question before relief from UK tax is given.

Under many DTAs a person may be able to claim exemption from UK tax on: earnings from an employment; and profits or earnings for independent, personal or professional services, carried on in the UK, if he or she is a resident of the overseas country for the purposes of the agreement. (Note that the exemption may not apply to entertainers or sportsmen and women.)

The usual conditions to be met are as follows. In the case of employments: the person must not be in the UK for more than 183 days in the period (often 12 months) specified in the agreement; and his or her remuneration must be paid by (or on behalf of) an employer that is not resident in the UK, and not be borne by a UK branch of his or her employer. In the case of independent, personal or professional services, the person must not: operate from a fixed base in the UK or, in the case of some agreements, spend more than a specified number of days in the UK.

Residence and ordinary residence – tax consequences

Stephen Asher, Frank Hirth plc

Although there is an important distinction between residence and ordinary residence, together they determine the charge to income tax of a person's earnings. However, neither is related to nationality and citizenship, nor to immigration issues.

It should be noted that it is possible to be resident (or ordinarily resident) in the UK and one or more other countries at the same time. However, if a person is resident both in the UK and in a country with which the UK has a double taxation agreement, special provisions in the agreement may treat him or her as a resident of only one of the countries for the purposes of the agreement.

The following describes the treatment of individuals coming to or leaving the UK in respect of their residence status and ordinary residence status for income tax purposes.

COMING TO THE UK

The residence and ordinary residence status of a person coming to the UK is determined by whether the person is coming to the UK permanently, indefinitely or as a short-term or longer-term visitor.

Note that initially a person may fall to be either a short-term or longer-term visitor but later move to another category, depending on circumstances.

A person coming to the UK should complete form P86, which will help HMRC determine his or her residency status.

Coming to the UK as a longer-term visitor

A longer-term visitor is treated as resident in the UK from the day he or she arrives to the day he or she leaves, if he or she comes to the UK for a purpose (eg employment) that will mean he or she remains in the UK for at least two years. The same treatment will apply if he or she owns or leases accommodation in the UK in the year he or she arrives.

In all other cases he or she is treated as resident for the tax year if he or she: spends 183 days or more in the UK in the tax year; or owns or leases accommodation in the UK.

A longer-term visitor is treated as ordinarily resident in the UK from the date he or she arrives, whether to work in the UK or not, if it is clear that he or she intends to stay for at least three years. However, a student who comes to the UK for a period of study or education and who will be in the UK for less than four years is treated as not ordinarily resident, providing that: he or she does not own or buy accommodation in the UK or acquire such accommodation on a lease of three years or more; and on leaving the UK he or she does not plan to return regularly for visits that average 91 days or more in a tax year.

A person is treated as ordinarily resident from the beginning of the tax year after the third anniversary of his or her arrival if he or she comes to, and remains in, the UK, but originally intended to stay for at least three years and does not buy accommodation or acquire it on a lease of three years or more.

A person who, after coming to the UK, decides to stay for at least three years from the date of his or her original arrival is treated as ordinarily resident from: the day he or she arrives if the decision is made in the tax year of arrival; or the beginning of the tax year in which he or she makes the decision, when this is after the year of arrival.

A person who comes to, and remains in, the UK is treated as ordinarily resident from either:

▪ the day of arrival, if he or she:
  – already owns accommodation in the UK; or
  – buys accommodation during the tax year of arrival; or
  – has or acquires accommodation on a lease of three years or more during the tax year of arrival; or

▪ 6 April of the tax year in which such accommodation becomes available, when this occurs after the year of arrival.

A person who is treated as ordinarily resident solely because he or she has accommodation in the UK may be treated as not ordinarily resident for the duration of his or her stay if:

▌ it is to his or her advantage; and

▌ he or she disposes of the accommodation; and

▌ he or she leaves the UK within three years of his or her arrival.

Coming to the UK as a short-term visitor

A short-term visitor to the UK is treated as resident for a tax year if he or she:

▌ is in the UK for 183 days or more in the tax year; or

▌ visits the UK regularly and, after four tax years, his or her visits during those years average 91 days or more a tax year, in which case the person is treated as resident from the fifth year. However, the person is treated as resident from 6 April of:
  – the first year, if it is clear when he or she first came to the UK that he or she intended making such visits and actually carried out his or her intention; or
  – the tax year in which he or she decided that he or she would make such visits, where the decision was made before the start of the fifth tax year and was actually carried out.

A person is treated as ordinarily resident if he or she comes to the UK regularly and his or her visits average 91 days or more a tax year. The date from which the person is treated as ordinarily resident depends upon his or her intentions and whether he or she actually carries them out. He or she will be ordinarily resident from 6 April of:

▌ the tax year of his or her first arrival, if it is clear when he or she first comes to the UK that he or she intends visiting the UK regularly for at least four tax years;

▌ the fifth tax year after he or she has visited the UK over four years, if he or she originally came with no definite plans about the number of years he or she would visit;

▌ the tax year in which he or she decides that he or she will be visiting the UK regularly, if the decision is made before the start of the fifth tax year.

Coming to the UK permanently or indefinitely

A person is treated as resident and ordinarily resident from the date he or she arrives in the UK if his or her home has been abroad and he or she intends to come to the UK to live in the UK permanently or remain in the UK for three years or more.

LEAVING THE UK

The residence and ordinary residence status of a person leaving the UK is determined by whether the person is leaving the UK permanently, indefinitely or to work abroad. In addition, the treatment is affected by special rules that apply to:

▌ employees of the Crown (eg civil servants, diplomats, members of the armed forces, etc);

▌ employees of the European Union;

▌ employees working in gas and oil exploration and extraction industries (where the employer is not resident in the UK);

▌ employees who are Merchant Navy seafarers.

When a person leaves (or is about to leave) the UK (other than for short trips) he or she should complete form P85, which is then used by HMRC to help determine the person's residence status. Alternatively, form P85(S) is used where a person who is not a UK citizen is leaving after completing an assignment in the UK.

Leaving the UK for employment abroad

Where a person leaves the UK to work full time abroad under a contract of employment, he or she is treated as not resident and not ordinarily resident in the UK if all the following conditions are met:

▌ The person's absence from the UK and his or her employment abroad both last for at least a whole tax year.

▌ During the period of the person's absence any visits he or she makes to the UK:
  – do not total more than 182 days in any tax year; and
  – average less than 91 days a tax year.

Where all the above conditions are met, the person is treated as not resident and not ordinarily resident in the UK from the day after he or she leaves the UK to the day before he or she returns to the UK at the end of his or her employment abroad. He or she is treated as coming to the UK permanently on the day he or she returns from his or her employment abroad and resident and ordinarily resident from that date.

However, where all the conditions above are not met, the person remains resident and ordinarily resident unless he or she has left the UK either permanently or to live abroad for three or more years.

Where there is a break in full-time employment, or some other change in the person's circumstances during the period in which he or she is overseas, HMRC will need to review the position to decide whether the conditions were met. Where at the end of one employment the person returned temporarily to the UK, but with the plan to go abroad again after a very short stay in the UK, HMRC may review the person's residence status in the light of all the circumstances of his or her employment abroad and his or her return to the UK.

Leaving the UK permanently or indefinitely

Where a person has left the UK permanently or for at least three years, he or she is treated as not resident and not ordinarily resident from the day after the date of departure, providing that: his or her absence from the UK has covered at least a whole tax year; and his or her visits to the UK since leaving do not total more than 182 days in any tax year and average less than 91 days a tax year.

Where a person goes abroad permanently, he or she is treated as remaining resident and ordinarily resident if his or her visits to the UK average 91 days or more a year.

If a person claims that he or she is no longer resident and ordinarily resident in the UK, HMRC may ask for evidence that he or she has left the UK permanently, or to live outside the UK for three years or more. This evidence might be, for example, that he or she has taken steps to acquire accommodation abroad to live in as a permanent home.

If the person does not have this evidence, but has gone abroad for a settled purpose (which includes a fixed object or intention in which he or she is going to be engaged for an extended period of time), he or she is treated as not resident and not ordinarily resident from the day after the date of departure providing that: his or her absence from the UK has covered at least a whole tax year; and his or her visits to the UK since leaving total not more than 182 days in any tax year and average less than 91 days a tax year.

If the person has not gone abroad for a settled purpose, he or she is treated as remaining resident and ordinarily resident in the UK. However, this can be reviewed if: the absence actually covers three years from his or her departure; or evidence becomes available to show that he or she has left the UK permanently and, in either case, his or her visits to the UK since leaving do not total more than 182 days in any tax year and average less than 91 days a tax year.

However, if during the person's absence the pattern of his or her visits varied substantially year by year, it might be appropriate to look at the absence as being made up of separate periods for the purpose of calculating average visits. This might be necessary if, for example, a shift in the pattern of the person's visits suggested a change of circumstances that altered how HMRC viewed his or her residence status.

3.9

Outline of National Insurance contributions framework

Stephen Asher, Frank Hirth plc

Liability to Class 1 National Insurance contributions (NICs) arises only where a person is in employed earner's employment in Great Britain. Note that, although liability to secondary (employer) Class 1 NICs usually follows the liability to primary (employee) Class 1 NICs, there are circumstances where a liability only to primary Class 1 NICs arises. There is also the possibility that in certain circumstances a person who has left the UK may wish to make voluntary NICs to protect his or her entitlement to state benefits.

There may also be certain and fairly unusual circumstances in which an employee's earnings are to be apportioned on a daily basis between UK and non-UK employment for NICs (Class 1 and Class 1A). (Details with examples of these circumstances are given in HMRC's *Tax Bulletin* 79, which can be accessed at www.hmrc.gov.UK/bulletins/tb79.htm#b.)

CLASS 1 NICS

Strictly, liability to Class 1 NICs arises only where a person is in employed earner's employment in Great Britain and is resident or present or ordinarily resident in Great Britain or Northern Ireland. This means that liability to Class 1 NICs does not arise where these conditions are not present, such as where, for example, a person leaves the UK permanently to work and live abroad.

However, legislation, treaties and conventions modify liability to pay Class 1 NICs in circumstances where a person is seconded by a UK employer to work abroad or an overseas employer to work in the UK.

The legislation, treaties and conventions serve to retain a person within the social security provisions of his or her originating country for a prescribed period. Typically, this period is one year (ie 52 weeks) but can be up to five years (eg in the case of the United States and Germany).

Coming to the UK

Where an overseas employer seconds a person to work in the UK, Class 1 NICs may or may not be payable immediately, depending on whether the person comes from a country: within the European Economic Area (EEA); or with which the UK has either a reciprocal agreement or a double contributions convention.

Countries outside the EEA or with which there is no reciprocal agreement or convention

Class 1 NICs (primary and secondary contributions) must be paid from the date the employee starts work in the UK if: the employee comes from a country outside the EEA or with which there is no reciprocal agreement or a double contributions convention; and the employer is resident or present or has a place of business in the UK.

However, note that there is no Class 1 NICs liability in the first 52 weeks starting from the Sunday following the employee's arrival in the UK if he or she does not normally live or work in the UK and he or she has been sent to work temporarily in the UK by an overseas employer.

Countries with which there is a reciprocal agreement or convention

Class 1 NICs are not payable on the earnings of an employee coming from a country with which the UK has a reciprocal agreement or a double contributions convention if he or she holds a valid certificate of coverage issued by the other country. Therefore, if there is no valid certificate, Class 1 NICs are payable.

The period for which Class 1 NICs may not be payable is determined in accordance with the terms of the agreement. Table 3.9.1 shows the various countries with which the UK has an agreement and the period for which Class 1 NICs may not be payable.

Table 3.9.1 Countries with which the UK has double taxation agreements

Antigua and Barbuda	Iceland	Papua New Guinea
Argentina	India	Philippines
Australia	Indonesia	Poland
Austria	Ireland (Republic of)	Portugal
Azerbaijan	Isle of Man	Romania
Bangladesh	Israel	Russian Federation
Barbados	Italy	Serbia and Montenegro
Belarus	Ivory Coast	Sierra Leone
Belgium	Jamaica	Singapore
Belize	Japan	Slovak Republic
Bolivia	Jersey	Slovenia*
Bosnia-Herzegovina	Jordan	Solomon Islands
Botswana	Kazakhstan	South Africa
Brunei	Kenya	Spain
Bulgaria	Kiribati	Sri Lanka
Burma (Myanmar)	Korea (Republic of)	St Kitts and Nevis
Canada	Kuwait	Sudan
Chile	Latvia	Swaziland
China	Lesotho	Sweden
Croatia*	Lithuania	Switzerland
Cyprus	Luxembourg	Taiwan
Czech Republic	Macedonia*	Tajikistan
Denmark	Malawi	Thailand
Egypt	Malaysia	Trinidad and Tobago
Estonia	Malta	Tunisia
Falkland Islands	Mauritius	Turkey
Fiji	Mexico	Turkmenistan
Finland	Mongolia	Tuvalu
France	Montserrat	Uganda
Gambia	Morocco	Ukraine
Georgia	Myanmar (Burma)	United States
Germany	Namibia	Uzbekistan
Ghana	Netherlands	Venezuela
Greece	New Zealand	Vietnam
Grenada	Nigeria	Yugoslavia*
Guernsey	Norway	Zambia
Guyana	Oman	Zimbabwe
Hungary	Pakistan	

Notes:
– For a guide to the possible entitlement to double taxation relief for certain types of UK income received by the above territories see the *Digest of Double Taxation Treaties* published by HMRC.
– The UK's agreement with Yugoslavia is to be regarded as in force between the UK and the former Yugoslav states marked *. The position with regard to the remainder of what was Yugoslavia is undetermined.

Once the period of exception shown on the certificate has elapsed: Class 1 NICs (both primary and secondary contributions) must be paid if the employer is resident or present or has a place of business in the UK; or primary Class 1 NICs (but not secondary Class 1 NICs) must be paid if the employer is not resident or present or does not have a place of business in the UK. The latter gives rise to a problem of making payment of the primary Class 1 NICs. The primary Class 1 NICs could be paid by an associate of the employer or by the employee.

Where the associate pays the primary Class 1 NICs, records, including end-of-year returns, are to be kept separate from any other records or returns. Where the employee pays the primary Class 1 NICs he or she must record the details.

Countries within the EEA

Class 1 NICs are not payable on the earnings of an employee if he or she holds a valid certificate, form E101, issued by the other country in the EEA, which shows that social security contributions for him or her are being paid in that country. Those countries are listed in Table 3.9.2. Note that: if there is no valid certificate E101, Class 1 NICs are payable; and a valid form E101 received some time after the person has started work in the UK has to be accepted and, where appropriate, retrospectively applied.

Typically, form E101 is valid for a specified period of 12 months in duration. However, there are circumstances where a longer period, up to a maximum of five years, may be agreed between the social security authorities of the two countries, where certain conditions are met. The authorities may also agree an extension of the initial 12 months specified in the form E101, with form E102 being issued.

Once the period of exception shown in the form E101 (or form E102) has elapsed: Class 1 NICs (both primary and secondary contributions) must be paid if the employer is resident or present or has a place of business in the UK; and primary Class 1 NICs (but not secondary Class 1 NICs) must be paid if the employer is not resident or present or does not have a place of business in the UK. The latter gives rise to a problem of making payment of the primary Class 1 NICs. The primary Class 1 NICs could be paid by an associate of the employer or by the employee.

Where the associate pays the primary Class 1 NICs, records, including end-of-year returns, are to be kept separate from any other records or returns. Where the employee pays the primary Class 1 NICs he or she must record the details.

Table 3.9.2   Countries of the European Economic Area (EEA)

Country	Comments
Austria	
Belgium	
Bulgaria	
Cyprus, Republic of	But not Northern Cyprus.
Czech Republic	
Denmark	Excluding Faroe Islands.
Estonia	
Finland	
France	Including Corsica, French Guyana, Guadeloupe, Martinique, Réunion and Saint Pierre et Miquelon.
Germany	
Gibraltar	The other EEA countries treat Gibraltar as part of the UK.
Greece	Including Crete and the Greek islands.
Hungary	
Iceland	Part of the European Free Trade Area (EFTA), but not part of the European Union; it has a separate agreement with Switzerland.
Ireland, Republic of	
Italy	Including Elba, Sardinia, Sicily and Trieste. Excluding San Marino and the Vatican City.
Latvia	
Liechtenstein	Part of EFTA, but not part of the European Union; it has a separate agreement with Switzerland.
Lithuania	
Luxembourg	
Malta	
Netherlands	
Norway	Part of EFTA, but not part of the European Union; it has a separate agreement with Switzerland.
Poland	
Portugal	Including Azores and Madeira.
Romania	
Slovakia	
Slovenia	
Spain	Including Balearic Islands, Canary Islands, Ceuta and Melilla.
Sweden	
Switzerland	Included by virtue of a special EC agreement that took effect on 1 June 2002.
UK	The other EEA countries treat Gibraltar as part of the UK, but the UK treats Gibraltar as a separate EEA country. Excluding Channel Islands and the Isle of Man.

Leaving the UK

Where a UK employer seconds a person to work abroad, Class 1 NICs may or may not be payable immediately, depending on whether the person goes to a country: within the EEA; or with which the UK has either a reciprocal agreement or a double contributions convention.

Where an employer is sending an employee to work abroad in a country within the EEA or with which the UK has an agreement or convention, the employer should complete form CA3821 and form CA3822. Form CA3821 is a questionnaire about the employer. Form CA3822 is a questionnaire about the employee and the assignment.

Countries outside the EEA or with which there is no reciprocal agreement or convention

Where an employee is sent by his or her UK employer to work in a country that is outside the EEA or with which there is no reciprocal agreement or convention, Class 1 NICs are payable for the first 52 weeks if certain conditions are met. The conditions are that: the employer has a place of business in the UK; and the employee is ordinarily resident in the UK and was resident in the UK immediately before starting the work abroad.

If any of the conditions are not met, liability to Class 1 NICs ceases immediately from the date of departure from the UK.

Countries with which there is a reciprocal agreement or convention

Where an employee is sent by his or her UK employer to work in a country with which the UK has a reciprocal agreement or convention (other than Switzerland and countries within the EEA), Class 1 NICs may or may not be payable depending on the terms of the particular agreement. Table 3.9.3 shows the various countries with which the UK has an agreement and the period for which Class 1 NICs can continue.

The employer is required to use forms CA3821 and CA3822 to apply for a certificate confirming that Class 1 NICs can continue to be paid while the employee is working in the other country.

Once the period shown in the certificate has elapsed, the employer should cease Class 1 NICs.

Table 3.9.3   Countries with which the UK has a reciprocal agreement or double contributions convention

Country	Comments
Barbados	Initial certificate covers three years.
Bermuda	Initial certificate covers 12 months.
Canada	Initial certificate covers five years.
Guernsey	Initial certificate covers three years.
Isle of Man	This agreement is limited, and liability is generally determined under place of residence. There are no time limits.
Israel	Initial certificate covers two years.
Jamaica	Initial certificate covers three years.
Japan	Initial certificate covers five years.
Jersey	Initial certificate covers three years.
Korea, Republic of	Initial certificate covers five years.
Mauritius	Initial certificate covers two years.
Philippines	Initial certificate covers three years.
Turkey	Initial certificate covers three years.
United States	Initial certificate covers five years.
Yugoslavia	Initial certificate covers 12 months. Yugoslavia comprises the Federal Republic of Yugoslavia (Serbia and Montenegro), Bosnia-Herzegovina, Croatia and the former Yugoslav Republic of Macedonia.

Countries within the EEA

Class 1 NICs continue to be payable on the earnings of an employee who is an EEA national if his or her UK employer holds a valid certificate, form E101.

Note that: if there is no valid certificate E101 Class 1 NICs are not payable; and a valid form E101 received some time after the person has started work in the other country has to be accepted and, where appropriate, applied retrospectively.

Typically, form E101 is valid for a specified period of 12 months in duration. However, there are circumstances where a longer period, up to a maximum of five years, may be agreed between the social security authorities of the two countries, and certain conditions are met. The authorities may also agree an extension of the initial 12 months specified in the form E101, with form E102 being issued.

The employer is required to use form CA3821 and form CA3822 to apply for a certificate confirming that Class 1 NICs can continue to be paid while the employee is working in the other country.

Once the period of exception shown in the form E101 (or form E102) has elapsed, Class 1 NICs (both primary and secondary contributions) must cease to be paid.

Modified NICs arrangement

Employers can formally apply to HMRC to enter into an agreement to operate modified arrangements for calculating and paying NICs for tax-equalized employees and/or employees assigned from the UK to work overseas. There are similarities between the procedures to be followed for each.

Tax-equalized employees

Employers who obtain the agreement of HMRC to operate a modified PAYE arrangement for tax-equalized employees can also apply to enter into a formal agreement with HMRC that will allow them to account for NICs based on a best estimate of the earnings and then submit the correct figures, on an 'NIC Settlement Return', by 31 March following the year end, without incurring interest and penalties.

To be eligible for inclusion in the agreement, the employee or employees must:

- be subject to a modified PAYE arrangement; and

- be assigned to work in the UK from abroad and have an employer or host employer in the UK liable for secondary UK NICs liabilities; and

- pay NICs on earnings above the annual upper earnings limit for the year, or on earnings at or above the upper earnings limit in each earnings period throughout the year.

If an employee joins, commences liability part-way through an earnings period, or leaves the employment part-way through an earnings period, this does not invalidate the agreement, provided that: for employees with monthly pay periods, NICs are calculated and paid on earnings at or above the upper earnings limit in all months other than the month in which the employee joined or left; and, for employees with an annual pay period, those NICs are calculated and paid on earnings to the person's pro rata upper earnings limit.

Employees assigned from the UK to work overseas

Employers can, subject to certain conditions, enter into an agreement with HMRC that will allow them to account for NICs based on a best estimate of the earnings and then submit the correct figures, on an 'NIC Settlement Return', by 31 March following the year end, without incurring interest and penalties.

The arrangement applies only to those employees who:

▌ are employed by a UK employer and are assigned to work abroad for a period of limited duration, but for more than a complete tax year;

▌ have an ongoing liability to UK NICs whilst abroad;

▌ earn above the upper earnings limit in every earnings period throughout the tax year (but see note below);

▌ are not resident and ordinarily resident for tax purposes and not liable for tax in the UK on the earnings from the relevant employment;

▌ receive some earnings and benefits derived from the employment from sources other than the UK employer.

Note: Where an employee earns less than the upper earnings limit in the pay period he or she joins the employer, or in the pay period in which he or she leaves, if in all other pay periods during the year the upper earnings limit is exceeded he or she can still qualify. However, in the case of employees with annual earnings periods, to be within the agreement their earnings must exceed the annual upper earnings limit.

CLASS 1A NICS

Liability to pay Class 1A NICs in respect of benefits and so on provided to or for the benefit of the employee continues while he or she is abroad while liability to pay Class 1 NICs continues.

CLASS 2 AND CLASS 3 VOLUNTARY NICS

A person who leaves the UK to work abroad and is not liable to pay Class 1 NICs while abroad can make voluntary Class 2 or Class 3 NICs. The purpose of paying such voluntary contributions is to maintain entitlement to certain benefits, for example UK retirement benefit. However, voluntary

NICs do not give cover for health care abroad in any circumstances. The individual uses form CF83 to apply to pay voluntary NICs. A person can choose to change from one class to the other by completing form CF83, but he or she cannot change from Class 3 to Class 2 if he or she is not working.

RESIDENT, ORDINARILY RESIDENT AND PRESENT

Although residency has a bearing on liability to NICs, it does not have the same degree of significance as it does in the income tax treatment of the person's income. However, it has relevance where a person leaves the UK to work abroad or is seconded by an overseas employer to work in the UK. However, the liability (and, indeed, the right) to pay NICs is subject to other factors.

Employer's residency status

Generally, an employer can be said:

▪ to be resident or present if its registered office is in Great Britain or Northern Ireland; or

▪ to have a place of business in Great Britain or Northern Ireland if:
 – it has a fixed address or occupies premises where it is, or is present with the consent of, the lawful owner or tenant;
 – an activity takes place that need not necessarily be remunerative in itself but is in furtherance of the purposes of the business. The business does not need to be of a trading or commercial nature.

Indicators of a place of business include:

▪ a nameplate displayed on the door or premises;

▪ headed letter paper;

▪ a listing in a telephone directory;

▪ a lease or rent agreement, or some sort of financial transaction for the use of the premises;

▪ a registered office;

▪ other premises in Great Britain or Northern Ireland.

Leaving the UK

Whether a person who goes abroad remains ordinarily resident in the UK depends on the circumstances. The following is a list of some of the factors that need to be taken into account:

- If the person maintains a home in the UK during his or her absence, this indicates he or she retains an ordinarily resident status in the UK. However, if the person's home has been rented out on a long lease this will not indicate that he or she is ordinarily resident.

- If the person will be returning to the UK after his or her employment abroad this will indicate that ordinary residence continues. The earlier the return, the more likely it is that ordinary residence status is maintained in the UK.

- Where the person's partner (and/or children, if any) also goes abroad with him or her, it is more likely that ordinary residence in the UK will not be maintained, particularly where a home is not retained in the UK or they make occasional visits to the UK.

- If the person will be returning to the UK from time to time during the period of employment abroad and he or she makes frequent and lengthy returns, it is more likely that ordinary residence continues.

- If the purpose of the person's visits to the UK are to visit his or her family who have remained at the person's home (or to spend holidays there) this will indicate continuing ordinary residence. However, visits solely for the purpose of carrying on duties incidental to the work overseas (such as briefing, training or making reports) will not be such a strong indicator.

Multi-state employment

Where an EEA citizen is employed concurrently in two or more EEA member states, he or she is treated as subject to the social security contribution law of the country in which he or she is resident if he or she works partly in that member state.

An EEA citizen who is employed concurrently in two or more EEA member states, and does not work in the member state in which he or she resides, is subject to the social security contribution law of the country either in which he or she resides or in which his or her employer's registered office or place of business is located.

Part 4

Immigration and employment law

4.1

Obtaining UK work authorization

Alex Paterson and Owen Davies, Fragomen LLP

INTRODUCTION

Immigration has often been considered the 'poor relation' of expatriate management, thought of, at best, just before the planned start date in the host location or, all too frequently, after arrival.

In a worst-case scenario, the first notification is when an emergency call comes in from the airport confirming that the assignee has been stopped at the border and legal advice is needed. It is fair to say though that immigration is moving up the corporate agenda in the majority of multinational companies, owing to an increasing focus on compliance and the need to track global staff movements. Governments are placing increased responsibility on businesses to comply with immigration legislation or face harsh penalties including significant fines, custodial sentences against culpable directors and managers and, in the case of the UK, removing the right to be able to sponsor any foreign workers in the future.

When considering the hire of any non-EEA national in the UK, whether on a local or an assignment basis, one of the first questions that needs to be asked is whether the individual has the ability to work in the UK legally. The immigration issue is likely to be one of the longest and most bureaucratic of all the processes involved. Therefore it is important to manage the expectations of the business and the individual from the outset. Otherwise the coordinator of the hire may not only be dealing with a loss of personal reputation, but also be placing the company and themselves at significant legal risk.

IS WORK AUTHORIZATION ALWAYS REQUIRED?

Not every non-EEA national requires permission to undertake work in the UK. Some may have obtained a self-sponsored immigration status that provides the freedom to work; others may have family connections to the UK that carry an automatic work authorization; still others may be students or have been sponsored by their home governments to spend a period of time in the UK.

The complexity of UK immigration law is such that a full list of who is and who is not required to obtain work authorization would not be possible, as the personal circumstances of the individual in question is often the defining factor.

The most common question asked of immigration lawyers is whether an individual who has no work authorization in the UK can carry out business activities as a visitor. Although an attractive option, given that a significant number of nationalities do not need immigration permission to visit the UK, it is unfortunately an area of constant abuse.

If the individual is to be paid an income from a UK source or is to have a UK employment contract or letter of assignment, employment authorization is always required. However, the fact that an individual is not paid an income from a UK source or is not to have a UK employment contract or letter of assignment does not always obviate the work authorization requirements. When considering whether an individual requires work authorization or can enter the UK as a visitor, four questions need to be asked, each of which is detailed below.

The answer to the first question will help to determine what should be done to ensure legal compliance. However, the answer is not always definitive and, where this is the case, the second to fourth questions should be asked, because the answers here will be determined by company policy and the employer's attitude to risk.

In addition, the immigration category of visitor is currently the subject of review by the UK government. It is important, therefore, to research the up-to-date position of visitors whenever carrying out an assessment.

1. What is the activity to be carried out in the UK?

A business visitor to the UK will be expected to meet all criteria for entry to the UK as a visitor. The immigration officer must be convinced that the business visitor continues to work outside the UK and has no intention to transfer his or her base to the UK, even temporarily. The business visitor will be expected to receive his or her salary from outside the UK but can receive reasonable expenses to cover costs of travel and subsistence whilst in the UK. He or she must not receive a salary or fee from a UK source and must not be involved in selling goods or services direct to the public.

It is not possible to give a comprehensive list of permitted activities that a business visitor can carry out in the UK or whether an activity will be considered to be 'productive work' that requires work authorization. The decision will depend, in part, on the particular circumstances of the individual. For example, gathering information in the UK is a permitted activity of a business visitor unless that visitor is an auditor, when gathering information is a duty of such a role and, as such, a productive activity that requires work authorization. Therefore, there is a grey area as to what is or is not permitted. However, the following are generally accepted as permitted activities:

- attending meetings and/or conferences;

- arranging deals, negotiating or signing contracts;

- coming to undertake fact-finding missions or check goods;

- coming for training in techniques and work practices used in the UK, provided the training is confined to classroom instruction or observation and familiarization;

- coming to speak at a conference, where the conference is a one-off and not run as a commercial concern;

- advisers, consultants and trainers, provided they are employed outside the UK, either directly or under contract by the same company (or group of companies) to which the client company in the UK belongs. This must not extend to project management or providing advice or consultancy services direct to clients of the UK company. Training should be for specific, one-off purposes. It should be restricted to classroom training.

Accordingly, the activity that the individual will carry out in the UK will determine whether work authorization is required. However, because the meaning of 'productive activity' is such a grey area, the following three questions may be asked to determine whether work authorization should be obtained to minimize risk and protect the individual and company from potential criminal liability for illegal work.

2. How long will the person spend in the UK?

If an individual has entered the UK as a business visitor, he or she will routinely be granted permission to remain in the UK for six months, as the law allows for a foreign national to spend six months out of every 12 months in the UK as a visitor. However, an immigration officer must be convinced that the individual is a genuine visitor and, if an individual wished to spend six months in the UK, the question would arise as to whether such a visit is genuine. In short, the longer the time that a person plans to spend in the UK, the more likely it is that he or she will be carrying out activities that are not permitted to a visitor and, therefore, the chances of refusal of entry are increased.

Companies have different policies on what length of time is acceptable for a business visitor depending on attitudes to risk. In general, however, a planned visit that is to exceed six weeks at any one time raises serious questions of genuineness and, therefore, even if the planned activities in the UK are within the visitor criteria, work authorization should be obtained to minimize the risk associated with the travel.

3. How many times will the person be travelling to the UK?

Whether an individual should be allowed to enter the UK as a business visitor is a decision taken by an immigration officer on the individual's entry to the UK. Accordingly, although there is the risk that the company may be visited during the course of the individual's time in the UK, the main immigration risk associated with business travel exists when the person arrives in the UK. Thus, a high number of entries to the UK will, itself, increase the risk of being refused entry to the UK.

The number of entries to the UK is difficult to control or follow. However, if it is known from the outset that an individual will be making regular trips to the UK over a relatively short period of time, work authorization should be obtained to minimize the risk associated with the travel. This is particularly so because a special type of work authorization exists within the UK system, specifically for the scenario where regular travel to the UK is required but a person's place of work will continue outside the UK.

4. How senior is the individual travelling to the UK?

The seniority of an individual is not a factor that will determine whether an immigration officer allows or does not allow entry to the UK as a business visitor. However, an individual's seniority should be taken into consideration when deciding upon whether work authorization is required for several reasons. If a senior individual is denied entry to the UK as a business visitor:

▌ the potential cost impact for the company may be significantly higher than if a more junior staff member is denied entry;

▌ the potential embarrassment to the company is increased (for example, if a meeting is missed with a client);

▌ the potential for adverse publicity is increased;

▌ the potential negative impact on others within the company, for example those within an HR department who allowed the travel to the UK as a visitor, is increased.

Accordingly, the more senior the individual who is travelling to the UK, the better it is to obtain work authorization for that individual to minimize risk and increase protection, particularly where the answers to questions 2 and 3 are such that the risk involved is relatively high.

Obtaining work authorization: the UK points-based system

Alex Paterson and Owen Davies, Fragomen LLP

The UK Border Agency (UKBA) has led a recent reform of the UK immigration system and the implementation of a new Points Based System (PBS). The roll-out of PBS began on 29 February 2008 and should be completed by April 2009; it sits alongside ongoing activity to tighten up the UK's immigration controls.

Based on the Australian immigration system, the PBS has been developed to provide a simpler, more objective and more transparent immigration system by replacing the 80-plus worker and study entry routes into the UK with a five-tiered Points Based System (see Table 4.2.1).

Tiers 1, 2 and 5 have sub-categories that reflect the different circumstances of both the applicant (for Tier 1) and the sponsor (for Tiers 2 and 5).

The biggest impact on the employer will be the introduction of Tier 2 (the replacement of the current UK work permit scheme) and, as such, the remainder of this chapter will concentrate on this tier.

TIER 2 OF PBS

Tier 2 is an employer-led based system for medium- and high-skilled migrants that in 2008 will replace the UK work permit scheme.

Applicants will need to have a job offer from an employer that has been issued with a sponsorship licence by the UKBA. The licensed employer

Table 4.2.1 The UK five-tiered points based immigration system

Tiers	Type of Worker	Government Implementation Timeline	Sponsor Needed	Work Authorization	Leads to Permanent Residency
Tier 1	Highly skilled migrants with no job offer	From February 2008	No	Yes, in most cases, for any employer	Yes, in most cases
Tier 2	Skilled workers with job offer	From October 2008	Yes, employer	Yes, in all cases, for specified employer	Yes, in all cases
Tier 3	Low-skilled workers with job offer	No timeline	Yes, employer	Yes, in all cases, for specified employer	No
Tier 4	Students	April 2009	Yes, educational institute	Yes, in all cases, for any employer but with restrictions on hours	No
Tier 5	Visiting workers, youth mobility and cultural exchange	From October 2008	Yes, sponsor depends on sub-category	Yes, in most cases, for both any and specified employer depending on sub-category	No

will issue a certificate of sponsorship that the applicant will need to incorporate into his or her Tier 2 immigration application. Each of these three stages is detailed further below.

1. Employer obtains a licence to sponsor from the UKBA

If a UK company wishes to sponsor non-EEA national employees in the UK, a sponsorship licence will be needed.[1] Even if no new non-EEA national employees are to be employed, a sponsorship licence will be required if current non-EEA national employees who have work permits will require a renewal process during their stay in the UK.

The sponsorship licence is obtained through application to the UKBA. The sponsor will register online, with supporting documentation being submitted in paper format within 14 days.

The UK employer, and not a third-party legal representative, should submit the online application form. However, when submitting, the UK employer can detail the name and contact details of a legal representative who will be dealing with the day-to-day issues of Tier 2 on behalf of the UK employer. Only one legal representative can be detailed.

Before issuing the licence, the UKBA will investigate applicants to ensure that they are bona fide organizations that are likely to comply with the conditions of sponsorship and general duties of an employer under current UK immigration legislation and PBS.[2]

Once the licence is obtained, it will be valid for four years before a renewal will be required.

2. Employer issues a certificate of sponsorship

Once the employer is a licensed sponsor, the employer[3] will issue a certificate of sponsorship for a non-EEA national whom the employer wishes to employ. The non-EEA national can then use the certificate to obtain the relevant immigration permission.

In effect, the certificate of sponsorship replaces the work permit of the work permit scheme. Thus, the criteria to be met before the employer should issue a certificate of sponsorship will be almost identical to the criteria to be met for the UKBA to issue a work permit. In short, the following will be measured:

▌ that the position on offer in the UK is at least at NVQ Level 3;

▌ that the applicant intends and is able to carry out the duties of the position on offer;

▌ that the salary offered for the UK position is at market rate;

▌ that the applicant is an intra-company transferee (through at least six months' employment with a group company overseas) or the position is listed as a shortage occupation or has been advertised in line with the resident labour market test.

However, a duty of sponsorship is to only issue certificates of sponsorship to migrants who, to the best of the sponsor's knowledge and belief, meet the requirements of Tier 2 and are likely to comply with the conditions of their immigration permission. Therefore, the employer should also ensure that the conditions of the immigration application (see the next section) are met before issuing the certificate of sponsorship.

Unlike the work permit, the certificate of sponsorship will not be a physical document but a pin number that the individual can then use to support his or her immigration application. The pin number is generated by entering the relevant data within the new UKBA online Sponsorship Management System (SMS), which the employer will have access to once the sponsorship licence has been issued. The UKBA will be using the information inputted into the SMS to monitor activity and carry out risk assessments.

3. Individual submits the immigration application

The non-EEA national will not be able to submit his or her immigration application without the certificate of sponsorship. However, the certificate of sponsorship alone will not be sufficient for the immigration application to be successful. The applicant will still need to score sufficient points for the application to be successful. Table 4.2.2 identifies the point-scoring areas.

In addition, applications will be successful only where:

▌ the applicant has no adverse UK immigration history that would warrant a refusal of the immigration application;

▌ the applicant has no criminal record that would warrant a refusal of the immigration application;

▌ the applicant has no medical history that would warrant a refusal of the immigration application.

At present the maintenance test requires the individual to have a minimum credit bank balance of £800 for a period prior to submission of

Table 4.2.2   Points-scoring areas for UK entry

At least 70 points are required from this table (including 10 for maintenance and 10 for English).

All jobs must be at or above NVQ3 skill level and salary must be at or above the appropriate rate.

Section	Certificate of Sponsorship		Qualifications (or NARIC equivalents)		Prospective Earnings (£)[1,2,3]	
A	Offer of job in shortage occupation	50	No qualifications	0	17,000–19,999	5
(50 points needed)	Offer of job that passes Resident Labour Market test	30	NVQ3	5	20,000–21,999	10
			Bachelor's or Master's	10	22,000–23,999	15
	Intra-company transfer	30	PhD	15	24,000+	20
B	Maintenance requirement					10
C	Competence in English					10

Source: UK Border Agency

the immigration application, with additional funds being required if the applicant is to be accompanied by family members.

The Competence in English test will be based on the individual's circumstances, with type of certificate of sponsorship, nationality and education being reviewed to ascertain whether the test has been met.

The immigration application will involve three stages: an initial online submission of data; a biometrics appointment that requires the applicant and every family member at and over five years old to attend so that a digital photograph and fingerprints can be taken; and the physical submission of documentation to the relevant government agency. The documentation to be submitted will all need to be original and translated into English where needed for the government agency to ascertain whether the applicant meets the relevant criteria.

WHAT IF I GET IT WRONG?

Although PBS has significant benefits in that the employer, rather than the UKBA, will issue the UK work authorization, there will also be new requirements for the UK employer to monitor closely, report on and audit its non-EEA national workforce. To ensure that these obligations are met, the UK government is introducing or has introduced new penalties for non-compliance. These include:

- New criminal penalties if any UK employer *knowingly* employs a foreign national in the UK without the requisite immigration permission. In such circumstances, the UK employer could face an unlimited fine or up to two years' imprisonment.

- New civil penalties if any UK employer *negligently* employs a foreign national in the UK without the requisite immigration permission. In such circumstances, the UK employer could face a fine of up to £10,000 per illegal worker.

- New automatic bans from entering the UK for non-EEA nationals who have been refused entry to the UK or found to be breaching their conditions of entry (eg a visitor found to be working in the UK). These automatic bans range from 1 to 10 years depending on the severity of the breach.

- The UK employer being downgraded from 'A' to 'B' rating and possible removal from the sponsorship register. Such action would have the following consequences:
  - Given that the sponsorship register is a public document, the UK employer being 'B' graded or ungraded would have a significant impact on recruitment, as the UK employer would be less attractive to possible recruits if 'B' graded or would not be able to sponsor non-EEA nationals if ungraded.
  - The UKBA might suspend the UK employer's recruitment of foreign nationals during any period of 'B' grading.
  - All foreign nationals employed by the UK employer in the UK on the basis of work permits or certificates of sponsorship would need to be dismissed within 60 days of the UK employer becoming ungraded.
  - The grading of the sponsorship register, as a public document, might affect the share price as an indicator of the UK employer's ability to employ foreign nationals in the UK.

WHAT CAN I DO TO MAKE MY LIFE EASIER?

The benefits of migrants to the UK economy are well recognized, albeit not well publicized. Official statistics show that migrants contribute 10 per cent of GDP despite making up only 8 per cent of the workforce. At a corporate level, 60 per cent of companies regard human resources as the most important factor in future competitiveness and, with increased global competition and the rise of the knowledge economy, eight in 10 UK employers are looking beyond the domestic market and are actively recruiting staff from overseas.

Accordingly, the sourcing, mobility and retention of quality human resources are paramount, and the immigration issue is now a commonplace factor within the everyday activities of UK companies. Therefore initiating and developing a corporate immigration strategy is a simple way of documenting processes and maximizing compliance whilst communicating to the business as a whole what is acceptable and what is not acceptable from a company perspective.

What is corporate immigration strategy?

Simply put, corporate immigration strategy is a coherent corporate approach to ensuring that immigration is a business tool rather than a business impediment. It can be domestic in approach but, depending on the organization involved, most effective when regional or even global in nature. It defines what is acceptable from a corporate risk standpoint whilst also introducing policies that will best benefit the company now and in the future. As it relates to the interpretation and implementation of law, it requires buy-in at the appropriate level of an organization and needs to be properly communicated throughout the organization to have maximum effect.

How does it work in practice?

Any corporate immigration strategy will be unique to the organization involved. There are, however, common themes.

The UK immigration authorities are extremely commercially aware. However, their resources are limited and, therefore, the most respected and well-known service users will be at an advantage. Branding and representation, both at corporate and at legal representative level, are, therefore, key to immigration. Whilst pigeon-holed and/or under-represented, the leverage available to obtain concessions, exceptional treatment and better turnaround times is limited.

Then there are costs. A coherent and comprehensive corporate immigration strategy may immediately save some money. In the future, however, a carefully planned corporate immigration strategy introduced now, in anticipation of the employer accreditation scheme, could potentially save some organizations hundreds of thousands of pounds.

The final common theme is the willingness of the vast majority of UK companies to be compliant. In most cases, compliance is directly related to control. A review of organizational structure from an immigration perspective and the authority to deal with an increasingly complex area of law typically identifies weaknesses. This, in turn, can assist in policy drafting to strengthen the company and maximize leverage benefit.

The thread that runs through all themes is the need for companies to be able to monitor, track and connect with their migrant population. The need to produce and review reports is, therefore, paramount, and the days of the Excel spreadsheet with expiry dates should be long gone. The intelligent company should have access to reports both in the UK and internationally that can detail all immigration aspects of an expatriate assignment or new hire. Only in this way can a company truly calculate movement to maximize branding, manage costs and ascertain compliance levels.

UK immigration law has become a fundamental consideration for any UK company. With the current overhaul of the UK immigration system, this will become even more so as companies are obliged to monitor their migrant population. For those companies that already have a corporate immigration strategy in place, it is a good time for review in light of the UK government's overhaul of the UK immigration system. For those that don't, an immediate discussion may prove vital.

What is clear is that now is the ideal opportunity to consider where companies are at present in terms of their immigration policy and where they would like to be when Tier 2 of the PBS is implemented. The key under the new system is to put into practice a cohesive and manageable process, practical to operate and robust from an audit and compliance perspective.

If you would like to discuss roll-out of PBS further and how Fragomen LLP can assist you, please send your enquiry to pbs@fragomen.com or call +44 (0)20 3077 5130 or visit https://pbs.fragomen.net.

NOTES

1. Group versus Individual licence. If a UK employer has a number of legal entities in the UK, the entities can apply for individual sponsorship licences or an application can be made for one group licence, incorporating all or a number of UK legal entities. The advantages of the group licence are: 1) Only one application fee is incurred. 2) With PBS focusing on compliance, a group licence may allow the group to control better the activity of its workforce through the introduction of group-wide policies and procedures rather than each individual company being left to implement its own process or no

process at all. Thus a group licence should maximize compliance in the group as a whole through central control. A group licence, therefore, assists in protecting the organization as a whole. 3) A group licence will allow the UK employer's employees to transfer between group companies within the UK without the need for the issue of a further certificate of sponsorship. The disadvantage of the group licence is that the group is at risk if there is non-compliance within an individual company. However, this risk is tempered by the advantages of control and representation at 2) above.

2. Conditions of sponsorship and general duties of the sponsor. The conditions of sponsorship and general duties of the sponsor in obtaining the sponsorship licence are: 1) to carry out pre-employment checks on every employee working for the company in the UK to ensure that they have the relevant immigration permission to take the employment in question; 2) to record the contact details (residential address, telephone number, mobile telephone number) of each sponsored migrant; 3) to carry out an annual audit of all non-EEA national employees to ensure that their immigration permission remains valid for the employment in question, in terms both of expiry and of conditions attached to that immigration permission; 4) to inform the UK government whenever the employee changes his or her contact details or whenever there is a significant change in circumstances (such as change of job or salary) or a prolonged leave of absence during the employment life cycle; 5) to report any suspicions that the migrant is breaching the conditions of his or her immigration permission; 6) to inform the UK government when the employee leaves the employment or no longer requires sponsorship; 7) to inform the UK government if there is a change in corporate structure that affects the sponsorship licence; 8) to issue a certificate of sponsorship only if the relevant criteria are met; 9) to pay at least the salary specified on the certificate of sponsorship; and 10) to maintain records as evidence that the above duties are being carried out.

3. The legal representative can issue the certificate of sponsorship on behalf of the employer, but the generic term 'employer' is used here.

Digest of employment law

Jonathan Exten-Wright and Paul Thompson,
DLA Piper UK LLP

This chapter covers the essential aspects of employment law when appointing employees on short- and long-term international assignments. It covers contractual issues such as choice of law and jurisdiction, and considers benefits and practical advice. It is primarily aimed at UK-based employers planning to appoint staff to roles outside the UK, but issues for inbound appointments are also covered.

KEY LEGAL FEATURES OF AN INTERNATIONAL CONTRACT OF EMPLOYMENT

When drafting any international contract of employment (or a service agreement for senior employees), it is necessary to consider the following:

- the applicable law of the agreement;
- where any disputes will be resolved – the country of jurisdiction;
- the mandatory local laws that must prevail in any event.

One important point to note is that in Europe the Posted Workers Directive may apply if an employee is sent for a limited period by an employer based in one EU member state to work for a company based in another. This requires the company in the host state to apply certain local minimum terms and conditions, including minimum wage, holidays and equal treatment. When seconding or temporarily posting a worker, employers must ensure that the contract complies with local minimum terms and conditions. By way of example, if a full-time UK worker is seconded to the Paris office, he or she would have a 35-hour working week, which is the maximum in France.

The extent to which local rules can continue to apply can conflict with the principle of freedom of movement of workers within the EU. A recent European Court of Justice decision in *Dirk Rüffert* v *Land Niedersachsen* has held that foreign companies bringing construction workers to another member state can ignore collective agreements in force in that Member State and pay workers at rates below prescribed industry minimum wages there. This tension has not yet been fully resolved by the court.

What protection applies to UK employees working overseas?

Employees are primarily protected by the terms of their contract. Should an employer breach these terms, employees may obtain remedies such as damages in a court or employment tribunal.

Employees also receive statutory protection in the form of both domestic and European legislation. The most important remedy is the right not to be unfairly dismissed. The exclusion of the right to bring a claim for unfair dismissal in the UK for those who ordinarily worked outside the UK was removed in 1999 and so, along with employees who were employed in Great Britain at the time of the dismissal, certain types of employees who work abroad will be covered.

The case of *Lawson* v *Serco Ltd* considered the scope of section 94 of the Employment Rights Act 1996, which governs unfair dismissal in this context. It set out the following categories of employees who would also be able to bring a claim for unfair dismissal:

▌ peripatetic employees (such as pilots) if Britain was their 'base' at the time of dismissal;

▌ expatriate employees working wholly abroad if they:
   – were posted abroad by a British employer for the purposes of a business carried on in Britain; or
   – worked for a British employer in an extraterritorial base abroad (such as a military base or embassy); or
   – can demonstrate equally strong connections with Britain and British employment law.

The scope of domestic legislation that can potentially be enforced by UK employees overseas has recently been developed further in case law. In

Duncombe v *Department for Education and Skills*, the court held that employees who worked abroad were entitled to bring claims under the Fixed-term Employees (Prevention of Less Favourable Treatment) Regulations 2002.

There has been another important development in terms of when an employee's rights under European Union-inspired legislation can be enforced, seen as distinct from when rights under domestic legislation can be enforced. In the case of *Bleuse* v *MBT Transport Ltd*, the court extended the scope of claims that overseas workers can bring in the UK. The employee failed in his unfair dismissal claim, as he did not meet the *Lawson* v *Serco* criteria set out above, but he did have jurisdiction, the right to bring a holiday pay claim under the Working Time Directive, as this was a directly effective right conferred by European Union law. The correctness of this judgment has been questioned, but it is clear that this is a complex and fast-developing area of case law. UK-based employers with overseas workers are currently finding that the range of potential claims that can be brought against them in the UK by expatriate workers is widening.

Can you choose the law that will apply to the contract?

As a basic rule, parties may select the law that they would like to apply to a contract. Special rules apply to contracts of employment, however, and an exception to the freedom to choose the applicable law of the contract is set out at Article 6 of the Rome Convention. This aspect of European Union law was brought into UK domestic law by the Contracts (Applicable Law) Act 1990 and, as with other European Union-derived laws, the European Court of Justice has authority on questions of interpretation.

Article 6 provides that the choice of law clauses in contracts of employment cannot exclude or waive the protection of mandatory rules. This means parties cannot contract out of the application of certain statutory rules that ordinarily apply to protect employees in the country in which the contract is being performed.

It follows that, wherever an employee habitually works in the European Union, he or she will get the protection of the mandatory laws of the host state. An example for inbound employees is that, even if Russian law is chosen as the applicable law of the contract, Article 6 will ensure that, if the employee is wholly or mainly based in the UK, he or she will receive UK statutory protection, such as anti-discrimination laws.

The Article 6 exception to the Rome Convention does not cover arbitration clauses. A company is free to contract with an employee to include a clause to arbitrate a dispute in an agreed jurisdiction. The subject matter of the dispute will have to be identifiably separate from the contract of employment, but could potentially include certain incentive agreements.

What if there is no choice of law?

If there is no express choice of law in the contract, Article 6(2) states that the contract will be governed a) by the law of the country in which the employee habitually carries out work in performance of the contract (even if he or she is temporarily employed in another country) or b) if the employee does not habitually carry out work in any one country, by the law of the country in which the place of business through which he or she is engaged is situated (unless the circumstances show that the contract is more closely connected with another country, in which case the law of that country will apply).

Can you choose which courts will have jurisdiction?

Separate from the issue of which law applies, it is also possible to choose, in the contract, the country where any dispute that may arise will be heard. This is, however, also subject to the limitations of Article 6. In other words, if an employee based in Spain has a contract giving exclusive jurisdiction to the courts of England and Wales, he or she will not be deprived of his or her mandatory Spanish law rights at the UK hearing.

By way of example, in the case of *Harada Ltd (t/a chequepoint)* v *Turner*, the UK court was awarded jurisdiction to hear a contractual claim by an Englishman employed in Spain by an Irish offshore entity, as the central management and control of the company were exercised in England.

As another illustration, the case of *Samengo-Turner* v *Marsh McLennan (Services) Limited* held that long-term incentive and stock award plans awarded to employees in the UK working at an English insurance broker, which were said to be subject to the law and jurisdiction of New York, were part of the employees' contracts of employment. Accordingly, jurisdiction was awarded to the UK courts.

Restrictive covenants are often the subject matter of disputes. In *Duarte* v *Black & Decker Corporation* an employee based in the UK had a long-term incentive plan including post-termination restrictive covenants that was subject to the law and jurisdiction of Maryland, United States. Even though the obligation to work was contained in a separate contract of employment, the UK Court of Appeal held that the terms of the incentive agreement were part of an overall package of UK employment terms and conditions. That being the case, it held that it would not allow employers to circumvent Article 6 by hiving off certain aspects of an employment relationship into a side agreement that, standing alone, would not amount to an individual employment contract.

These cases could have repercussions for employers that provide equity benefits to senior employees who have contracts of employment and/or incentive arrangements expressed as subject to one law and one jurisdiction but actually worked upon in the UK. These may be subject to challenge should they breach the laws of the UK, despite what is said in the documentation.

No matter what law is chosen to apply to a contract, remedies such as damages are assessed by the rules of the courts of the country with jurisdiction. This means that employers should always consider the potential remedies they may require when deciding which jurisdiction they specify will apply if there is a dispute. If the procedural law of the state whose courts have jurisdiction to hear the matter does not provide a certain remedy (such as a type of injunction or other court order to stop an employee committing a particular act), this remedy cannot be achieved. (In matters relating to tort, ie a civil wrongdoing as opposed to a contractual claim, such as negligence committed by an overseas employer, a defendant can be sued in the courts of the place in which the harmful event occurred.)

Can employees be given dual contracts?

Dual contracts are used where an employee is not domiciled in the UK but carries out duties of employment both in and outside the UK.

In most cases, with non-domiciled status, an employee's overseas work can attract lower tax rates. Indeed, for this reason many City of London non-domiciled employees try to structure their role so that some of the performance of their identifiable duties is for the part of the business outside the UK so as to achieve more favourable tax treatment of that part of their reward structure.

An example is where non-UK domiciled employees come to work in the UK for UK resident employers. In such an instance, the employee may be offered two employments instead of one: 1) covering the performance of duties in the UK; and 2) covering duties performed outside the UK, usually with an associated company resident offshore.

Dual contracts such as these can be very effective, but it is often difficult to separate two employment roles, especially for senior employees. HMRC looks closely at such arrangements and will study the actual commercial situation of the employee's arrangements. If the non-UK remuneration is not compatible with the actual role or duties carried out in the other country, HMRC is likely to challenge the arrangement. It is often difficult to prove that there are two separate employment roles in each country, as employment abroad must be performed wholly outside the UK and that contract must be with a 'foreign employer' – this is usually another employing entity within the same group structure.

Helpfully, HMRC has issued guidance on the components of dual contract arrangements that they may challenge. Examples range from identical contracts and means of communication to unrealistic weighting of remuneration to the offshore employment. Employers must be able to show a distinct role in each territory and have two separate payrolls and expense procedures and even sets of business cards. It is worth noting that, if HMRC deems there to be just one employment, the UK employer could be liable for PAYE (income tax) and National Insurance contribution liabilities for the non-UK employment, plus penalties and interest.

It is also possible to have a dual contract by maintaining an existing contract as a base, but suspending it for the length of the overseas role, which would then be covered by a separate contract.

CONSIDERATIONS APPLYING TO SHORT- AND LONG-TERM EXPATRIATE APPOINTMENTS

Staff employed in one country may be asked to go on secondment, make a short visit or undertake a long-term assignment in another country. The employee will usually remain employed by the original employer, which will retain the power to dismiss or discipline the employee or vary the contract. Daily activities will normally be directed by the host employer. For short visits and most secondments, whether into or from the UK, it is normal for a company to pay all travel expenses (subject to company policies on receipts, mode of travel, etc). Other potential considerations are:

▌ work permit and visa;

▌ additional medical insurance cover;

▌ provision of accommodation;

▌ daily allowance or temporary increase in salary due to relocation or enforced absence;

▌ personal or out-of-pocket expenses.

Most employees will have a mobility clause, but an employee's consent to a longer-term appointment will usually be necessary. Along with country-specific tax requirements, components of a service agreement for a longer-term international appointment will be:

▌ commencement and termination dates of the assignment (and provisions for extension);

▌ medical examination;

▌ salary (home country plus usually a mark-up or allowance, or host country package, often to include a relocation package);

▌ pension and share options provisions if the employee cannot stay in the home company schemes;

▌ relevant adjusted working hours;

▌ additional family benefits, such as school fees;

▌ rules covering local laws and customs where necessary.

Secondments – who pays the employee?

Usually the seconding entity will continue to pay the secondee's wages and all other costs (including income tax and National Insurance contributions). If the secondment is a commercial arrangement, however, then the host will usually reimburse these costs. Parties should clearly agree who will be paying any additional costs (for example overtime, bonuses, expenses especially relocation and travel expenses), training and membership fees; and what occurs if the secondee is absent for a substantial period (for example, maternity leave or long-term absences due to illness).

EXTENDING OR TERMINATING CONTRACTS AND OTHER PRACTICAL TIPS

Expatriate assignments are, at times, brought to an end prematurely. Costs can be significant and range from wasted training, cancelled leases and lost deposits to reduced goodwill and cooperation from customers and international colleagues. Whether premature or not, repatriation and new roles should be planned in advance to minimize risk.

It is important to insert a power-of-recall clause in any agreement if it is possible that the worker will be needed back in the country of origin during the term of the secondment or assignment or if it is easier or more appropriate to effect termination there.

Many companies have template or pro forma assignment agreements or secondment agreements. Any international agreements should still be 'health checked' and adapted to local conditions, and each specific contract should be tailored every time a worker is posted abroad.

When extending or varying an overseas assignment, it is important to keep a record of renewal documentation, especially if this is a continuing series of appointments. This is especially important if the roles are located in numerous jurisdictions and there is potential for a dispute over which rights apply. Each renewal or relocation should not be done simply as a matter of course. Care should be taken to assess whether there are any continuing or accumulating rights, in the original home country, the employee's country of origin, the new host country or even former host countries, despite employees moving on. These points need to be addressed each time and properly canvassed in the paperwork.

Lastly, during a long-term assignment, decide if and when full employment may commence with the host country. It may be costly to the business or inappropriate to keep an employee on secondment terms if the assignment lasts for a period of years. Any localization of terms and conditions should be planned well in advance.

Part 5

Practical problem areas

60 Second Interview with Dale Collins, CEO of an International Moving & Relocation Company

We asked Dale Collins,
CEO of Interdean International Relocation,
about his company.

Tell us a bit about Interdean

Interdean is a global move management company. Quite simply this means we help organisations to relocate their staff anywhere around the world by providing household goods moving services and supporting relocation programmes.

Who are your customers?

Interdean's clients tend to be those people who have responsibility within organisations for the relocation of staff between their business' various locations and the costs involved in these processes.

We aim to help our customers by working with them to design a moving or relocation policy that suits the needs of their business and the individuals being moved.

In terms of the type of organisations Interdean works for, we cover just about every geographic location, size and industry sector. The fact that we have such a diverse client base means that our service needs to be extremely flexible, delivered to a high standard and at the same time be totally consistent.

What does "global move management" involve?

Moving people involves having the vehicles, warehouses, systems, specialist equipment and experienced staff to handle each of the elements of a relocation programme. However most of what we do involves managing and co-ordinating hundreds of other service providers across the world for each part of the relocation service. Interdean's ability to control each of these elements is where I believe we really stand out.

What makes Interdean different?

Interdean offers excellent service in terms of consistency and quality, but where I think we are different is in our customer service approach.

Interdean has experienced account management teams in locations that are convenient to our customers. Each is capable of managing global contracts and provides a continual source of feedback for the client and their relocating employees. This makes a lot of sense in terms of communication and quality control. It also makes things a lot simpler for our customers.

Interdean's philosophy is that our service should support both the business and the people we move.

What do you value most in your company?

I am really proud of the fact that we have such diversity in our company. I feel that our range of skills and cultural mix as a business is a real strength and continues to drive us forward.

I am also very proud of the work Interdean is doing towards the environment at the moment. As a father of two I feel that we all have a responsibility towards society and the world that we live in.

Where is Interdean based?

Interdean has offices throughout Europe and in to Asia, in fact we have 45 service centres in over 33 countries. Interdean covers all of the places you are familiar with and those that represent the largest emerging markets.

Which countries have the most relocation activity?

The United States remains the dominant market, with the UK remaining in the top three. Unsurprisingly China and India are fast growing destinations. Dubai represents a lot of our traffic along with Australia, Hong Kong and Singapore. The growth areas most wouldn't think of are the Eastern European states such as Kazakhstan and Russia, whilst South America continues to show potential.

How to Contact Interdean International Relocation

If your business moves employees between locations, then you may wish to speak Interdean.
+44 (0)20 8961 4141
www.interdean.com

Moving employees

Philip Pertoldi, Abels Moving Services

Getting what you want from service suppliers when organizing international moves for your company employees can seem to be a complex process. The aim of this chapter is to offer some tips and guidance in selecting a company to provide hands-on move management services, making sure it delivers the required service levels at your behest and at optimum cost – in a nutshell, how to obtain cost-effective solutions whilst avoiding upsetting valuable staff when moving them around the globe.

SELECTING THE RIGHT COMPANY

In selecting the right moving company for the job there are a few key indicators to look for in any supplier's credentials. Assuming you are not delegating responsibility for moving services to a relocation company or international van line, you will find specialist international movers are members of the FIDI Global Network, whose major criterion for membership is its FAIM quality accreditation, which is audited by an external body to a demanding industry-prescribed standard. Added to this is the ISO 9001:2000 international standard for quality management systems, whose criteria again receive annual testing by a recognized outside organization like the BSI. In the UK, insurance services can be offered only by companies that are authorized and regulated by the Financial Services Authority (FSA), which tests a company's financial stability, insurance knowledge and suitability of management.

Once the credentials of potential suppliers have been checked, the tendering process needs to be selected. Let us examine briefly the benefits and disadvantages of four alternative tender processes: three supplier quotes; exclusive supplier agreements; fixed panel; and two global suppliers.

Three supplier quotes

In the case of organizations having a large number of staff making international moves, getting three supplier quotes for each is not recommended. This can involve excessive administration, with the purchasing officer having to deal with three quotes for each move, seasonal price fluctuations and other issues such as companies making local agreements and expats making private arrangements at company expense.

Exclusive supplier agreements

Exclusive supplier agreements can offer the benefit of a streamlined purchasing process, often via website bookings, uniform service, and cost savings due to the discounts available on high volumes of business. But the lack of competitive pressure on pricing once the tender process has been completed is a major disadvantage, and it may be unwise to have all your eggs in one basket.

Fixed panel

Alternatively, a fixed panel of suppliers could be used to provide competition. The difficulty with this approach is that it requires a dedicated in-house move management team to compare the quotes and services of each company.

Two global suppliers

Appointing two global suppliers combines the advantages of exclusive agreements and a fixed panel of suppliers, with work allocated on the basis of competitiveness and quality of service. Alternative suppliers can also be regionalized to suit a company's own buying areas.

Other criteria in selecting a move management provider include price, network coverage, IT support, innovation, past performance and experience, appropriate references, environmental awareness, and health and safety standards. Each criterion can be given a weighting, and the weighted criteria together will determine the final selection.

REQUEST FOR QUOTATION (RFQ) – TELLING THE SUPPLIER WHAT YOU WANT TO GET A SENSIBLE AND ACCURATE QUOTE

Once companies are selected based on a criterion other than price and in order for the supplier to draw up as accurate a quote model as possible, it is essential that they are provided with sufficient information. The more accurate and relevant this is, the closer the quote will be to the actual cost and the lower the risk of a premium over the budgeted cost of the move. It is also important at this stage to define additional costs, such as insurance, that have a major impact on the overall fees.

As an outline guide an RFQ needs to contain:

▌ the routes most used, often called customer traffic lanes, and their volumes of business (number of moves), based on recent historical data;

▌ allowances for different transferee groups, such as single persons, couples and families;

▌ a comprehensive request for the rates for different traffic lanes;

▌ levels of transparency relating to a breakdown of costs such as management fees and freight booking fees;

▌ management of shipping and airfreight costs;

▌ the required service levels.

Additionally, the purchaser must understand what is excluded from and included in the fixed price of the move and make sure that the RFQ takes account of any additional charges, currency fluctuations, insurance and liability coverage.

Detailed RFQ quotation requirements

History of traffic lanes and allowances

A history of traffic lanes is simply a record of the past movements of people. The record needs to be broken down into routes, frequency of travel and traveller identification – whether singles, couples or families. For example, of a total of 30 international moves of company employees in a year, 27 (90 per cent) of them were between London and New York, of which 12 were couples (40 per cent) and 15 were single (50 per cent), with the remaining 3 (10 per cent) being couples moving between London and

Beijing. Although the history of business moves may not accurately reflect the future, it is better to use some relevant information than a sweeping global wish list, which can mean little.

Freight allowances for company employees need to be detailed, such as single people being allowed a volume of say 15 cubic metres, couples 30 cubic metres and families 60 cubic metres. These allowances are used as an average to calculate the quote. Obviously, the lower the allowance the lower the average and total volume of the moves. US companies often use the weight, not volume, for an allowance, whilst the rest of the world calculates costs on volume. It may also be split as a percentage allocation between sea and air.

To avoid nasty surprises it is important to get a quote for all the normal traffic lanes. A few suppliers are tempted to quote a very attractive rate on a small number of traffic lanes, such as London to New York, and make up the losses on others that were not specified in the original quote, for example London to Sydney.

Understandably, it may not be possible to predict the addition of a new traffic lane generated, for example, by a new business win and the need to send an employee to a new destination. If this occurs, it is important when adding this to the contract that the rate quoted is benchmarked for competitiveness.

Breakdown of costs – how much transparency?

Within RFQs it is a good idea to outline how much transparency is required in fees such as management fees, freight booking fees and shipping and airfreight costs.

Because freight costs are significant in any move and have many variable components, they require special attention. If it is demanded that within the contract they are fixed for a long period of time, the supplier will charge a higher rate to cover the risk of any cost increases. To avoid this, freight costs should be quoted separately and reviewed either every six months or annually, with certain parameters of variation for currency and fuel cost adjustment that are reviewed monthly by the operators.

When a customer requests a detailed breakdown of costs, it is important to balance the need for sufficient information for effective monitoring with what is practical administratively for the supplier. For example, stipulating the labour cost of packing based on time and hourly rates will present the supplier with an onerous administrative burden, which in itself will be cost-generating.

Defining quality of service

In the RFQ, it is essential to define the level of performance required from the supplier. Obviously, the shorter the time for the delivery of an employee's household goods abroad and of the move notice period, the greater the cost of the quote. Supplier performance levels are outlined in the service level agreement (SLA). Because of the cost to organizations of delays or other related performance issues, the SLA is very important and is discussed in more detail later.

Currency rates, additional rates, insurance and liability

Currency rates fluctuate, so, if the supplier fixes the rate in US dollars, euros, pounds sterling or some other currency, a premium may need to be added for the supplier to take account of the risk. The longer the period, the greater the risk. To limit this it is best to provide a mechanism within the contract to apply periodically the actual currency level operating at a particular time. Alternatively, rates can be quoted in multiple currencies, although freight rates are usually quoted by the operator in US dollars or euros.

The insurance premium for items in transit and storage must also be examined thoroughly, as it can have a considerable impact on the overall cost. This is particularly important in the case of those suppliers that use the insurance premium to recover a profit on the move.

It is also essential that various additional moving costs, such as storage fees, store handling charges, ferry crossings, parking, any outside elevator, poor access for loading or unloading and other costs incurring standard additional charges, should be clarified in the quote to avoid substantial mark-ups.

Inclusions and exclusions

Within the RFQ it is important to request what is to be included and what excluded from the cost of the move. This will not only help when comparing quotes, but also help to avoid shocks when the invoice arrives.

Typically, a supplier should provide at the point of origin:

▪ a survey of the items to be moved;

▪ one-time delivery of packing material, if required, for some owner packing;

▪ disassembly of normal furniture if necessary;

▪ packing of all small items into boxes;

- wrapping of furniture;
- fumigation (if applicable);
- moisture absorption pack (if applicable);
- supply and loading of the transport unit;
- transport to the air- or seaport of departure;
- terminal handling charges (THC) and other port charges at origin;
- export customs clearance formalities;
- all export documentation.

And standard inclusions at the destination are:

- THC and other port charges;
- transport from the air- or seaport of entry to the residence;
- unloading of the transport unit at the residence;
- placing of all items in appropriate rooms;
- unpacking of furniture;
- assembly of contractor-disassembled normal furniture (not new furniture);
- unpacking of contractor-packed boxes (not placing in cupboards);
- removal of debris (cartons, crates, etc) on the day of unpacking;
- return of the empty transport unit to the terminal or port;
- import customs clearance formalities;
- import permit charges (if applicable).

There are a number of other items that are recommended for inclusion in the overall costs: wooden crating of items, additional collection of debris, and various charges associated with bad access, for example parking permits, an outside elevator and above-second-floor delivery.

Generally, the following service costs should be quoted separately:

- storage;
- store handling;

■ tax and duties;

■ third-party services;

■ extraordinary items such as special tools or tradespeople services, customs inspection, an additional delivery or pick-up address, demurrage (surcharge to cover delays in loading or unloading) caused by the employee, and new freight surcharges.

Rate structures

In response to an RFQ, companies will send their rate structures. This normally consists of a grid showing the change in rate with consignment size and distance transported. Each mode of transport – road, air and ship – will have a grid and set of units. Consignments taken by road will have a volume–distance rate matrix (in cubic metres and kilometres) for domestic and European cross-border journeys.

Airfreight is charged on gross size or weight, whichever is the greater, as directed by the airlines.

Shipping rates are based on steel container loads, with lengths of 20 feet, 40 feet and, to some locations, 45 feet; additionally, there are supercube containers that have extra height. Rates are charged for a full container load (FCL) or less than a container load (LCL).

To draw up a grid it is best to consult with experts from the supplier, as this will avoid potential misunderstandings. An example of a rate grid is given in Table 5.1.1.

The supplier would also provide the freight rates per destination for 20-feet and 40-feet container options.

Table 5.1.1   Seafreight rate grid

By seafreight in 20-feet FCL consignment	15 m^3	$16–20 \text{ m}^3$	$21–25 \text{ m}^3$	$26–30 \text{ m}^3$	over 30 m^3
Rate per cubic metre	€110	€108	€107	€106	€105
By seafreight in 40-feet FCL consignment	under 40 m^3	$41–45 \text{ m}^3$	$46–50 \text{ m}^3$	$51–55 \text{ m}^3$	$56–60 \text{ m}^3$
Rate per cubic metre	€103	€102	€101	€100	€99

In addition, there are destination service costs such as port handling charges, customs clearance, labour for unpacking and removal of waste materials, and the return of empty containers to port.

SERVICE LEVEL AGREEMENT – DEFINING THE QUALITY OF SERVICE REQUIRED

The service level agreement defines the levels of performance the customer requires from the supplier. Poor performance will not only affect the direct and indirect cost of a move, but will also have a hidden cost associated with it. For example, if there is a delay in delivery then there will be accommodation costs for the employee or even the employee's family, while they wait for their belongings to be delivered. Furthermore, there is the opportunity cost of the employee being less productive through spending time on activities such as buying essentials that should already have been delivered. This means that the cost of poor performance can have a major impact on the overall cost of the move.

To be effective, a service level agreement needs to be specific, measurable, acceptable, realistic and time bound, summarized by the acronym SMART. Its contents should include:

▌ the time limit in which to contact the transferee, for example 24 hours;

▌ the time limit in which to submit a budget and schedule, for example three days;

▌ the accuracy of the survey data;

▌ the maximum allowed transit time;

▌ the proportion of satisfied transferees – usually expressed as a percentage, for example 99 per cent;

▌ the proportion and severity of complaints;

▌ an insurance claim per value of consignment or a claims/value ratio;

▌ a performance score; invoicing accuracy, for example 100 per cent; and timely invoicing, for example 30 days.

The transit time must be carefully defined. To optimize load utilization, the supplier will consolidate a customer's LCL load with other customer loads. This presents the risk of the whole shipment being delayed if there is a delay or withdrawal of any of the other consignments. By defining the transit time, the supplier will be able to offer and cost the service to match the customer's requirements. Usually, the supplier will provide a grid of transit times against the variables of consignment size and distance for different moves, such as within Europe or overseas, of which Table 5.1.2 is an example.

Various industry surveys have shown that the added cost of delays can be as much as 43 per cent of the cost of the move for a four-day delay.

The proportion of satisfied transferees and the seriousness of complaints from them will also affect overall cost. Therefore the service level agreement needs to refer to the minimum level of satisfied transferees, the maximum acceptable level of complaints and the nature of their severity. Examples of complaint severity include the surveyor being half an hour late categorized as a light complaint, rising to mis-estimation classed as a medium level complaint, while, at the other end of the scale, not enough crew members being provided, leading to a delay, would be classed as a serious complaint.

Similarly, owing to hidden costs, the acceptable level of insurance claims per total value of the consignment, expressed as the claim ratio, needs to be defined. Otherwise there is less of an incentive for the supplier to take care in avoiding breakages and other incidents that lead to an insurance claim being made.

Proportion of satisfied transferees, levels of seriousness of complaints and insurance claims are important, as they all involve the cost of a transferee taking time off work to sort out the consequences of poor performance, for example having to phone various people because of missing or delayed items or insurance claims.

Table 5.1.2   Transit time (days) – Europe

| | Cubic Metres | | | | | |
Kilometres	0–5	6–10	11–15	16–20	21–25	Etc
0–100	1	1	1	1	1	
101–200	2	2	2	2	2	
201–300	2	2	2	2	2	
301–400	3	3	3	3	3	
401–500	5	5	5	4	4	
Etc						

WORKING TOGETHER

There are significant cost savings to be made by the client working together with the supplier. For example, giving as much notice of a move as possible will help reduce costs. Additionally, administrative savings can be achieved by making the checking and approval of invoices easier. This can be achieved by simplifying rate structures and including in the fixed charge the relatively small additional costs, such as bad access charges, that often arise from a move in a major city.

SUMMARY

To make quotations comparable and close to the actual cost of moving services, the supplier needs to have as accurate information as possible, that is a high-quality request for quotation. Within this, the quality of service needs to be clearly defined in the service level agreement, particularly the length of time to complete a job, as this will affect its cost. For example, if quality of service is not detailed, the extra hidden cost of failure to perform is the cost of an employee not being able to get on with his or her work, which can cause the organization almost to double its budgeted moving cost. But it must also be remembered that working in partnership with your supplier reaps rewards, not only of further cost reduction but also of improvements in service.

From Sausages to Sushi,
we know you have your plate full

Moving from Totteridge to Tokyo, Mumbai to Matlock or Cirencester to Sydney can seem like a daunting prospect. There are so many ingredients to think about: packing, transport, storage, shipping, customs, insurance, tracking and billing...

Fortunately Cadogan Tate has thirty years' experience of moving company executives, diplomats and private individuals round the world. Our Move Management team handles the entire process from collection to delivery, and provides progress reports every step of the way.

Leaving our clients free to enjoy the finer points of relocation.

For worldwide relocation at its best, visit: www.cadogantate.com or call 0800 988 6029.

Cadogan Tate
Everything, handled with care

Moving Storage Shipping

Making Employee Relocation Less Painful

Moving house within the UK is traumatic enough, but relocating internationally increases these stress levels threefold every 100 miles moved. People required to move abroad for their job may be wary about starting life in another country, so it is crucial that HR managers co-ordinate the move to be as smooth possible, leaving employees ready to do a great job in their new country of residence.

According to Frank McCluskey, chief executive of Cadogan Tate Worldwide, the process can be as stressful for HR managers as for their assignees, but can be made far easier if they remember three things: plan, plan, plan!

Cadogan Tate Worldwide is a market-leading provider of door-to-door moving services throughout the world for businesses and employees, as well as individuals, expatriates and diplomatic families. With 30 years of experience, the company has handled more than 2000 international moves in the past 12 months alone.

Frank advises that the success of an international move depends on how effectively time is used during the preceding eight to ten weeks. One of the most important stages in the planning process is for HR managers to work in partnership with the employee to compile a timetable of activity – this should include everything from arranging visas, to ensuring the staff member leaves time to say goodbye to family and friends.

Selecting a removal firm is often left at the bottom of this list but making the decision early in the process produces many benefits – a reputable company will be able to help with far more than just transportation and will ultimately make an HR manager's job easier. Cadogan Tate has developed a bespoke Move Management service, which provides HR departments with a single point of contact to manage the entire process for them.

"When choosing a removals firm, look for members of the British Association of Removers (BAR), as only BAR Overseas Group members are qualified to carry out international moves," says Frank. "Equally, check that companies are affiliated to FIDI and certified with the FAIM* quality standard. This is the accepted industry benchmark worldwide and will ensure the goods are being cared for by the very best moving companies.

"Another way of checking a company's credibility is to look at its longevity – as a guideline, removal firms that have been operating for more than 10 years will have had time to foster and develop relationships with overseas agents. We've carefully selected our partners abroad, making sure that we can rely on them to provide a premium quality service."

HR managers should obtain a number of quotations and moving firms should supply a fixed price for specific services, covering an agreed quantity of goods. Unless a limited service has been agreed, companies should request a door-to-door service, which will mean the price includes customs clearance, port handling and collection or delivery to the assignee's residence. It is also worthwhile and cost-effective to request details on the IMMI insurance backed advance payment guarantee scheme, which financially underwrites the costs associated with overseas shipment and is available exclusively from members of BAR. And, if relocation is a regular occurrence within a business, HR managers should highlight this on their quotation, as a discount may be available.

So what factors need to be considered when planning an international move? According to Frank, HR managers should evaluate the three stages of relocation: origin source (the assignee's home), freight and destination.

The first stage involves a pre-shipment survey that analyses the mover's requirements and involves a physical inspection of the goods. This will determine the cost of transporting the goods, usually calculated by weight and volume. At this point the moving company can also identify whether specialist crating is needed for fragile items, and can arrange competitively priced high-value insurance cover.

Items to be stored or discarded should be identified beforehand and if there is more than one shipment, each item should be clearly marked accordingly. Some assignees may prefer storage in the destination country so it is important to check that the moving company can provide such facilities.

When deciding what to send abroad, employees should bear in mind that depending on destination, they will be without most of their personal effects for up to 10 weeks if moving by sea freight. Generally there are certain items that should not be moved or should be transported in person. For example, if guns or alcohol are included in the shipment, this will normally result in delays, duties or confiscation. Equally, less obvious items such as jewellery, stamp or coin collections, negotiable securities and deeds may be uninsured if included with the household goods.

It can be very unsettling for an employee and his or her family to arrive in a new country and have nothing familiar around them. Because of transportation times, HR managers should make sure the assignee carries enough with them for the first few weeks, as necessary items may not be available in the destination country. Frank suggests assignees should keep a 'carry with me' list of all those essentials items, as well as the vital documents needed for the journey.

The next step is to prepare items for transit. A reputable company will advise on the different types of freight service available to meet deadlines and budget. The use of consolidated or "groupage" service in steel steamship containers is ideal for limited budgets but can result in much longer transit time.

If employees require personal or work items sooner, these can be air-freighted. This is a more expensive option, but because of the faster transit time (10 to 14 days or longer depending on destination, customs clearance and security) it may mean less in hotel expenses while employees wait for their goods.

Once the consignment has arrived in the country, a good moving company will ensure customs clearance and the safe transportation to the designated residence. They should also unpack the items, helping the assignee their family to settle into their new home and life as quickly and easily as possible.

"While it is important to keep within budget, it pays to use a reputable company," says Frank. "It is ultimately reassuring to receive a personalised service from a company which has proven knowledge and expertise, and which can provide an employee with ongoing support during what could otherwise be a difficult period of upheaval."

---

*FIDI, or Fédération Internationale des Déménageurs Internationaux, is the largest global alliance of independent quality international removal companies and FAIM (FIDI Accredited International Mover) is the first industry certification for international movers

Critical issues for employees

Stephen Gill, Stephen Gill Associates

THE BEST OF TIMES

'It was the best of times, it was the worst of times…'; so begins Charles Dickens's *A Tale of Two Cities*, one of his very few historical novels and one with a plot that centres on the period of the French Revolution. Circumstances today are very different, of course, and yet I have heard these same words used to describe many an expatriate experience. Whilst as employees we are not going to be dropped in the middle of 18th-century revolutionary France, the predicament of finding ourselves in an unfamiliar city in a foreign country is by its very nature a current and common occurrence for today's expatriate employee.

Just as no two cities or countries are alike, nor are any two work assignments; they can vary widely in task, duration, destination, employment or relocation package and, of course, employer. However, there are some general issues that remain relevant for all expatriates, and these will be covered here, based upon personal experience of some of those 'best and worst of times'.

Many of the practical issues are adequately covered elsewhere in this book; however, it is often the 'softer' issues such as 'cultural shock' and 'family-related issues' that are the most critical to the expatriate, assuming that the employer has taken care of the obvious welfare and travel arrangements. Therefore, it is these 'soft' issues that this chapter addresses.

Perhaps the biggest critical issue facing expatriates is one that doesn't spring immediately to mind when considering the prospect of a prolonged working period abroad: what happens when they return? Often over-looked, but perhaps the most critical career factor of all, can be successful repatriation. This issue is also considered at the end of the chapter.

Common sense

Whether it is due to over-excitement or simply to apprehension of the prospective 'overseas trip', it seems that common sense often deserts those involved, who arrive totally unprepared for living and working in a new country.

It is all too common to focus solely on the working environment and job or work-task element. Admittedly these work-related aspects shouldn't be taken for granted, but equally the essential issues of setting up daily lives, such as visas, finances, family and health care, require just as much careful consideration and planning if inconvenient situations or, sometimes, downright unpleasant experiences are to be avoided. Many, if not all, of the negative experiences come down to common sense in the end; so the first part of this chapter covers essentials that may seem obvious.

The cost of failure

It is human nature to view the world from one's own perspective and, in this respect, expatriates are no different from anyone else. Quite rightly we value our time and, as employees, place a value on the disruption of being transferred abroad.

However, we should also be aware that for our employers significant cost is involved. For most companies, the use of expatriates is limited to key positions, such as senior managers, high-level professionals and technical specialists, because the costs of employing an expatriate have been estimated as being three to four times as much as employing the same individual at home.

Furthermore, once the costs of lost potential business opportunities and loss of company image that may be the result of an assignment failure are added to the direct labour costs, the overall potential cost is so significantly high as to warrant special attention.

It is important that expatriates realize this, not so that undue pressure is exerted upon them regarding their performance, but to encourage them to be proactive in gaining the support that they need to make the assignment a success. So don't be shy about having an active involvement in requesting that all support mechanisms are in place for you.

FACT-FINDING TRIP

Rather surprisingly, a fact-finding trip before the main assignment is often not requested by an employee or, when granted, is treated as a free holiday. Of course, it is not always possible for a variety of reasons or simply will be inappropriate in a certain case. However, by and large, a pre-assignment fact-finding trip is both appropriate and reasonable and should always be considered.

A fact-finding trip is very different to a holiday, and the planning involved is also quite different. The focus of the trip must be to do the research that will make the move to the new location as smooth as possible, so plan around your own personal circumstances including those of family members who may be joining you.

What to take

If you are fortunate enough to be granted a fact-finding trip, it will be because it is considered important, so don't treat it lightly, and prepare yourself beforehand.

Apart from your detailed plan covering all the aspects of living in a new country environment that you need to 'tick off', the obvious items to take with you are the same standard essentials as for any overseas trip, which include travel documents, local currency, appropriate clothing and those miscellaneous items such as an informative travel guide, pocket-sized phrase book, insect repellent, hand sanitizer (if appropriate) and, depending upon the location, some toilet rolls and tissues. Read the advice in the travel guide for any additional items that may be required for the particular location.

The law of the land

A word of warning here; no one wants to end up in a foreign jail, or even on the wrong side of the law in any shape or form. Unfortunately, the popular beliefs that foreigners are excused from complying with local laws or somehow have immunity from prosecution are simply not true (excepting some diplomatic immunity).

It is common to hear of expatriates who flout the local law and get away with it. Unfortunately, it is also not uncommon to hear of those who don't escape the arm of the law, or even innocently and unwittingly fall foul of a (to them) unknown law and end up being interrogated like serious criminals. Hefty fines and confiscation of personal and business items are some of the milder consequences of even seemingly innocuous misdemeanours, such as staying past your visa expiration or working without the appropriate documents.

In short, no one appreciates foreigners breaking the law, and a foreigner is exactly what you are when you are in another country. So take care: the consequences can be frightening and far worse than you imagine.

CULTURE SHOCK

Many executives and managers choose potential expatriates under the assumption that, 'if employees can work well at home, they can also do well abroad'. Indeed, when many companies select potential candidates for expatriate assignments, they often place overemphasis on technical competence and disregard other important attributes. Unfortunately, cross-cultural differences may make such skills irrelevant in a new environment.

Culture shock caused by cross-cultural differences can have a negative impact on an international assignment if not appropriately managed. These cross-cultural differences can affect both the expatriate and his or her family.

Expatriates may find it difficult to work in a culturally different environment, which could make them lose motivation and patience at work, thereby adding to the stress level already experienced by living and working abroad. Moreover, this stress can increase when the family has difficulties adjusting to the new environment. Often in this situation, if the proper cultural training is not provided, the international assignment can turn into a failure, with resulting cost to the company and the potential to demotivate key staff; in turn, relationships with clients and other stakeholders can be damaged.

It is not uncommon for the inability of the most technically gifted expatriates to adapt to the foreign environment to result in failure when additional support and training are not provided.

PRE-DEPARTURE AND POST-ARRIVAL CROSS-CULTURAL TRAINING

Although the term 'culture shock' is fairly widely used and its meaning usually understood by even the first-time expatriate, something that is perhaps less known and appreciated by the expatriate is cross-cultural training (CCT). As a consequence, CCT is very seldom requested by an employee and almost as infrequently offered by an employer. However, some enlightened employers do now offer CCT to employees; it is worth taking a little time to appreciate the significance and value of CCT and to understand what it involves.

Pre-departure and post-arrival CCT is very important for expatriates and their families. The benefits can include maximum take-up of business opportunities, reduced expatriate failure rates, increased expatriate efficiency on arrival and the reduction of mental and physical health problems for the expatriates and their family members.

The principles of CCT are:

▌ *self-understanding:* understanding that people are all culturally bound and that behaviour is influenced by basic cultural assumptions, values and beliefs;

▌ *understanding others:* knowing that intercultural miscommunication happens as a result of people's different styles and that the difference does not necessarily imply inferiority;

▌ *different style of interaction:* learning to check and accept assumptions about behaviour that are different from what we might normally expect in a situation, learning different listening and responding styles, and preparing a range of options and choices to deal with different situations.

There are four distinct phases in the cross-cultural adjustment process of expatriates and their family members:

1. the ethnocentric phase, in which experiences in the host culture are interpreted as deviation from the 'correct' behaviour;

2. the culture shock phase, in which a defensive coping mechanism sets in;

3. the conformist phase, in which the individual starts to adjust more effectively to the host culture;

4. culturally adjusted.

It has been suggested that appropriate sequencing of training methods would make CCT more effective. For example, pre-departure CCT should provide the expatriates and their family members with the knowledge about the potential difficulties they may face in a foreign culture. Post-arrival CCT should enhance cultural awareness and lower ethnocentrism; it can highlight similarities and differences between the home and host culture by focusing on immediate implications of changes

Family issues and expats – education options

Employers and expatriate families face many decisions when they relocate to another country.

Concerns

One of the first issues many potential expat employees are going to raise is the impact of the upheaval on the rest of the family. It would therefore be lot easier for employers simply to select from the 'singles' pool, thus avoiding these problems. However, business requirements frequently involve sending experienced managers. This means that often it is executives in their 30s and 40s with family responsibilities who are most likely to fulfill the job specifications.

Once relocated, there are other issues for the family which can lead to problems; the breadwinner who becomes involved in his or her career while the partner is stuck at home. In a new culture with little or no social infrastructure with which they are familiar, the partner may not have enough worthwhile outlets. Boredom and loneliness are two of the biggest problems for partners isolated in the home in a strange environment.

Work life balance is also a major consideration, as HR Directors responsible for recruitment have had to initiate more family friendly policies to retain key people in the business. If the whole family is posted abroad, the spouse is more settled, and as a result, will be more likely to remain for the full term of his/her contract. This is well understood by HR Directors and managers responsible for expat families.

Education

One of the most important considerations if the whole family is relocating, is to ensure that the children continue to receive a good education. This factor alone can influence their decision on whether or not to go.

So what are the options? Most employers and relocation companies will initially think of International Schools. In many cases these *may* the best solution. However, supposing the local international school only offers American-based courses? The American system begins formal education at 6 years of age, one year behind the British system. Subjects, such as English and Maths will be tackled differently; History will have a different focus. Such anomalies can lead to problems on returning to the UK, when children slot back into school and find they are behind in key subjects.

Perhaps there aren't any International Schools and the only schools available - local state or private ones - might not reach the standard required. Boarding schools might be the next consideration. However, not all families wish to send their children away to be educated and it might not be appropriate, especially if the children are very young.

Home Schooling

There *is* another approach that might not immediately spring to mind - home schooling. Basically, home schooling involves parents teaching their own children at home, anywhere in the world, from the relative comfort of a Western European country, to a remote village in Africa, a war torn country, a Pacific island or even on board a yacht! Parents have a wide variety of roles, including diplomats, mining managers, aerospace engineers, operations managers, NGO workers and missionaries.

Benefits

Home Schooling is a practical, positive and flexible solution that allows families to stay together and children to benefit from the experience of living abroad, while at the same time keeping up with UK standards of education.

For many expat partners, who cannot find employment overseas, home schooling can provide a real focus and interest. It offers the perfect solution for parents who travel frequently and prefer to have their children accompany them. It gives employers and parents flexibility to organise short-term contracts while ensuring the continuity of the children's education. Unlike internet based home schools, parents can manage daily schedules to meet their own needs. They are also fully aware of what their children are learning, which might not always be the case when children are taught outside the home. Parent and child often find this a mutually rewarding experience.

Children with special learning needs, whether high fliers or slow learners, often blossom in home school with the one-to-one teaching which allows a child's individual needs, experience and potential to be developed in a settled and happy atmosphere. Coursework can be adapted to accommodate specific requirements and there is time to pursue special hobbies and interests. There is no school bell to determine when a lesson should end and time can be spent more productively.

Home schooling with WES

World-wide Education Service (WES), one of the leading providers in the field of home schooling was founded more than a 100 years ago, it offers structured yearly courses for children aged 4-14 in English, Maths, Science, History, Geography and RE. WES courses guide parents through their children's lessons in a logical and straightforward way and are designed for non-teachers to follow with ease. Courses can be started at any time so do not have to fit in with school term times – convenient if relocating at short notice.

Courses include:

- an initial assessment of the child's educational level
- a syllabus matched to the child's ability, based on the National Curriculum of England. This sets out a full daily schedule of what and how to teach
- up-to-date books and materials to support the subjects
- a WES personal tutor based in the UK to advise and support parents in their role of teacher

- regular assessments of the child's progress throughout the term
- a final report from WES detailing the child's educational level to hand on to future schools

A 'top-up service' where parents can combine enrolment at a local school with WES courses in other subjects is also available. In some cases companies have asked **WES** to provide curriculum to local schools which are setting up with a number of expat families.

Fees are directly related to the service provided, and offer excellent value for money compared with boarding and private schooling.

WES courses are accredited by the **Open Distance Learning Quality Council** and are regularly updated in line with the National Curriculum of England so children can slot back into UK or International schools with ease.

Summary

Home schooling enables employers to:

- attract a wide variety of highly qualified and experienced staff to more remote overseas postings
- send families abroad, either on long-term or short-term contracts
- relocate families at relatively short notice without interrupting their children's education
- offer a high quality and economic alternative to boarding school
- ensure continuity in children's education if families have to move from one country to another
- create the opportunity for parents to play a positive role in their children's education, providing a fulfilling alternative when the accompanying partner is not locally employed

to daily life at home and work. CCT should also provide situational exercises, role-playing simulations that help expatriates and their families learn how to adapt well, and as quickly as possible, to the culturally different environment.

Language training for expatriates and their families should also be provided after arrival if it is important for successful adaptation to the local culture. Learning even a few words of the local language can pay dividends in the most unexpected ways and usually enriches the experience of the expatriate and his or her family.

FAMILY ISSUES

Family-related issues often have a major influence upon the expatriate's own adjustment process and his or her ability to perform effectively on the assignment.

Difficulties regarding the children, language and spousal adjustment are likely to heighten the expatriate's level of stress and uncertainty. Those expatriates whose family members are struggling to adjust are likely to feel responsible for their unhappiness while, conversely, well-adjusted families are likely to provide support.

The family generally experiences a more difficult adjustment process than the expatriate, as expatriates continue to feel the familiarity of the work. It is therefore not uncommon for the family to experience a greater degree of culture shock than the expatriate. This may lead to the family facing challenges such as loss of self-worth, lack of contact with friends and family, social and cultural ostracism and also disruption of children's education.

An expatriate or a company that ignores family issues and excludes the family from CCT runs the very real risk of encountering serious problems at some point.

AFTERWARDS – COMING BACK

Repatriation is the process of bringing expatriates home from the international assignment, and it completes the expatriation process cycle. For many expatriates, this is both the most difficult part and the part for which they are the least prepared. Usually it is simply not given enough consideration by either expatriates themselves or their employers. Although repatriation may be the natural conclusion of the whole cycle, for many it is not a stage that is either easy or natural. On the contrary, it can be made all the more difficult as repatriates themselves experience unexpected 'reverse culture shock'.

There is often a huge difference between expatriates' high expectations prior to their return and the reality that they encounter after they return. Expatriates always expect that they will hold similar, if not higher, hierarchical positions upon their return, where there will be good opportunities to utilize the skills, knowledge and experience that they have acquired abroad.

Unfortunately, it is often simply unrealistic and sometimes impossible to guarantee expatriates a specific position upon their return. Consequently, it is crucial for companies to be honest to expatriates in an attempt to try to minimize any readjustment difficulties upon return.

One potential key ingredient for effective repatriation is to start early in making expatriates aware of all the potential possibilities open to them when they return. If handled badly, repatriation can cause expatriates to leave their companies or, at best, lower their morale and hence performance. Often the skills gained by expatriates abroad are not fully utilized by companies when the expatriates return and so the valuable experience that has been gained is wasted. It is an unfortunate truth that many companies do not value the competencies and wisdom that their repatriates have gained from their international assignments.

Expatriates' tolerance for ambiguity, intercultural understanding and ability to relate effectively to people of different cultures are commonly not used by the expatriates' home companies in the positions in which the repatriates are often placed. This lack of effective utilization and possibly understanding by the home company may unwittingly force repatriates to seek employment elsewhere and possibly even with the company's competitors. As companies invest significant sums of money training expatriates, it is sensible to try to retain their knowledge and experience within the organization.

So, strange as this may sound if you are on the verge of embarking on the new and exciting adventure of becoming an expatriate, be prepared to be unappreciated when you return. Discuss this aspect as early as you can with your employer and question its repatriation process.

CRITICAL ISSUES

Charles Dickens's *A Tale of Two Cities* ends with one of the main characters losing his head by the guillotine. Hopefully, nothing quite so drastic awaits the expatriates who don't perform or, for that matter, the team that supported them. The 'best of times' surely awaits those companies that can improve their expatriation programmes and policies to help expatriates and their family members to adapt and adjust so as to improve expatriate success. Nor can the importance of CCT provided to family members, including children, be neglected, as it can help them adapt quickly to the foreign environment, thereby reducing expatriate failure. These have been shown to be critical issues for expatriate success, but ones that are also often sadly overlooked.

Administration issues for employees

Geoff Davidson, Hessel

Jose was delighted when his boss confirmed that he had been appointed as Regional Finance Director EMAE and would be on a five-year expatriate contract from the New York office to London. Both Jose and his wife loved London and thought it was an exciting and vibrant city. The assignment could not have been more welcome.

It was about three months later that Jose received a call from his wife letting him know that the landlord had just changed the locks on the apartment for non-payment of rent. This was swiftly followed by a rather embarrassing conversation with the bursar of their children's school about the non-payment of the school fees. Jose began to reconsider the definition of 'exciting'…

WHY IT ALL GOES WRONG

For modern businesses above a certain size and with more than the most parochial of ambitions, recruiting the right people is going to involve relocation. This applies to both internal and external recruitment.

The way this usually works is that the business will start by either bringing somebody into the country or sending somebody out of the country, often on an extended business trip. As the company's business becomes more extensive, the trips will become longer and more convoluted until the point is reached when the company will be forced to admit that it needs to have some kind of international relocation or assignment programme.

If the company has good administrators who can run all this stuff on the corner of their desks as 'exceptions', the inevitable administrative meltdown can be delayed for quite a number of years. The trigger points for a meltdown are usually some kind of HMRC inquiry, the loss of a key administrator who has all the 'processes' in his or her head, or your new director of finance getting a county court judgment and the bailiffs at the door because of council tax arrears.

If this all sounds horribly familiar, don't worry: you are in the same boat as some of the best-run and most intelligently managed companies in the world. If it doesn't, you are ahead of the game and have the opportunity to save a lot of time, energy and money.

Going to the wrong place for help

Because relocation is a sub-function of recruitment, relocation and international assignments tend to be regarded as issues that belong to human resources. Frankly, this is as good a place as anywhere to try to control a process that runs so contrarily to every other business process. However, it is important to recognize that HR 'doesn't do money', in the same way that finance 'doesn't do people'.

In most organizations, the HR department will reach out to a relocation company as an external provider for moving services upon the assumption that the normal business processes can cope with the administration. After all, relocation applies only to a handful of employees compared to the total size of the payroll, doesn't it?

The truth is a little more complex. International relocation providers can be divided into three specialities: visa and immigration, moving services and destination services; the functions are fairly self-evident. What all of these specialities have in common is that they are concerned only with getting employees to their destination. They have no particular interest in the ongoing support. This means that, once they have performed their part of the relocation, they will send in their bill and wait for the next case.

Unless employees are going to be localized, they will need ongoing support. There will be rent to pay, utility costs, local property taxes, school fees, spousal support, car hire or purchase, driving and language training, storage costs, furniture rental, home leave trips... The list goes on and on. Even localized employees will probably have extra costs for tax services and medical insurance, and localization is often either not an option or not a practical reality. This means that the relocation provider is not going to have the skill or interest in the assignment support that employees will require.

The problem outlined

Here lies the administrative problem. First, at a practical level, how will the company actually go about the business of paying these suppliers and, secondly, how can this information be captured in a reliable way?

The payment issue arises because of modern supply chain management. We have procurement departments that vet suppliers and manage contracts and payment terms; we have payment processes that are often outsourced, involving purchase orders. None of these are particularly suited to paying a council tax bill within the next five days. The suppliers are not registered suppliers, they don't have a purchase order, they are not about to go through the procurement process and they are about to issue a summons for non-payment followed by a visit from the bailiffs.

The situation acquires yet another layer of complexity if the invoice originates from a vendor in another country, say a rent demand in Malaysia, a country with a closed currency.

Data management is probably a less understood issue. Everyone will be aware that providing benefits and expenses to employees is liable to generate a tax liability somewhere. Most people will tend towards the view that tax is a retrospective activity and that there is probably time enough to sort out the tax issues at a later date. They may well be right – the UK tax system allows benefits to be reported on an annual basis.

The UK is one of only a handful of tax regimes that provide this facility, and it is under review at the moment. Some relocation emoluments may be provided in the form of allowances, customarily grossed up, which will need to be put through a modified payroll process. While these can be trued up, it causes a considerable amount of handcrafted work and, in any event, social security payments for these allowances should be paid in real time.

A more pressing issue is cost centre recharging. Every modern business is under pressure to provide accurate and timely financial information to regulatory bodies, shareholders and stock markets. It is not often appreciated that moving an employee from one country to another is usually also moving the employee from one financial jurisdiction to another. This means that employee relocations and international assignments can become a source of financial leakage unless the costs are captured and recharged to the correct cost centres as soon as the organization becomes aware of them.

It is here that the problem of ad hoc vendors takes its toll. Because they are not a part of the supply chain management, their costs will not have been pre-agreed against a particular cost centre or a purchase order.

Furthermore, while finance is interested in seeing costs in terms of employees and cost centres, vendors will tend to think and invoice in terms of shipments or property-related billing.

This means that someone in your organization is going to have to translate, in real time, these costs into a format that can be assimilated by the finance department. That means tagging each and every cost with the cost centre and employee details that finance requires; it also means breaking down the invoices themselves into their component parts for tax analysis.

For example, a bill from a shipping agent for household goods removal services may include the cost of packing up at the old home location, the cost of shipment, the cost of transferring some of the goods into permanent storage at the destination and the cost of transferring some of the goods to the employee's long-term accommodation. While the bill represents one cost at cost centre level, each component potentially has a different tax impact.

GETTING THE BASICS RIGHT

The first thing is to recognize that the administration of a relocation or international assignment is probably not going to fit into your existing ways of doing things. The online travel desk is not going to be able to cope with distinguishing between home leave trips and ordinary business travel. But, believe me, the inspector of taxes can tell at a glance.

Take a long, hard look at your payment processes and talk to the people who run them. Within the existing protocols, can they pay an ad hoc vendor, say a landlord, within 12 hours of being asked to do so? Are cross-border payments something that the accounts payable department is happy about within existing protocols?

Understand that *someone* is going to need to track all this information for tax reporting (possibly in a number of jurisdictions), cost centre recharging and general management control. This may start as a corner-of-the-desk job for a well-intentioned body in HR, but if you do not put strict data quality controls in place you will never be certain about the quality of the data that you are reporting until the next audit.

These processes can be outsourced, but make sure that you look for a specialist. Relocation providers may indicate that they can handle expense management, but in reality they usually mean that they can pay some of the bills on your behalf. As relocation providers invariably subcontract the majority of the services that they offer, handing them the opportunity to pay their own bills is a total abdication of fiscal responsibility.

Be prepared

One thing you may well encounter is a surprising amount of inertia within your own organization. An organization that has just spent millions of euros outsourcing the payment system to an Eastern European country may not want to hear that it doesn't work for this particular group of employees. The finance department may not want to hear that the only way that the cost data for international assignments can be collected is by hand on a spreadsheet filled in haphazardly by a junior in the HR department.

When this happens, or the car parking scheme is given a higher priority, you may want to remind yourself that the search for and retention of talent is the single biggest guarantee of success that any company can have. Without a well-managed administrative process, your global search for talent is doomed to failure. You may consider that this advice is slightly over the top, but bear in mind that there is a catastrophic failure rate in international assignments. This is partly through the misguided selection of candidates but just as frequently through the ham-fisted handling of the employees and their family requirements. Watch out; the brightest and the best may be leaving your company to work for your competitors.

Part 6

Personal taxation and social security payments in key expatriate employment locations

The tax and social security data for each of the 14 jurisdictions surveyed in this final part of the book are drawn from a number of sources, including the website of Deloitte International. This information is dated January 2008. In the case of the UK, tax and NIC rates have been updated to include changes resulting from the 2008 Finance Act, and apply through the tax year ending 5 April 2009. Working conditions and useful information sections, included for all countries other than the UK, are taken from the country sections accompanying the current edition of *Working Abroad* (Jonathan Reuvid, 2008, also published by Kogan Page – for more details visit www.koganpage.com).

Business, Job, Family & Kids – Migrating to Australia

Twenty years ago, Britain's bad weather was the main reason why people wanted to migrate to Australia. Today, it's lack of economic opportunity and the desire for a better lifestyle that drives UK businesses, workers and their families to seek a new life down under.

Two decades ago, the UK was a leading powerhouse of growth and opportunity; today Australia has eclipsed Europe to become one of the world's top tiger economies.

During the boom and bust 1980's, British workers were urged by government ministers to, 'get on your bike' and go find work. Twenty years later, as European economies suffer slowdown, the cycle has returned with British workers, professionals and business investors queuing to migrate to Australia.

Over 425,000 Brits will leave UK in 2008, with another 2.25 million (at any one time) hoping to do the same thing. Australia is the Number Destination for migrants. 'It's not just about people wanting to get away from UK, it's more about the attraction of Australia – the sunshine, bigger houses, better schools, safer streets,' says Darrell Todd, ceo of thinking**australia**.com. 'It's a better job with more satisfaction for the parents and a better environment and lifestyle for the kids.

'For the business migrant or investor, it's a double-win situation: all of the above PLUS a wealth of attractive business and commercial opportunities across fast-expanding national markets and a wide range of exciting verticals.

'The number of business migrants and investors from UK to Australia that we have acted on behalf of has doubled every year since 2005,' says Todd. 'It's a major step. Professionals and executives are naturally cautious and well-prepared for the migration process – business investors even more so. Our expert personal service has guided thousands of clients to migration success while our comprehensive B2B network deliver opportunities and supports your business migration ambitions'.

Australia is growing fast and will continue, its economy expanding as an influx of millions of new workers generate greater GDP and create a fast-expanding national consumer and services market.

'Across Australia, there's currently an 12-month waiting list for a new house,' says Todd. 'Major national construction projects are being delayed because there are not enough workers and managers to do the jobs. Mining and export quota's are not being met because there's not enough truck drivers. There's a huge demand for skilled workers, trades-people, professionals, healthcare specialists, teachers – all key people needed to support a rapidly expanding economy'.

With current economic growth predicted to last for the next 20 years, there has never been a better time for skilled workers - and business migrants – to tap into the booming services markets such as IT and telecoms, property, finance, travel and leisure.

In the 1980's Australia lagged behind in terms of communications, IT and electronic commerce. Today, IT infrastructure and use of latest technology in business is equal to that of UK and Europe.

40% of Australian businesses plan to replace their fixed line network with an all-IP solution by 2010*. Internet-based VoIP services like Skype are seeing strong adoption in Australian companies, especially SOHO and small businesses. 'Greater availability of higher-bandwidth broadband and improved quality of internet-based VoIP services have lifted user confidence and are increasingly deemed acceptable by business,' says Samia Jawed, senior industry analyst at Telsyte.

In the Capital, Canberra, and in all major cities across Australia IT, Network infrastructure and telecoms professionals are in great demand, along with mainframe technicians, web developers, eCommerce specialists, integrators, software developers and B2B IT professionals.

And it's not just IT experts and white collar workers that are in high demand. There's currently a big shortage of truck drivers in the mines of Western Australia – annual salary $100k. 'In addition to skilled workers, the country needs project managers and administrators across all sectors such as IT, commerce, industry, health care, construction and central and local government departments,' says Darrell Todd.

Demand for workers is acute across all Australian States and now business and government agencies must compete to attract the number of workers needed for each State.

'State officials and local businesses are having to work harder and harder to attract the workers and skills they so desperately need', says Simon Kinsmore, head of marketing at the ACT Government in Canberra. 'We believe Australia's Capital city offers the most advantages for migrants: highest wages in the country, highest skills base, safest environment, most modern city in a beautiful location - and centre of government. We have it all'.

Bruce McFarlane, head of business development division, Western Australian Government, believes W.A offers most to migrants, not least its close traditional links to the UK. 'W.A. and especially Perth is where many of the original Poms settled from the 1950s onwards, so we've always had a good word-of-mouth migrant channel. Now, we need skilled workers across all sectors. W.A. offers probably the most attractive packages for business migrants and investors with a wide range of incentives and tax breaks'.

'In business Down Under a lot of things are similar but many things are very different, so seek expert help to find the right opportunity and the right team to support your ambitions'. Says David Neilson of Business & Investment ,the leading business sales specialist in Australia and N.Z.

'To reach the top in professional or business life takes focus, drive and skill. It also takes research, expert application and teamwork. To navigate the process involved in business migration requires similar expertise', says Neilson: 'We combine individual requirement with best possible opportunities to ensure success'.

Economic growth in Australia will continue unabated, fuelled and supported by the millions of migrant workers and families that, demographically, must swell the population by 20% over the next decade if Australia is to maintain its trading position in the world market.

This process will expand and remain self-supporting for many years to come, providing on-going opportunities for migrant workers, professionals and business investors from UK.

'If you have the skills, the business ambition and the ability to adapt – then we have a job, a lifestyle and a home for you,' says Darrell Todd. 'With opportunities to suit everyone, it's the perfect time to start looking at your current life and prospects - and compare it to what is possible in Australia'.

By 2009, the population of Australia is projected to be 21.4 million, with:

- one birth every 1 minute and 55 seconds,
- one death every 3 minutes and 57 seconds,
- a net gain of one international migrant every 2 minutes and 38 seconds leading to
- an overall total population increase of one person every 1 minute and 33 seconds.

Source: the Australian Bureau of Statistics (ABS).

State by State Growth

Western Australia and the Northern Territory recorded the fastest population growth at 2.4%, followed by Queensland, 2.3%, Victoria 1.6%, Australian Capital Territory 1.3%, New South Wales 1.1%, South Australia 1.0% and Tasmania 0.8%.

Net overseas migration contributed more than half the population increase (184,400 people or 56%), and natural increase (the excess of births over deaths) added a further 147,400 people (or 44%). The overseas migration increase represents an average of over 1,100 immigrant arrivals and 620 departures per day.

Queensland and Western Australia continued as the leaders in interstate migration, gaining 25,600 and 3,800 people respectively from the other states.

The Northern Territory (860), the Australian Capital Territory (350) and Tasmania (290) also grew from interstate migration, while New South Wales (-24,000), South Australia (-3,800) and Victoria (-3,100) lost people.

Source: the Australian Bureau of Statistics (ABS).

Average wages – July 2008

Full-time adult ordinary time earnings rose by 4.1% for males and 4.3% for females in the twelve months to July 2008. In the twelve months to July 2008, full-time adult total earnings rose by 4.4% for males and 4.3% for females.

Source: the Australian Bureau of Statistics (ABS).

The grey haired time-bomb

Australia's aging population is a demographic time-bomb; another reason why the country needs the skills, qualification and experience of British workers, managers and business migrants. The vast number of key workers, managers and top company execs due to reach retirement age in this decade is creating an annual rise in number of job vacancies - and that's in addition to the ongoing problem of jobs that can't be filled today. For the 5 years ending June 2007, the Australian population aged 60-64yrs recorded the largest growth, rising 4.7%. The population aged 85 and over also recorded large growth over this period, up 4.6%. These two age groups also recorded the largest growth for the year ending 30 June 2007 growing 7.6% and 6.8 % respectively. These trends reflect the ageing nature of Australia's population.

Source: the Australian Bureau of Statistics (ABS).

* Telsyte study, 'Australian Business Fixed Line Usage and Directions, 2008 End-User Survey'

All communications contained in this article are 'information 'only and should not be regarded as 'advice '. Our / your 'appointed' agent only provides advice as this is the requirements of the Australian Migration Act

Australia

WORKING CONDITIONS

Leave entitlements

At executive and professional levels, international standards and conditions of work apply. Holidays are normally four weeks a year, and some firms pay a holiday bonus. There is also often a form of sabbatical leave after 10 years' service with a company. Flexible working hours are quite common in Australia, particularly in the public sector.

The chief difference in working conditions between Australia and other countries is that the concept of status related to specific jobs – and, even more, the social and workplace behaviour associated with it – has to be discarded. Any tendency to 'give yourself airs' is fatal!

Recruitment

Australian employers will not usually recruit from a distance, but it is possible to get a good picture of the sort of employment opportunities available from Australian newspapers and particularly from the Australian migration authorities. In general, the demand is for specific skills and professional or managerial qualifications. Most British professional qualifications are recognized in Australia; however, accreditation from the appropriate licensing board may be required for certain professions.

Entry visas

There are a number of business visas available for individuals or companies wishing to set up a branch or representative office in Australia or to engage in business activities. The following is a brief summary of some of the more commonly used visas:

▮ *Business visit visa (456)/electronic travel authority (ETA).* The business visit visa/ETA allows for a visit of up to three months – no extensions can be made while the visa holder is in Australia. No work may be undertaken on this visa. The purpose is to attend meetings, hold discussions, participate in short-term training, etc. Nationals of certain countries can apply on the internet or through travel agencies or airlines for the ETA. Non–ETA-eligible nationals need to apply for the 456 visa through the nearest Australian diplomatic mission.

▮ *Business long-stay visa (457).* This temporary visa is granted for up to four years and can be renewed or extended. It is commonly known as the work visa, as it provides visa holders with permission to work – but only for the sponsoring company. This visa is commonly used by companies overseas looking to send staff to Australia to set up and run a branch or representative office, or to establish a company in Australia, for the purposes of engaging in business. This visa is also used by companies already operating in Australia that wish to bring in specialist staff from overseas. There are three stages to obtaining a 457 work visa: 1) Sponsorship – an overseas-based company must first apply for approval as a sponsoring company. Assessment looks at company background, financials, and proposed activities in Australia. 2) Nomination – this involves assessing the position that is to be filled by the visa applicant. The position must relate to an occupation on a list of skilled occupations. The salary for the position must meet minimum thresholds. 3) Visa – assesses the visa applicants and whether they have the formal skills and qualifications for the position.

▮ *Occupational training visa (442).* A temporary visa for up to two years that allows an Australian company to sponsor someone from overseas to undertake work-based training. A formal training programme is essential.

▮ *Employer nomination visa.* This is a permanent residence visa. It requires a company to sponsor someone and is similar to the 457, although the visa application requirements are different. It requires the sponsoring company to be established and operating in Australia.

▮ *Business skills visas.* There are a number of these visas – most are temporary visas for four years and are not renewable. They require visa holders to establish or purchase a business in Australia (a small business is usually sufficient) and manage that business. If that business achieves certain business outcomes in terms of turnover, equity, staffing, etc, then the visa holder may apply for permanent residence.

These visas target people who have successfully run their own businesses over the last few years, or who have had very senior executive positions in large corporations (non-government), or who have themselves actively managed a portfolio of investments over a number of years and who have a high net worth.

USEFUL INFORMATION

Financial year: The Australian financial year runs from 1 July to 30 June.

Electricity: Electrical goods should be checked with the maker to see if they will work in Australia, because the voltage systems differ (220–250 V, 50 Hz ac). Gas appliances are particularly tricky because of differences in pressure and gas composition. British TVs and video recorders do not function in Australia because of different signals and need to be professionally converted to be compatible with the Australian system.

Driving: A car, essential in Australia, is best bought there. If you import a car you will have to make sure that it meets the safety regulations of the state to which you are going. You can drive on a British licence for the first three months. After that you will have to take a local test, but this will only be an oral one if you already hold a British or international licence.

Transport: Interstate transport is usually by aeroplane, although there is also a large railway network.

Education: Education begins at the age of 5 or 6 and is compulsory up to age 15 or 16 (depending on the state). The school session starts early in February, not September as in the UK. It must be remembered that, in the southern hemisphere, the seasons are reversed; hence the Australian Christmas is in mid-summer. Tuition is free in government schools, but parents generally have to provide uniforms, books and other materials. As many as 25 per cent of pupils, however, attend private schools, particularly in the latter years of secondary education. Fees are reasonable because these schools are aided by government grants. Allow A$5,000–$8,000 a year for private secondary school tuition fees.

There are small tuition fees for university-level education, which is very well provided for in all states. Most Australians take a pass degree rather than honours. Standards are similar to those in the UK.

Useful contacts:

British High Commission, Commonwealth Avenue, Yarralumla, Canberra, ACT 2600 (tel: 612 6270 6666, website: www.uk.emb.gov.au)

Australian High Commission, Australia House, Strand, London WC2 (tel: 020 7379 4334)

Australian Tourist Commission (tel: 020 8780 2229, websites: www.aussie. net.au, www.australia.com)

PERSONAL TAXATION

Residence

Australian tax residents are taxed on their worldwide income, while non-residents are taxed only on Australian-sourced income, subject to the operation of double taxation agreements, which override domestic tax law.

An individual will be an Australian resident for taxation purposes if he or she ordinarily resides in Australia or if any of the following tests is satisfied:

▌ the individual's domicile is in Australia and he or she does not have a permanent place of abode elsewhere;

▌ the individual has physically been present in Australia for 183 days or more in the financial year (1 July to 30 June) and does not have a usual place of abode outside Australia; or

▌ the individual is a member of certain Commonwealth government superannuation schemes.

A place of abode is the place where the taxpayer adopts a habitual mode of living. Where an individual is a dual tax resident, double taxation agreements may apply to demarcate the taxing right of each country in respect of the income derived.

Taxes on income

Taxable income for personal income tax purposes includes income from employment, business income, certain capital gains and passive income such as dividends, interest and rental income. Tax rates are progressive up to 45 per cent. A 'temporary' resident (one who holds a temporary visa, is not a resident within the meaning of the Social Security Act 1991 and does not have a spouse who is an Australian resident) is granted exemption for most foreign-source income and capital gains and for interest withholding tax obligations associated with foreign liabilities.

Deductions and allowances

Business expenses are deductible if they are necessarily incurred in gaining or producing assessable income. Expenses of a capital, private or domestic nature are not deductible. Residents are allowed some tax rebates, including rebates for dependants and certain personal expenses.

Social security

Employers contribute to the mandatory superannuation pension scheme on behalf of their employees at 9 per cent of the employee's gross income or salary. In addition to income tax, a 1.5 per cent Medicare levy is payable on the taxable income of Australian residents. Relief is available to low-income taxpayers. A further 1 per cent surcharge may be imposed on taxpayers who have no private hospital cover.

Capital gains

Gains derived from the disposal of assets acquired after 19 September 1985 are included in assessable income. For assets acquired after 1 October 1999 and held for more than one year, individuals are taxed at their marginal rate on half the gain, setting a maximum effective capital gains tax rate of 22.5 per cent. For assets acquired before that date, individuals may choose between the new system and the pre-September 1985 system, under which they are taxed at their marginal rate on the whole gain, indexed for inflation. Indexation of the cost base of existing assets was frozen at 30 September 1999. Capital gains tax applies only to taxable Australian property disposed of by foreign investors as from 12 December 2006.

Real property tax

The states and territories impose stamp duty at varying rates up to 6.75 per cent on the transfer of real property.

Other taxes

There is no net wealth/net worth tax, inheritance/estate tax, capital acquisitions tax or capital duty.

Double taxation agreements

Australia has double tax agreements with more than 40 countries, including both the United States and the UK.

Filing and payment

Joint tax returns for a spouse are not permitted. Every individual with assessable income in excess of the tax-free threshold of A$6,000 is required to file a tax return for each year ending 30 June by 31 October of that year, unless the individual is on a tax agent lodgement programme and is eligible for an extended deadline.

Penalties and interest may be applied for late filing, failure to file, failure to exercise due care, and tax evasion.

To access a fuller range of country profiles, available to download as part of the Kogan Page title *Working Abroad*, please go to www.koganpage.com/workingabroad (password: WA50571).

Belgium

WORKING CONDITIONS

EU nationals with valid passports are free to come and go, but they must register at a local police station or town hall within eight days of arrival. Children must also be registered. The period of their stay (more or less than three months) in Belgium and their capacity (employee, student, family member) will determine if a residence permit needs to be issued.

The level of managerial and executive salaries is higher than in the UK. An upper middle-ranked executive could expect to earn at least £55,000 gross a year. Increasingly, a company car could be provided in addition to the basic salary.

USEFUL INFORMATION

Banking hours: 9.00 am to 3.30 or 4.00 pm Monday–Friday, 9.00 am to 12.00 pm on Saturday; banks close during the lunch hour.

Post office: 9.00 am to 12.00 pm and 2.00 pm to 4.00 pm or 5.00 pm Monday–Friday.

Shopping hours: 10.00 am to 6.00 pm Monday–Saturday.

Electricity: 220 V, 50 Hz ac.

Driving: Speed limits are 30 km/h in school areas, 50 km/h in built-up areas, 90 km/h on overland roads, and 120 km/h on motorways. Front and back seat belts compulsory. Maximum blood alcohol level 0.5 mg/l. Children (up to age four or 18 kilos) need to be placed in a child seat.

Transport: Distances are so short that most travel is done by train or car. Rail services are efficient and there is a good network of roads and autoroutes, with ring roads round the large towns. Urban transport in Brussels is adequate, but buses and trams get very crowded.

Health care: The health services are part of the general social security system, which is a very comprehensive one. Everyone has to belong to a *mutualité/mutualiteit* (sickness insurance fund). You have to pay for a visit to a doctor and for prescriptions, but about 75 per cent of the cost of medical treatment may be reimbursed by the *mutualité*. Many hospitals and clinics are run by different denominational groups. People who are currently insured under the UK social security scheme should obtain the necessary forms for reciprocal treatment before leaving the UK.

Education: Education, both primary and secondary, is free and compulsory for all Belgian children between 6 and 18. As well as the state schools there are many Catholic and independent schools in Brussels and elsewhere. There are a number of European and international schools. The International School of Brussels takes in children from 3 to 19 (a 13th year is possible) in kindergarten, elementary and secondary schools and has over 1,000 boys and girls, the majority being from the United States. There is a smaller international school at Antwerp. The British School of Brussels, which is co-educational and follows the UK National Curriculum, has over 1,000 students aged 2 to 11. There is also a school in Antwerp offering a British curriculum. The small British Primary School in Brussels caters for children from 3 to 11. The St John's English-speaking school at Waterloo, near Brussels, caters for children between 3 and 19 (a 13th year is possible).

There are French- and Dutch-speaking 'free' universities at Leuven and Louvain-la-Neuve, state universities at Ghent, Brussels and Liège and university centres at Antwerp, Mons and Diepenbeek. Education is free, and standards are high.

Useful contacts:

British Embassy, 85 Rue d'Arlon, 1040 Brussels (tel: 32 2 287 6211, website: www.britishembassy.gov.uk/belgium)

Belgium Embassy, 103–104 Eaton Square, London SW1W 9AB (tel: 020 7470 3700, website: www.diplobel.org/uk)

Belgium Tourist Offices (Brussels-Wallonia), 217 Marsh Wall, London E14 9FJ (tel: 0800 9545 245 (brochure line), website: www. belgiumtheplaceto.be)

Tourism Flanders-Brussels, 1a Cavendish Square, London W1G 0LD (tel: 0800 954 5245 (brochure line), website: www.visitflanders.co.uk)

Websites:
www.visitbelgium.com
www.belgique-tourisme.net

Expatriate information:
www.expatsinbrussels.com
www.xpats.com
www.expatriate–online.com

PERSONAL TAXATION

Residence

Belgium taxes income on the basis of residence. In general, individuals are considered to be resident in Belgium for income tax purposes if their established 'domicile' (*domicile/domicilie*), their established place of residence or the centre of their wealth (*siège de fortune/zetel van fortuin*) is in Belgium. Physical presence is not conclusive. They are taxed on worldwide income, whereas non-residents are taxed on Belgian-source income. Persons in the national register are deemed to be resident unless there is evidence to the contrary. However, executives on temporary assignment to Belgium may apply for the special expatriate regime.

Taxation of personal income

Residents are subject to income tax on their worldwide income, divided into four categories:

1. (deemed) rental income from real (immovable) property, reduced for owner-occupied dwellings;

2. income from movable property, including dividends, interest and royalties (investment income);

3. earned income, including business income, professional income, employment income and pension income;

4. miscellaneous income.

The net taxable income for each category amounts to the gross income less expenses incurred in acquiring or preserving the income and is computed according to each category's own rules. Certain additional deductions can be made from this total net income before applying the progressive tax rates, ranging from 25 per cent up to 50 per cent.

Income from employment

Employment income (salary, benefits in kind, termination payments and so forth) is fully taxable. However, employment income from a treaty country is exempt from tax for a Belgian resident, although it is added to the taxable income when determining the rate of income tax to be applied to the taxable income (this method is known as 'exemption with progression').

A tax credit of 50 per cent is available for employment income from a non-treaty country, provided that the income was taxed abroad, no matter at what rate. Foreign income is subject to income tax for its net amount (less expenses, including withholding and income taxes, regardless of the availability of any other relief).

Professional expenses are deductible, either on a lump-sum basis or on the actual amount incurred, provided this can be substantiated. Employees can also benefit from a number of tax-free 'social benefits' (such as meal tickets, hospitalization insurance and sick-pay arrangements), provided that the related requirements are met.

Expatriates temporarily residing in Belgium can benefit from a privileged tax regime, provided that a number of conditions are satisfied, allowing them to be taxed as if they were non-resident. They are taxed on their remuneration, which is pro-rated on the basis of the number of working days spent in Belgium. Moreover, certain expenses borne by the employer (moving costs, housing allowance, costs of a yearly trip to the home country, tax equalization, cost-of-living allowances, etc) are considered as expenses proper to the employer and are, within certain limits, exempt from tax for the employee. The expat status must be specifically granted by the tax authorities.

A system of withholding tax operates on earnings.

Real property tax

Annual tax, not deductible from personal income tax, is levied on the presumed annual rental income of owned land, buildings and industrial equipment, assessed at 1.25 per cent for buildings in the Brussels and Walloon region and 2.5 per cent in the Flemish region.

Capital acquisition tax

Tax is levied on the acquisition of real estate in Wallonia and the Brussels region at 12.5 per cent and in Flanders at 10 per cent. In certain cases, a reduced rate of 6 per cent in Wallonia and the Brussels region and 5 per cent in Flanders may apply.

Capital gains

As for corporations, capital gains realized by individuals engaged in business activities are regarded as business income and taxed accordingly at the ordinary individual income tax rate, although special rules and separate tax rates apply. Capital gains on shares in an enterprise, qualifying as professional income, are normally taxed at the individual income tax rate, unless the shares were acquired more than five years earlier, in which case the gains are taxed at 16.5 per cent. The same rate is charged on capital gains realized on fixed assets that have been used for more than five years.

Capital gains of individuals not engaged in business activities are not taxable unless the capital gain is related to a speculative transaction, the sale of immovable property within five years of acquisition, the sale of a substantial shareholding in a non-EU-based company, or the sale of rights in intangible property.

Wealth tax and capital duty

There is no wealth tax or capital duty in Belgium.

Inheritance/estate tax

Spouses and direct descendants are liable at rates ranging from 3 to 30 per cent in Wallonia and the Brussels region and at 3 to 27 per cent in Flanders. Higher rates apply to gifts and higher rates to more distant and unrelated beneficiaries (up to 80 per cent in Wallonia and Brussels and 65 per cent in Flanders).

Double tax treaties

Belgium has concluded more than 80 comprehensive treaties to avoid double taxation, among which are treaties with the UK and the United States.

Filing and payment

The tax year is the calendar year. Annual tax returns must generally be filed by 30 June of the year following. Salaried persons may prepay estimated income tax. Although taxes are normally withheld at source, individuals on a split payroll may need to pay additional taxes. Self-employed individuals are required to prepay estimated tax.

To access a fuller range of country profiles, available to download as part of the Kogan Page title *Working Abroad*, please go to www.koganpage.com/workingabroad (password: WA50571).

Canada

WORKING CONDITIONS

The general working atmosphere and corporate style in Canada closely resemble those of the United States, but Canadian society is more stable, with lower crime figures. If you go to Canada intending to stay more than three months, you have to register this fact on arrival. You cannot change your status from visitor while in-country. Applications for visas or permanent residency must be made abroad.

By and large, executive salaries are higher than in the UK, becoming more equal going down the scale. Professional groups that are in demand include mathematicians, sales and advertising personnel, chemists and physicists. It is also possible to immigrate if you have capital available or intend to run a business in Canada under the Business Immigration Program. Other schemes include Temporary Employment Authorization and Live-in Caregiver Program, as well as work opportunities for foreign students.

In the public services, preference is given to Canadian citizens and here, as well as in many private sector jobs, a knowledge of French is essential. It should not be assumed that the status of French in Canada is merely a nationalistic gesture. It is the mother language of many Canadian citizens. However, people who do not speak it may still enter public service, as provision will be made for them to learn the language subsequently.

People who want to exercise professional skills will have to apply to the appropriate professional bodies and institutes to make sure that their qualifications are recognized and that they possess the appropriate licence. In some cases where training to achieve the qualifications in question is substantially different in Canada, further examinations may have to be taken to achieve recognition. In all instances, though, documentary proof of degrees, etc should be taken with you, as well as such personal documents as birth and marriage certificates.

Anyone who is not a Canadian citizen or a permanent resident who wishes to work in Canada requires authorization. In certain cases an individual is authorized by virtue of the regulations, but in most cases the individual must obtain a work permit from Citizenship and Immigration Canada. A work permit can only be issued for a temporary position. In order to reside and work permanently in Canada, the applicant must qualify as a skilled worker.

For detailed information, visit the website at www.canada.org.uk.

USEFUL INFORMATION

Climate: Canadian winters are much colder than anything one is accustomed to in temperate zones, although similar to those of Scandinavia. This is true even in the population centres in the southern part of the country. If you are to arrive in Canada any time between October and March make sure you have plenty of warm clothes. On the other hand, the summer (June to September) can be very warm, with temperatures averaging around 32°C in midsummer in southern places like Toronto.

Electricity: 120 V, 60 Hz; conversion from other voltages is not really possible.

Health care: Canada operates a national health insurance programme, which is administered by the provinces, for both hospital and ordinary medical (though not dental) care. In all provinces except Quebec and British Columbia, which impose a brief residence qualification (though in the case of Quebec only for hospital insurance), this is available to immigrants immediately on arrival, and you should be sure to obtain details of registration and premium payments as soon as possible. Many employers pay the employee's contribution as part of the remuneration package, and this is a point worth checking in any job offer.

Education: Education is compulsory from 6 or 7 to 16 (15 in some provinces) and is free to the end of secondary schooling. Educational methods are progressive and similar to those in primary and comprehensive schools in the UK. There are also a small number of private schools. For registration you will need a birth certificate, visa, vaccination certificate and previous school records. In Quebec and French-speaking Canada the medium of instruction in many schools is French, and the teaching of French is an important part of the curriculum.

Post-secondary education is not free, but repayable loans are available from the province, and there are various other forms of monetary assistance including scholarships for able students. University fees vary but are mainly low.

Useful contacts:

British High Commission, 80 Elgin Street, Ottawa K1P 5K7 (tel: 1 613 237 1530, website: www.britainincanada.org)

Canadian High Commission, Macdonald House, 38 Grosvenor Street, London W1K 4AA (tel: 020 7258 6600, website: www.canada.org.uk)

Canadian Tourism Commission, 62–65 Trafalgar Square, London WC2N 5DV (tel: 020 7389 9988)

PERSONAL TAXATION

Residence

Like many countries, Canada taxes on the basis of residence. Tax legislation does not specifically define residence, although it does include several rules under which an individual may be 'deemed' to be resident. Generally, residence is determined by common law principles. Under these rules, an individual is generally considered to be resident if he or she has a 'continuing state of relationship' with Canada, as evidenced by a dwelling held for year-round use, the presence of a spouse or other family members in Canada, or the maintenance of personal property or other social ties in Canada, such as bank accounts, furniture and club memberships. An individual is also deemed to be resident if he or she stays in Canada for 183 days or more in a calendar year.

Taxation of personal income

Canadian residents are subject to tax on their worldwide income. Taxation can also arise in respect of investments in foreign investment entities and certain non-residential trusts. Non-residents are subject to tax on income earned from Canadian sources. The federal tax rates rise progressively up to 29 per cent (or 24.215 per cent for residents of Quebec). In addition, each province or territory imposes an income tax, with the maximum rate ranging from 10 per cent to 24 per cent.

Employment income (including most employment benefits), certain investment income and profits earned from a business or a profession are taxable at the individual's applicable personal tax rate. Dividends received from Canadian corporations are subject to a more favourable tax regime.

Social security

Employed persons, as well as their employers, are required to make employment and government pension plan contributions.

Capital gains

One-half of capital gains realized are included in taxable income.

Real property tax

Municipal authorities levy taxes on the occupation of real property.

Other taxes

There is no net wealth/net worth tax, formal inheritance or estate tax, capital duty, stamp duty or capital acquisitions tax in Canada.

Double taxation treaties

Canada has concluded more than 90 income tax treaties or conventions in force with other countries for the elimination of double taxation on income, including treaties with both the UK and the United States.

Filing and penalties

There are no family income tax returns in Canada. The tax year is the calendar year. The deadline to file an individual tax return and to pay the outstanding tax liability is 30 April of the year following. Individuals and their spouses or common law partners who operate a business or profession have an extended filing deadline of 15 June, but the tax liability is still due by 30 April. Penalties are applied for late filing, and interest is payable on any late balance owing, compounded daily.

To access a fuller range of country profiles, available to download as part of the Kogan Page title *Working Abroad*, please go to www.koganpage.com/workingabroad (password: WA50571).

6.4

France

WORKING CONDITIONS

European Union citizens do not require work permits. At the end of 2003 a law was passed by which residence permits were no longer required by EU citizens subject to certain conditions. The 35-hour week is standard, but this is under review. French workers are entitled by law to five weeks' annual leave. Many firms and offices are shut for much of August.

The level of managerial salaries is around 30 to 40 per cent higher than in the UK. Employers' contributions to social security are among the highest in Europe, but direct taxation is relatively low. Secretarial salaries are much the same as in the UK.

Most wages are fixed by collective bargaining at national level. Equal pay is theoretically obligatory – the gap between men's and women's pay is narrower than in most EU countries. There is also a minimum legal wage. Given the current economic problems, these areas are under a great deal of pressure for change.

Many fringe benefits are provided, and most employers have to contribute to housing and welfare. The practice of a 13th-month bonus is widespread, and most manual workers are now paid monthly, instead of fortnightly, and enjoy staff status. French workers attach as much importance to social security and fringe benefits as to salary.

USEFUL INFORMATION

Banking hours: 9.00 am to 4.30 pm weekdays (closed in the afternoon before a public holiday), some closed on Saturdays. May be closed for lunch in provincial towns and villages.

Post office: 8.00 am to 7.00 pm weekdays, 8.00 am to 12.00 noon Saturdays.

Shopping hours: 10.00 am to 7.00 pm Monday–Saturday, closed 1.00 to 3.00 pm and all day Monday outside Paris.

Electricity: 220 V (may vary).

Driving: Driving is on the right. Paris is congested and parking difficult, but the traffic flows. If you take your own car, you are obliged to have it fitted with seat belts back and front; yellow headlamps are no longer compulsory for cars.

Transport: The main centres are linked by internal airways, and there are airports at Lyon, Marseille, Nice, Bordeaux, Strasbourg and Toulouse, as well as two in Paris: Charles de Gaulle and Orly. The railway network is highly efficient, with a number of express and TGV (260 km/h) trains. Fares are cheaper than in the UK. A direct rail link with the UK is via the Channel Tunnel. The roads are good, and there is a network of motorways, on which tolls are payable. These can be expensive on a long journey.

Health care: There was a reciprocal health agreement with the UK, but the French government has withdrawn benefits for UK expatriates domiciled in France from 2008. Medical attention is expensive, but 75 per cent of the fees for doctors and dentists working within the French sickness insurance scheme can be reimbursed. A proportion of the cost of prescriptions can be refunded (40–70 per cent), as well as outpatient hospital treatment (80 per cent), although this system is under review and may face cuts. Private treatment is costly. There is a British hospital in Paris, the Hertford, and a more expensive US one.

Education: Some expatriate parents send their children to local schools, which are of a high educational standard and where they can acquire a good knowledge of French. There is free compulsory education from 6 to 16, and for children below that age there are many crèches and nursery schools. Secondary education is in two cycles, from 11 to 15 and from 15 to 18. Those who complete the second cycle can take the baccalaureate examination, before proceeding to university or institutes of technology. US and British schools in Paris cater for children of diplomats and business people. The British School of Paris is geared to the UK system; it takes pupils from 4 to 18 and offers boarding facilities.

Useful contacts:

British Embassy, 35 Rue du Faubourg St Honoré, 75383 Paris, Cedex 08 (tel: 44 51 31 00, website: www.amb-grandebretagne.fr)

French Consulate General, 21 Cromwell Road, London SW7 2EN
(tel: 020 7838 2000)

French Tourist Office, www.franceguide.com, www.maison-de-la–france.fr

Country information:
www.paris-anglo.com
www.parisfranceguide.com

Further information: Living and Working in France, by Genevieve Brame
(published by Kogan Page; www.koganpage.com), provides in-depth
information for expatriates living in France.

PERSONAL TAXATION

Unless otherwise stated, all figures relate to 2007 income.

Territoriality and residence

An individual is considered to be French resident if one of the following
three criteria is met:

1. The individual's permanent home (*foyer*) is in France or, if the
   permanent home cannot be determined, the individual's principal
   place of stay, regardless of permanency, is in France.

2. The individual carries out an occupation or employment in France,
   unless subsidiary to a main occupation carried out elsewhere.

3. The individual's place of economic interest (main investments and
   their management) or main source of income is in France.

A French resident is subject to French tax on his or her worldwide income,
while a non-resident is subject to French tax only on French-source income.

Taxation of personal income

Individuals are subject to income tax on their annual taxable income.
Taxable income is determined by adding together the various categories
of income and deducting losses, expenses and relief.

Categories of income include:

▌ industrial and commercial profits;

▌ non-commercial profits;

▌ rental income;

▌ employment income;

▌ financial income;

▌ agricultural income.

The tax year for income tax purposes is the calendar year, and the yearly taxable income is determined for the whole household, that is, husband, wife and dependent children. Income tax is computed by the French tax authorities on the income of the preceding year (eg in 2008 taxpayers must complete and lodge their tax return for income received during 2007). Income tax is levied at progressive rates from 5.5 per cent. From 1 January 2008, the maximum rate is 40 per cent for 2007 income, to which miscellaneous social taxes must be added (different from social security taxes), amounting to up to 11 per cent, applicable on certain income (investment income, rental income and so on) for residents. In return for the reduction in the tax rates, taxpayers are no longer entitled to benefit from the 20 per cent supplementary deduction, which has been incorporated by the Finance Bill 2006 in the new progressive income tax rates.

Employment income

Employment income includes all benefits in cash or in kind received by an individual. Professional expenses are deductible, with taxpayers choosing between a standard deduction of 10 per cent and a deduction of actual professional expenses. Social security contributions around 15 to 20 per cent for the employee are also deductible from gross income. Pensions are taxed in the same way as employment income.

Financial income

Share dividends and bond interest are subject to income tax at the progressive rates.

Capital gains

Capital gains from the sale of securities and real estate property are taxed at 16 per cent plus a special social security surcharge, bringing the total to 27 per cent.

Other taxes on capital

There is no capital duty or capital acquisitions tax. Transfers within a family are mostly exempt from inheritance/estate tax.

Net wealth/net worth tax

Households, rather than individuals, pay a wealth tax on worth more than €760,000. Some types of asset are exempt, and small deductions are allowed for dependants. Non-residents must pay tax on their property in France unless they are exempt under a tax treaty. The tax is levied on a sliding scale from 0.55 per cent on assets of €760,000 to €1.16 million rising to 1.8 per cent on assets exceeding €25.81 million.

Real property tax

Owner-occupants are liable for tax on developed real property based on the rental value of the property assessed by the tax authorities.

Tax treaties

France has signed tax treaties with more than 110 countries, and this includes the entire developed world.

Filing and penalties

Married persons must file a joint tax return. The tax return must generally be filed by 1 March after the end of the tax year. Late payments and filing are subject to a 20 per cent penalty. Interest is charged at 9 per cent per year. Employment income of individuals is taxed by advance payments of tax.

To access a fuller range of country profiles, available to download as part of the Kogan Page title *Working Abroad*, please go to www.koganpage.com/workingabroad (password: WA50571).

Germany

WORKING CONDITIONS

British and other EEA nationals with valid passports/identification cards are free to enter and move about the country. However, all residents must register in the local community at special registration offices (*Einwohnermeldeamt*) in Germany. If an EU national intends to stay for more than three months, he or she will need to apply for a residence permit at the foreign nationals authority (*Ausländeramt*), which is valid for five years. Free entrance to the German labour market is being applied in stages to nationals of the new EU member states during a transitional period of seven years.

At managerial level, the Germans do considerably better than the British. Secretarial and skilled worker salaries are slightly higher than in the UK. The cost of living is lower in Germany than in the UK. The British Chamber of Commerce publishes annual surveys of salaries and fringe benefits.

The standard working week is 36–40 hours for five days. There is a minimum of 25–30 days' holiday, plus 10–13 public holidays (depending on the federal state).

Wages and salaries are determined by collective bargaining, which usually has the force of law. There are separate arrangements for senior executives (*leitende Angestellte*). Individual contracts are usually for an indefinite period and terminated by written notice, with compensation according to age and length of service.

Employers may provide, by law or by custom, additional benefits, for example a 13th-month bonus and group/performance bonuses, and help towards housing, meals, transport and recreation.

There is a long-established and comprehensive system of social security, with benefits related to earnings. The public social security system includes the old-age pension, unemployment insurance and health and nursing insurance. The employee and the employer both pay 50 per cent of the respective contributions in principle. The employer withholds social security contributions from the salary. For 2006, contributions amounted to 19.5 per cent for old-age pension, 6.5 per cent for unemployment insurance, 1.7 per cent for nursing insurance (1.95 per cent for childless individuals having reached the age of 23 years) and approximately 15 per cent for health insurance (depending on the chosen health care insurance company). There are certain ceilings beyond which no further contributions need to be paid. If the remuneration exceeds the obligatory health/nursing insurance ceiling, the employee is not obliged to choose one of the public health insurance companies; the employee can opt for private health insurance. In such a case, health and nursing insurance contributions will differ from the public rates depending on the chosen programme and insurance company, and the employer will be obliged to pay the employer's portion based on the average public insurance company's rate.

Under certain conditions, individuals who are seconded to Germany can apply to remain in their home country's social security system, and German social security contributions will not become due.

USEFUL INFORMATION

Banking hours: 8.30 am to 1.00 pm, 2.30 to 4.00 pm weekdays.

Shopping hours: 9.00 am to 8.00 pm weekdays, 9.00 am to 7.00 or 8.00 pm Saturday; closed Sunday and public holidays. Hairdressers and restaurants closed Mondays.

Driving: Speed limits are 50 km/h in built-up areas, 100 km/h on overland roads, and 130 km/h on motorways; cars with trailers 80 km/h. Driving is on the right. Breakdown emergency number: 01 8022 22.

Transport: There is a highly sophisticated network of air, rail and road transport, serving all parts of the country. All major cities are linked by motorways *(Autobahnen)*.

Health care: Medical treatment is of a high standard, and most costs are met through insurance funds. Charges are made for dentistry, medicine, drugs and medical aids. Refunds are possible if you exchange your Form E128 for a *Krankenschein* certificate issued by the German health insurance companies through the Local Sickness Fund.

Education: Education is compulsory from 6 to 18 (including three years at a vocational school on a part-time basis). A monthly fee is charged for nursery education between the ages of 3 and 6. The standard is high and thorough, and many expatriate parents send their children to local schools. Others want their children to continue education in the UK. There are international schools at Düsseldorf, Frankfurt, Hamburg and Munich. The British Embassy runs a preparatory school in Bonn for children from 4 to 13. Fees vary, so it is necessary to check. Schools for the children of British military personnel sometimes admit children of civilians.

Useful contacts:

British Embassy, Wilhelmstr 70–71, 10117 Berlin (tel: +49 302 0457 0, website: www.britischebotschaft.de/)

German Embassy, 23 Belgrave Square, London SW1X 8PZ (tel: 020 7824 1300)

German National Tourist Board, PO Box 2695, London W1A 3TN (tel: 020 7317 0908, website: www.germany-tourism.de/)

Expatriate information:
www.german-way.com

PERSONAL TAXATION

Residence

An individual who resides in Germany is subject to taxation on his or her worldwide income (unlimited tax liability) unless a double taxation treaty disallows the taxation of an income portion. Non-residents are subject to taxation on certain German-sourced income (limited tax liability) only.

To be considered a resident of Germany for tax purposes, an individual needs to maintain a permanent home or his or her habitual abode in Germany. The domicile-of-origin concept and citizenship have no impact on a person's tax status in Germany. A permanent home exists where an individual has possession of a house or apartment under circumstances that indicate he or she intends to stay not just temporarily in Germany. The German tax rules assume a habitual abode if the individual stays more than six months continuously in Germany. Short interruptions, such as for holidays or business trips, are disregarded. The unlimited tax liability arises (respectively ceases) in Germany as soon as the individual meets (respectively breaks) these residence criteria. Generally, married couples who are subject to unlimited taxation can elect to file jointly.

Taxation of personal income

German residents are subject to income tax on seven categories of income, which include:

▮ income from employment;

▮ income from a trade or profession;

▮ income from agriculture and forestry;

▮ income from rent and leasing;

▮ income from investment including capital gains;

▮ other income.

For these income categories, taxable income is computed by deducting income-related expenses from gross income. The cash receipts and disbursements method is used to calculate taxable income. There are no special rules for expatriates.

Income tax rates

Income tax is levied at progressive rates up to 45 per cent plus a solidarity surcharge of 5.5 per cent (resulting in a top rate of 47.5 per cent) and a church tax of 9 per cent (Bavaria and Baden-Württemberg 8 per cent) levied on the income tax.

Capital gains

The sale of real estate and rights to private property is subject to tax if the taxpayer has owned the property for less than 10 years. The sale of other assets is taxable if the taxpayer has held the assets for less than one year. The normal tax rates apply. For capital gains from the sale of shares, 50 per cent (60 per cent from 2009) is taxable at the normal rates if the taxpayer holds a direct or indirect interest of 1 per cent or more. As from 2009, such taxpayers will be subject to a flat rate of 25 per cent (26.375 per cent including the solidarity charge).

Inheritance/estate tax

Inheritance and gift taxes range from 7 per cent to 50 per cent, with various exemptions. The rules are currently under revision.

Other taxes

There is no capital duty, stamp duty, capital acquisitions tax or net worth/wealth tax in Germany.

Social security

Employed individuals are required to make a contribution for pensions and health and unemployment insurance. The employer bears 50 per cent of the total contribution.

Tax treaties

Germany has 88 income tax treaties and 6 inheritance and gift tax treaties.

Tax administration

The tax year for income tax purposes is the calendar year. In principle, income tax returns must be filed by 31 May following the tax year; however, extensions to 30 September will be granted automatically if the tax return is prepared by a professional tax adviser. A further extension may be available on application. A married couple living together may opt for joint or separate assessment.

Domestic employers are obliged to operate the pay-as-you-earn system, ie the employer withholds wage tax on behalf of the employee and transfers it to the respective tax office. To meet this rule the employee needs to provide a wage tax card to the employer that indicates the necessary tax information. The tax withheld is credited against the income tax liability levied on the basis of the filed income tax return.

The income tax liability is levied through an income tax assessment notice issued by the tax authorities. Income tax payments are payable within one month of the assessment's receipt. Refunds are paid out immediately after the issuance of the assessment. A protest against the tax assessment can be filed only within one month after the assessment's receipt.

The tax authorities can levy a penalty for delayed filing at a rate of 10 per cent of the tax liability. Furthermore, a late payment penalty of 1 per cent of the tax liability per month arises automatically on late payment.

To access a fuller range of country profiles, available to download as part of the Kogan Page title *Working Abroad*, please go to www.koganpage.com/workingabroad (password: WA50571).

Hong Kong

WORKING CONDITIONS

There are no exchange controls in Hong Kong, and money can be remitted into and out of the former colony. In the days prior to the handover, an expatriate employee in the private sector could expect to be earning 40 to 50 per cent more than his or her gross UK pay. On top of this, an expatriate employee could expect to get free or heavily subsidized accommodation, medical and dental coverage, an education and holiday visits allowance for his or her children, and possible further fringe benefits such as a car, servants and a good gratuity at the end of the contract. Since 1997 job opportunities for UK expatriates have dwindled as multinational corporations have moved their regional headquarters to Beijing or Shanghai. Public sector positions are no longer open to UK nationals.

Hong Kong's largely Chinese population (98 per cent) is impressively well educated, skilled and hard-working, so opportunities for expatriates are limited. A work permit is required for all foreign nationals in Hong Kong. However, work permits are hard to come by, and it is the policy of the Hong Kong government to recruit locally wherever possible. Employees living and working in Hong Kong for more than 180 days must have a Hong Kong identity card and carry it at all times.

USEFUL INFORMATION

The feature of Hong Kong life that strikes a newcomer most forcibly is the population density, impressive even by Asian standards. The population density for Hong Kong Island is 5,380 persons per square kilometre, including barren areas (three-quarters of the whole). So Hong Kong is no place for people who feel the need for wide open spaces or who are bothered by crowds.

Climate: The climate of Hong Kong – warm and humid for most of the year but with a brief cool winter – makes air conditioning and some heating facilities a necessity.

Driving: There are very few straight roads in Hong Kong and distances, in any case, are short, so a big car is a status symbol that attracts a higher rate of registration tax and annual licence fees. UK driving licences are valid for a stay of up to a year, but can be exchanged for a local licence without a test. Bringing a new car into Hong Kong is hardly cheaper than buying one locally; a first registration tax is charged. However, good second-hand cars are reported to be readily available.

Transport: Public transport and taxis are inexpensive but apt to be over-crowded, and many expatriates have cars, which in many cases are not provided as a perk that goes with the job.

Education: Education in Hong Kong can be a problem, and expatriates are advised to make arrangements for schooling as soon as they arrive there, or preferably before arrival. Prior to arrival it is worth notifying the Education Department (9–16th Floors, Wu Chung House, 197–221 Queen's Road East, Wanchai, Hong Kong) or the English Schools Foundation (43b Stubbs Road, Hong Kong) to ask about places. This is because most of the schools cater for the predominantly Chinese population, so the medium of instruction is either Chinese or, if in English, with the emphasis on English as a foreign language. There are several independent schools offering a UK curriculum, at both primary and secondary level.

Media: Hong Kong has two TV stations and two main radio stations providing services in both Chinese and English. There are two English-language TV channels and three English-language radio channels, two of which combine, from midnight to 6.00 am, to provide a 24-hour service; there is a BBC World Service relay on another channel at night. Satellite television offers a 24-hour global news service, and a cable TV channel carries locally produced programmes.

Useful contacts:

British Consulate General, No 1 Supreme Court Road, Central, Hong Kong, PO Box 528 (tel: 852 2901 3000, website: www.britishconsulate.org.hk/)

Hong Kong Government Office, 6 Grafton Street, London W1X 3LB (tel: 020 7499 9821)

Hong Kong Tourist Association, 6 Grafton Street, London W1X 3LB (tel: 020 7533 7100, website: www.hkta.org, US website: www.hkta.org/usa/)

PERSONAL TAXATION

Residence

The Hong Kong tax system adopts a source concept on taxability of income, and residence is therefore not relevant. However, for the purpose of the personal assessment option (see 'Filing and payment' below), the terms 'permanent resident' and 'temporary resident' are defined as follows. 'Permanent resident' means 'an individual who ordinarily resides in Hong Kong'. 'Temporary resident' means 'an individual who stays in Hong Kong for a period or a number of periods amounting to more than 180 days during the year of assessment, or for a period or periods amounting to more than 300 days in two consecutive years of assessment, one of which is the year of assessment in respect of which the election [of personal assessment] is made'. An expatriate employed by a non-resident company and staying in Hong Kong for less than 60 days is not liable to tax on his or her employment income. Where an expatriate is employed by a Hong Kong company and stays for more than 60 days, all Hong Kong income is taxable.

Taxes on personal income

Individuals are taxed on their total Hong Kong income from employment, less deductible expenses, charitable donations and personal allowances. The source of employment income is determined by where the contract was negotiated and concluded and where enforceable; the residence of the employer; and where the salary is paid. Income from non-Hong Kong employment is deemed to be sourced in Hong Kong if it is attributable to services rendered in Hong Kong. Taxable income includes commissions, bonuses, cost-of-living allowances, stock option gains, awards, gratuities, allowances (including those for education) and other perquisites derived from employment. Dividend income is not taxed, but gains from exercising share options are taxable. Personal income is taxed at progressive marginal rates ranging from 2 per cent to 17 per cent, with a standard rate of 16 per cent.

Deductions and allowances

Expenses incurred wholly, exclusively and necessarily for employment, and charitable donations, are deductible. Mortgage interest paid on a property used as the taxpayer's principal residence is deductible up to a prescribed limit. Allowable deductions also include mandatory contributions to a recognized occupational retirement scheme, self-education expense and elderly residential care expenses. There are a number of personal allowances, depending on the taxpayer's personal circumstances.

Social security

Employed and self-employed people are required to make contributions to a mandatory provident fund (MPF), which also benefits from contributions from employers. The employee must contribute 5 per cent of his or her salary to a chosen MPF account, and this amount must be matched by the employer. Additional contributions can be made by both parties.

Taxes on capital

There are no taxes on capital in Hong Kong.

Double taxation treaties

Hong Kong has concluded tax arrangements with mainland China for the avoidance of double taxation on income and has tax agreements with Belgium, Thailand and Luxembourg.

Filing and payment

A married couple may opt for joint or separate assessment. The tax year is 1 April to 31 March. Employment income of individuals is not taxed by withholding, but provisional salaries tax may be payable. A tax return is issued on 1 May following the tax year, and a final assessment to salaries tax is made based on the information in the return. Any provisional salaries tax paid is creditable against the final salaries tax for the year upon final assessment.

To access a fuller range of country profiles, available to download as part of the Kogan Page title *Working Abroad*, please go to www.koganpage.com/workingabroad (password: WA50571).

India

WORKING CONDITIONS

Anybody coming to India to take up employment needs a valid passport and a visa application form completed and signed, along with the necessary formalities for a work permit.

The working week is usually from Monday to Friday, 9.30 am to 5.30 pm, Saturday until 2.00 pm. However, in some offices, there is a five-day week.

USEFUL INFORMATION

Time zone: India is five and a half hours ahead of GMT.

Language: India has 16 officially recognized languages, of which Hindi is the official language of the republic. English is extensively used and understood almost everywhere.

Population: India is the second most populous country in the world, with over 1 billion people, which is about 16 per cent of the world population. There are 23 cities with a population of over a million. Mumbai, the largest city in India, has a population over 12.6 million.

Education: Education in India is of international standard. There are international-standard schools, colleges and universities. Various types of scholarships and loan facilities are provided. The government has also introduced employment exchange programmes all over the country to facilitate the recruitment of deserving candidates into various sectors. The literacy rate in India is 65 per cent, with a vast degree of regional variation.

Climate: Owing to the great size of the country and differences of altitude, there are various climatic zones in the country. However, India has three main seasons in the year:

▌ rainy: mid-June to mid-October;

▌ winter: mid-October to mid-March;

▌ summer: mid-March to mid-June.

Political structure: India is the largest democracy in the world and has adopted a parliamentary system of government with a federal structure. The central government in Delhi has exclusive jurisdiction over all matters of national interest, and consists of a Council of Ministers headed by the prime minister. The country is administratively divided into 29 states and six union territories. The state government has primary responsibility for matters like law and order, education, health and agriculture. The parliament comprises two houses, the lower house (the Lok Sabha) and the upper house (the Rajya Sabha).

Currency and banking: The Indian rupee (INR) is the country's currency. Transactions on capital account are still regulated, but the rupee is convertible on current account. The country's banking system is monitored and controlled by the Reserve Bank of India (RBI). The primary functions of the RBI are issuing currency, and regulation and supervision of Indian banks and banking. The commercial banking system in India is fully developed, and most of the large banks are state owned. Private and foreign banks also participate in the Indian banking sector.

Judiciary: India has a well-established and independent judiciary system. The Supreme Court of India is the highest court of appeal, in New Delhi. High courts in the states, along with supplementary district courts, enforce the fundamental rights of citizens that are guaranteed by the constitution.

Transport: All modes of public and private transport are usually available across India at reasonable rates.

Accommodation: India is witnessing increased urbanization. International-standard living accommodation can easily be rented or purchased by foreigners in major cities in India.

Health and health care: Generally, health standards are extremely good in India. Government and private bodies have set up various hospitals and private nursing homes. These hospitals provide international-standard facilities at competitive costs. Various types of medical insurances are also available in India. Medical insurance for employees and their families is also provided by employers through group insurance or for each individual.

Media: Media are widely spread and are operated by both government and private organizations. There are radio and TV stations such as All India Radio (AIR), Doordarshan News and the Press Information Bureau providing 24-hour service and offering global news through satellite links.

PERSONAL TAXATION

Residence

An individual is said to be resident in India if he or she satisfies either of the following basic conditions: 1) he or she stays in India for a period of more than 182 days; or 2) he or she stays in India for a period of 60 days or more during the year and 365 days or more during the four years immediately preceding.

A 'not ordinarily resident' individual is one either who has not been a resident in nine of the preceding 10 years or who has been in India for less than two years during the preceding seven years.

Taxes on income

Residents of India are normally taxed on worldwide income. Persons not ordinarily resident do not pay tax on income earned outside India unless it is derived from a business controlled in India or the income is accrued or first received in India or is deemed to have accrued in India.

Tax rates are progressive up to 30 per cent plus applicable surcharges.

Income from employment, including most employment benefits, is fully taxable. Profits derived from carrying on a trade or profession by an individual are generally taxed in the same way as profits derived by companies (ie at 30 per cent for domestic companies).

Deductions and allowances

Deductions are granted for medical expenses and insurance, retirement annuities, mortgage interest, education loans, etc. For most senior citizens (65 and older) the first INR145,000 is tax exempt for resident women and INR110,000 for men.

Social security

Employees contribute 10 to 12 per cent of wages per month towards a provident fund.

Capital gains

Gains are long-term if the asset is held for more than three years (one year in the case of shares and specified securities). Long-term gains on listed shares and specified securities are exempt, while gains from other long-term assets are taxed at 20 per cent. Short-term gains on listed shares and other specified securities are taxed at 10 per cent, and gains from other short-term assets are taxed at the normal income tax rates. A surcharge and cess are also imposed.

Net wealth/net worth tax

Wealth tax is levied on individuals only in respect of specified non-productive assets. Debts incurred for acquiring the specified assets are deductible in arriving at net taxable wealth. Net wealth up to INR1.5 million is exempt from wealth tax, and net wealth in excess of this amount is taxable at a flat rate of 1 per cent.

Other taxes

There is no inheritance/estate tax, capital acquisitions tax, real property tax or capital duty. Stamp duty is levied on financial instruments and transactions according to the Indian Stamp Act and the Stamp Acts of the various states.

Double tax treaties

There are double taxation avoidance agreements with more than 70 countries.

Filing and payment

Individuals are required to file tax returns separately and are assessed separately. The tax year runs from 1 April to 31 March. Employers withhold tax on salary income. Individuals must prepay at least 90 per cent of the final tax due by the end of the fiscal year, with interest payable on underpayment. Returns are due by 31 July. Penalties apply for failure to file a return.

To access a fuller range of country profiles, available to download as part of the Kogan Page title *Working Abroad*, please go to www.koganpage.com/workingabroad (password: WA50571).

6.8

Japan

WORKING CONDITIONS

An expatriate executive will need to double his or her UK salary to maintain standards, entertain as his or her job may require, and provide UK schooling for any children. Tokyo has consistently been one of the world's most expensive cities, and a senior expatriate executive should strive for US$180,000–$230,000, plus 15–20 per cent overseas loading. Japanese indigenous salaries, once relatively low, are also now in the upper quartile and well above UK levels. It is advisable to arrange for some salary to be paid elsewhere to ease the tax burden and facilitate the transfer of funds to the UK.

The majority of expatriates working in Japan are employed by foreign companies, particularly as representatives; otherwise, the main source of employment is as English language teachers. EFL teachers are likely to be recruited by Japanese language schools. Bona fide students in Japan can appeal for permission to work a limited number of hours per week (teaching EFL); pay is from £16 to £25 an hour. Some language schools underpay their full-time staff. Even a primary school teacher should be earning at least £16,000 a year, bearing in mind the cost of living.

A person wishing to enter Japan for the purposes of employment, training or study must apply for a visa. Requirements are: a valid passport; one visa application form completed and signed; one passport-sized photograph; and a certificate of eligibility (original and one photocopy). The certificate of eligibility is issued by the Ministry of Justice in Japan. It is provided by a future employer or sponsor in Japan. In certain cases additional support documents may be required.

Employment patterns in Japanese firms differ from those in the West – recruitment is on traditional paternalistic lines from families with loyalty to the company – and a knowledge of Japanese would be a prerequisite.

Holders of UK passports require no visas for tourist visits of less than 90 days, which period may be extended to a maximum of 180 days at the discretion of the authorities. A work visa is required by those who have already obtained a post. To obtain a work visa you must first have a definite job appointment in Japan. Your employer should then apply to the Ministry of Justice for a certificate of eligibility. Once this is received you must submit, in person, a visa application to the Japanese Consulate, together with the certificate. Provided the documents are all in order a visa can normally be issued fairly quickly. Information is available from the Visa Section, Consulate General of Japan, 101–104 Piccadilly, London W1V 9FN. Temporary work is not permitted but, if when visiting as a tourist you receive a written offer of a permanent post, a working visa may be obtained by leaving the country and applying from outside (Korea, for example).

Booklets outlining Japanese business practices and attitudes are available for business people from JETRO London, Leconfield House, Curzon Street, London W1Y 8LQ, and may be useful for other visitors. For points on etiquette and survival tips, three useful publications for intending expatriates in Japan are *Living in Japan*, *A Consumer's Guide to Prices in Japan* and *Finding a Home in Tokyo*, published by the American Chamber of Commerce in Japan, Bridgestone Toranomon Building, 3–25–2, Toranomon, Minato-ku, Tokyo 105 (tel: 03 3433 5381, fax: 03 3436 1446).

USEFUL INFORMATION

Commercial organizations: Office hours are usually 9.00 am to 5.00 pm; many companies operate a five-day week.

Banking hours: 9.00 am to 3.00 pm Monday–Friday, 9.00 am to 12.00 noon Saturday.

Shops: Shops and department stores are usually open on Sundays and public holidays, but most other businesses are closed then. There are public holidays throughout the year.

Duty: The expatriate who will be staying longer than a year may bring in household effects, including a car and/or boat, duty-free within limits considered reasonable by the customs authorities. The car (or boat) sales receipt must be presented to show that it has been in use for more than one year before its arrival in Japan.

Driving: An international driving licence is valid for one year, after which a Japanese licence must be obtained. This involves both practical and written tests, which may be taken in English. Traffic drives on the left, and tolls are payable for motorway use. The volume of traffic is immense, but Japanese drivers are patient and disciplined, and accidents are consequently few. Signposting is inadequate (assuming an ability to read them), and a compass might be useful.

Transport: All the usual forms of public and private transport are available.

Health care: Medical insurance for employees and their families is provided by either a government-managed scheme or a health insurance society. There are a number of English-speaking doctors in major cities, and Western brands of drugs are available.

Education: There are many schools for English-speaking children, but they are not geared to UK education. Most expatriates leave their children to be educated in Britain.

Media: Four English-language newspapers are published daily: the *Japan Times*, the *Yomiuri Daily*, the *Asahi Evening News* and the *Mainichi Daily News*.

Useful contacts:

British Embassy, No 1 Ichiban-cho, Chiyoda-ku, Tokyo 102–8381 (tel: 813 5211 1100, website: www.uknow.or.jp/)

Japanese Embassy, 101 Piccadilly, London W1V 7JT (tel: 020 7465 6500)

Japan National Tourist Organization (website: www.seejapan.co.uk)

PERSONAL TAXATION

Residence

A permanent resident is liable for tax on worldwide income; a temporary resident is liable for income tax on Japan-sourced income and foreign-sourced income to the extent that it is paid in or remitted to Japan; non-residents are liable on Japan-sourced income only.

A permanent resident is an individual who is either 'domiciled' in Japan or has lived in Japan for at least one year and is not a 'non-permanent resident'. A non-permanent resident is an individual who has been living in Japan for less than five years in the preceding 10 years.

Taxes on income

Most income, including employment income and investment income, is taxable. Specified deductions, allowances and credits are available to reduce tax. Progressive tax rates up to 50 per cent apply.

Deductions and allowances

Deductions are allowed for social insurance premiums paid to the government, life insurance premiums, earthquake insurance premiums, qualified medical expenses, charitable contributions, etc. There are personal allowances for the individual, a dependent spouse and children under the age of 23. There are also exemptions for the disabled and elderly.

Social security

The employee's share of social security contributions is currently 12.813 per cent, which is withheld by the employer.

Capital gains

Capital gains from the disposal of real property and of shares are subject to separate rules. Gains from the sale of shares are taxed at 20 per cent. However, through to December 2008, subject to certain conditions, a reduced rate of 10 per cent applies to the sale of listed shares. Long-term gains of individuals from the sale of land are taxed at 20 per cent. Short-term gains are generally taxed at 39 per cent.

Net wealth/net worth tax

There is no wealth tax in Japan.

Inheritance/estate tax

Progressive tax rates up to 70 per cent are applied.

Real property tax

Fixed assets are subject to a municipal levy at an annual rate of 1.4 to 2.1 per cent of assessed value. Additionally a real estate acquisitions tax of 3 per cent applies at the time of purchase, and there is a real estate registration tax imposed at rates ranging from 0.4 to 2 per cent, depending on the type of transfer.

Other taxes

There is no capital duty. Stamp duty of JPY200 to JPY600,000 is imposed on the execution of taxable documents.

Double taxation treaties

Japan has concluded 44 comprehensive income tax treaties, including those with the UK and the United States.

Filing and payment

Joint filing is not permitted; the tax rates are uniform and are not dependent on marital or other status. The tax year is the calendar year. Tax is withheld at source from the employment income of individuals. Where an individual needs to file a tax return, this is due by 15 March following the end of the calendar year.

To access a fuller range of country profiles, available to download as part of the Kogan Page title *Working Abroad*, please go to www.koganpage.com/workingabroad (password: WA50571).

The Netherlands

WORKING CONDITIONS

Executive salaries are about 30 per cent higher than in the UK; administrative salaries are roughly comparable.

A legal minimum wage is fixed for all workers aged 23 to 65 and is reviewed at least once a year in the light of movements in average earnings and the cost-of-living index. Apart from this, wages are determined by collective agreements – the practice of plant agreements has grown with the increase in the size of firms.

Collective agreements usually lay down procedures for dealing with disputes and provide for reference to arbitration boards in the event of failure to settle. The country has been relatively strike-free. Most contracts are written and provide for a two-month trial period. Dismissals and resignations come under government supervision; length of notice is governed by the terms of individual contracts and length of service – for managers the notice period is usually three months. In most industries the 40-hour week has become standard.

Workers are entitled to three weeks' paid holiday and most get more through collective bargaining. Five weeks is normal for managerial staff.

USEFUL INFORMATION

Banking hours: 9.00 am to 5.30 pm Monday–Saturday.

Shopping hours: 11.00 am or 12.00 noon to 5.00 pm Monday, 9.00 am to 5.30 or 6.00 pm Tuesday–Friday.

Transport: Internal and urban transport is very efficient. Frequent train services link the main centres, and there are country-wide bus services. The roads are good and not over-congested. Nearly everybody in The Netherlands cycles, and there are special cycle paths on the main roads.

Health care: The Dutch health service is based on a mixture of compulsory and voluntary schemes. The compulsory scheme covers about 70 per cent of the population. Private medical treatment is expensive. The Dutch, on the whole, are health-conscious, and have the longest life expectancy of any EU nationals. There is a reciprocal health agreement with the UK.

Education: Education is free (though some schools may request a voluntary contribution) and compulsory from 5 to 16, with part-time schooling for a further year. The British School in The Netherlands is in the vicinity of The Hague and provides for children between 3 and 18 years. The fees compare favourably with those of other international schools in The Netherlands. There is a British primary school in Amsterdam and a number of other international and US schools in the major cities – details of these can be obtained from the European Council of International Schools (ECIS) and the Council of British International Schools (COBIS).

Useful contacts:

British Embassy, Lange Voorhout 10, 2514 ED, The Hague (tel: 31 70 427 0427)

Dutch Embassy, 38 Hyde Park Gate, London SW7 5DP (tel: 020 7590 3200)

Netherlands Board of Tourism, PO Box 30783, London WC2B 6DH (tel: 020 7539 7950, website: www.goholland.com)

PERSONAL TAXATION

Residence

In the Netherlands residency is based on facts and circumstances. Court rulings indicate that the place where the spouse and children live is the main criterion for the determination of residency.

The Dutch tax system – highlights

Dutch residents are subject to Dutch income tax on their worldwide income. Declared income consists of the following categories:

- *Box 1:* taxable income from work and home ownership (progressive rate up to 52 per cent). Wage tax on employment income is credited against income tax.

- *Box 2:* taxable income from a substantial (business) interest (fixed rate of 25 per cent). In general a 'substantial interest' refers to a shareholding of at least 5 per cent in a capital divided into shares.

- *Box 3:* taxable income from savings and investments (a deemed income of 4 per cent of the savings and investments taxed at a fixed rate of 30 per cent; effective rate 1.2 per cent).

Non-resident individuals are subject to income tax on specific sources of remuneration, such as employment income (Box 1). Tax is assessed on a calendar-year basis.

Special features include the following:

- *Treated as resident taxpayer:* qualifying non-residents may choose to be treated as resident taxpayers. In that case they enjoy the same deductions as resident taxpayers. However, their worldwide income is taxable in The Netherlands, taking into account the provisions of the tax treaty of The Netherlands with the country of actual residence.

- *Tax credit:* after calculating the total income tax payable (Boxes 1, 2 and 3) a tax credit is granted. Non-resident individuals are only granted the social security part of the tax credit provided they pay social security premiums in The Netherlands.

- *Foreign employees '30 per cent ruling':* if certain requirements are met, Dutch employers may grant a special tax-exempt allowance of 30 per cent of the wage income. When the foreign employee lives in The Netherlands there is the possibility of electing for deemed non-residency for tax purposes. A deemed non-resident taxpayer is considered as a non-resident taxpayer with regard to his or her income in Boxes 2 and 3. For those boxes, he or she is taxable in The Netherlands on Dutch sources of income only. However, any Box 1 income remains subject to Dutch income tax, as for a regular resident taxpayer.

Deductions and allowances

In general, all expenses that are necessary to generate taxable income in Boxes 1 and 2 are deductible. In relation to Box 3, expenses are treated as liabilities deductible from the taxable base. Certain expenses of a mixed character are not deductible, or are deductible subject to limits.

Social security

State social security contributions are payable by all individual Netherlands residents. Employees and the self-employed pay additional social security contributions.

Capital gains

In principle, capital gains are taxed at progressive rates. If the gain is related to a substantial interest, a flat rate of 25 per cent applies. If the gain relates to an investment, it is not taxed as such under Box 3.

Inheritance/estate tax

Inheritance tax, at rates varying from 5 per cent to 68 per cent, is charged on inheritances received from Dutch residents, unless the donor is an emigrant for Dutch tax purposes and has emigrated within 10 years before his or her death.

Capital acquisitions tax

Transfer tax of 6 per cent is payable by the purchaser on the acquisition of real property or certain related rights.

Real property tax

Taxes at varying rates are imposed by municipalities on owners of real property on an annual basis. Real property tax is not deductible for individual income tax purposes.

Other taxes

There is no net wealth/net worth tax, capital duty or stamp duty.

Double taxation treaties

The Netherlands has an extensive tax treaty network with more than 80 countries, including the UK and the United States. If no treaty is available there is a unilateral rule to avoid double taxation.

Filing and penalties

A couple (married or unmarried) living together for the majority of the year may file a joint assessment. The tax return is due for filing before April of the next calendar year (tax year). Payment must be made on assessment.

To access a fuller range of country profiles, available to download as part of the Kogan Page title *Working Abroad*, please go to www.koganpage.com/workingabroad (password: WA50571).

Singapore

WORKING CONDITIONS

Singapore's expatriate community is quite large, with all of the world's key nationalities represented. Jobs are advertised in the appropriate sectors of the overseas press and are usually on a contract basis with a salary plus fringe benefits, as indicated in the 'Personal taxation' section below. The major Singapore professional bodies are affiliated to, or otherwise closely connected with, their global counterparts. People going to work in Singapore must have an employment pass, which has to be obtained by the prospective employer. Dependants must also obtain a pass that has to be applied for by the employer. There are various immigration schemes for those with proven technical, professional or entrepreneurial skills.

USEFUL INFORMATION

Climate: Singapore is less than 137 kilometres from the equator and is hot and humid for most of the year.

Transport: The importing of cars is discouraged, and there is a duty of 45 per cent on imported cars on top of a basic additional registration fee of 150 per cent of the value of any new car, imported or otherwise. Thus it is not advisable to bring a car into Singapore from abroad, even though buying one locally is very expensive. Second-hand cars are advertised for sale in the *Straits Times*. The government is trying to limit car ownership on the island, both by fiscal policies and by placing restrictions on the use of cars in the central business district. On the other hand, both taxis and public transport are correspondingly inexpensive, and indeed are among the world's cheapest.

Health: Singapore has a good health record, and the government wages a keen cleanliness campaign, which includes hefty fines for dropping even a bus ticket in the street.

Health care: There are no free medical facilities, but treatment in government clinics is very cheap, though most expatriates prefer to use private doctors, who charge between S$25 and S$50 (specialists S$45–$80), depending on their qualifications and what sort of treatment is involved. Surgeons' and obstetricians' fees start at around S$2,100, and a private room in a hospital costs about S$180 a day. Medical fees, or insurance premiums to cover them, are often, in the case of expatriates, met by employers.

Education: As with many other jobs overseas, education can be problematic, and arrangements to send children to local schools should be made as soon as possible. Government schools are very cheap, with only nominal fees for the children of Singapore residents. There are three good British private primary schools. The Singapore American School takes all ages up to 18, and there is also the United World College of South East Asia, which has facilities for A level teaching. There is an excellent university in Singapore, at which the standards of entry and the level of the courses are equivalent to UK universities. Fees vary depending on the nature of the course being taken.

Useful contacts:

British High Commission, 100 Tanglin Road, Singapore 247919 (tel: 656424 4200, website: www.britain.org.sg/)

Singapore High Commission, 9 Wilton Crescent, London SW1X 8SA (tel: 020 7235 8315)

Singapore Tourism Board, 1st Floor, Carrington House, 126–130 Regent Street, London W1R 5FE (tel: 020 7437 0033)

Expatriate contacts:
www.expatsingapore.com

PERSONAL TAXATION

Residence

A Singaporean is tax resident if he or she normally resides in Singapore except for temporary absence. A foreigner is regarded as resident in Singapore if, in the calendar year preceding the year of assessment, he or she was physically present in Singapore or exercised employment in Singapore (other than as a director of a company) for 183 days or more.

Taxes on income

Singapore tax residents are subject to income tax on income accrued in or derived from Singapore. Since 1 January 2004, foreign-source income has been exempt from income tax in Singapore. Certain investment income derived from Singapore sources by individuals on or after 1 January 2004 is also exempt. Non-resident tax individuals are subject to Singapore income tax only on the income accrued in or derived from Singapore.

Taxable income includes gains or profits from a trade or profession and earnings from employment (including the value of employer-provided benefits). Residents are taxed at progressive rates ranging from 3.5 to 20 per cent. Non-residents are taxed on employment income at a higher rate, at a flat rate of 15 per cent (without any deduction of personal reliefs and allowances). All other non-residents' income sourced in Singapore, including directors' and consultants' fees, is taxed at a flat rate of 20 per cent. A non-resident individual (other than a director) on short-term employment in Singapore for less than 60 days may be exempt from tax in Singapore.

Deductions and allowances

Personal reliefs and tax rebates against assessable income are granted only to resident individuals.

Social security

Only employees who are Singapore citizens or permanent residents are required to contribute to the Central Provident Fund (CPF), at a rate of 20 per cent. Graduated rates may apply for the first three years, when the employee first attains permanent residence.

Capital gains

Singapore does not tax capital gains.

Inheritance/estate tax

An individual domiciled in Singapore at the time of his or her death is liable to estate duty on all movable and immovable assets in Singapore and movable assets outside Singapore at 5 per cent on the first S$12 million and 10 per cent thereafter. A person neither domiciled nor resident in Singapore at the time of death is liable to estate duty only on immovable assets in Singapore.

Other taxes

There is no net wealth/net worth tax, capital acquisitions tax or capital duty.

Double taxation treaties

Singapore has signed 55 comprehensive tax treaties.

Filing and payment

There is no provision for joint filing, including married couples living together. The tax year is the calendar year. Individual tax returns and computations are due by 15 April each year following the end of the tax year, and an assessment is raised on the basis of this return. There is no system of deduction of tax from employment income. Penalties and interest are provided for late filing or failure to file.

To access a fuller range of country profiles, available to download as part of the Kogan Page title *Working Abroad*, please go to www.koganpage.com/workingabroad (password: WA50571).

South Africa

WORKING CONDITIONS

Fringe benefits are not a significant part of remuneration, although managerial jobs generally provide a car and holidays tend to be generous, six weeks a year being frequently quoted. Free or subsidized medical aid schemes are frequently offered to more senior people. If these are not available such costs, and they are considerable, should be borne in mind in assessing the true value of the remuneration package.

There are no restrictions on the amount of foreign currency you can bring into the country, but strict exchange control regulations are in force on taking money out of South Africa. For this reason, it is advisable to transfer no more of your assets than you need to South Africa unless you are absolutely sure you want to stay there.

At executive and professional level, working conditions (ie hours and leave) are very similar to those in the UK. There has been little industrial unrest in South Africa, though it has increased recently. Wages are fixed by industrial councils and vary according to occupation and region. Welfare benefits are minimal compared with the UK, although health care is now free, and there are numerous private schemes for medical care, pensions and disability.

Visitors to South Africa are required to have a visa upon arrival and valid international health certificates. Enquiries can be directed to South African diplomatic missions or to the Department of Home Affairs in Pretoria. Visas specifically for business purposes are available, although nationals from Canada, the EU and the United States are not required to have them. An application for a business visa must include the application form, a valid passport and a letter on the parent company's letterhead that undertakes financial responsibility for the applicant during his or her stay in South Africa. It is also necessary to provide flight details and addresses of businesses to be visited. Current legislation makes provision for no fewer than 13 types of temporary residence permits, and a foreigner has the option of no fewer than four types of work permit.

The main consideration in dealing with work permits is whether a South African citizen/permanent resident cannot perform the employment task to be undertaken. Work permits are therefore issued to foreigners only where South African citizens with the relevant skills are not available for appointment. Having said that, however, in some instances international concerns with branches/affiliated companies in the republic may from time to time decide to transfer existing personnel from a foreign branch to a branch in the republic. As these employees will be key employees they must apply for intra-company transfer work permits, in which instance no proof of steps taken to obtain the services of a South African citizen/permanent resident will be required.

A foreigner may only change his or her status while inside South Africa. This implies that a foreigner may only change from a temporary residence permit to a permanent residence permit within the country, as status has been defined as temporary or permanent residence. Any foreigner who therefore wishes to enter the Republic of South Africa must apply for the appropriate temporary residence permit at the South African diplomatic representative in his or her country of origin. Travellers entering South Africa from countries where yellow fever is endemic are often required to present their yellow World Health Organization (WHO) vaccination record or other proof of inoculation. If they are unable to do so, they must be inoculated at the airport in order to be permitted entry.

USEFUL INFORMATION

Climate: South Africa's climate is excellent, though by no means uniform. There is quite a difference at all times of the year between semi-tropical Kwazulu-Natal, the Mediterranean climate of the Western Cape and the dry, cold winters and hot, stormy summers of Johannesburg. Most of South Africa has elevations of over 914 metres (3,000 feet), and Johannesburg is 1,829 metres (6,000 feet) above sea level.

Education: According to the Bill of Rights contained in the Constitution of the Republic of South Africa, 1996 (Act 108 of 1996), everyone has the right to a basic education, including adult basic education and further education, which the state, through reasonable measures, must make progressively available and accessible. Education in state schools is free, but schools are allowed to charge a small fee to cover miscellaneous expenses. There are, of course, plenty of private fee-paying schools as well. Children who will not have reached the age of six before 1 July of the year of admission will not be allowed to attend school, even if they have done so previously. The school year begins after the Christmas holiday. It should be noted that the syllabus and atmosphere of South African schools are markedly more traditional and restrictive than is the case in most other countries. University education is not free. The British International College at Bryanston is well regarded (e-mail: bic@global.co.za).

Money: The local currency is the rand (ZAR) = 100 cents. Traveller's cheques and credit and charge cards are widely accepted, including American Express, Bank of America, Diners, MasterCard, Standard Bank Card and Visa. Most banks are open 9.00 am to 3.30 pm Monday–Friday, and 9.00 to 11.00 am Saturday. ATMs are found in most towns and operate 24 hours.

Local time: South Africa is two hours ahead of GMT.

Language: Afrikaans, English, Ndebele, Pedi, Sotho, Swazi, Tsonga, Tswana, Venda, Xhosa, Zulu.

Capital: Pretoria.

Transport: South Africa has international airports at Johannesburg, Durban and Cape Town. All major cities are connected by domestic flights. The railway system is well established and mostly privately run. All major towns are connected. The 'Blue Train' is famous for its sheer luxury, and you can also experience a steam train tour on the 'Apple Express', 'Outeniqua Choo-Tjoe' and 'Banana Express'. A number of bus coach operators run an inter-city service. All major international car rental companies are represented in South Africa, and the road network is of a high quality throughout the country.

Communications: South Africa's communication system is well developed, with 5.5 million installed telephones and 4.3 million installed exchange lines. The network is almost entirely digital, with digital microwave and fibre optics serving as the main transmission media. Internet access is widely available. State-controlled Telkom is responsible for the installation and maintenance of these facilities. South Africa is the world's fourth-fastest-growing GSM market, with a growth rate of 50 per cent per annum. There are three operators in the country: MTN, Cell C and Vodacom. Vodacom and MTN report more than 7 million and 5 million subscribers respectively. There are a large number of internet providers in the country.

Health and health care: The Department of Health is the government body responsible for the country's health facilities, which include well-equipped hospitals and primary health care clinics. The government has placed much emphasis on the primary health care sector specifically in rural and poorer areas. Treatment for TB is available free of charge at all clinics. Malaria is endemic in the low-altitude areas of the Northern Province, Mpumalanga and north-eastern KwaZulu-Natal, and the highest risk area is a strip of about 100 kilometres along the Zimbabwe, Mozambique and Swaziland border.

Costs for admission to private and provincial hospitals vary, and private hospitals usually require proof of membership of a medical scheme or medical aid.

The Department of Health has initiated the extended expanded programme on immunization, which aims to make immunization facilities available to all children and women of childbearing age. Immunization against TB, whooping cough, tetanus, diphtheria, poliomyelitis, hepatitis B and measles is available free of charge to all children up to the age of five years.

Useful contacts:

British High Commission, 256 Glyn Street, Hatfield, Pretoria 0083 (tel: 012 421 7802, website: www.britain.org.za/)

South African High Commission, South Africa House, Trafalgar Square, London WC2N 5DP (tel: +44 020 7589 6655)

South Africa Tourist Board, 5–6 Alt Grove, Wimbledon, London SW19 4DZ (tel: +44 0870 155 0044, websites: www.satour.co.za/, www.satour.org)

Worldwide Medical Consultants, Dr Albie De Frey (tel: +27 11 888 7488, website: http://www.traveldoctor.co.za, e-mail: wtmc@global.co.za)

Elliott Relocations, Paolo Longo (tel: +27 11 256 3097, e-mail: paolol@elliott.co.za, website: http://www.elliott.co.za/relocations.htm)

Worldchoice Travel Airscape, Ken Brown (tel: 27 11 475 2902, e-mail: kenb.travelair@galileosa.co.za, websites: www.acitravel.co.za, www. africanleisure.co.za)

PERSONAL TAXATION

Residence

The worldwide basis of taxation of residents of South Africa came into effect on 1 January 2001 and applies to years of assessment commencing on or after that date. Critical to the application of the tax system is a definition of residence, because the residential status of a person will determine his or her tax liability in the future. The tax year in South Africa runs from 1 March to 28/29 February.

A natural person will be resident if he or she is 'ordinarily resident' in South Africa, which means that it is the country he or she regards as home and to which he or she naturally and eventually returns from any travelling. If the person is not ordinarily resident, a time-based rule (physical presence test) applies: if a person is physically present for more than 91 days in the current tax year and more than 915 days in aggregate in the preceding five years, then such a person is classified as a South African.

Important considerations for the time-based rule are: if a person is present for less than 91 days in the current year, there is no South African residency.

Non-residents

Non-residents are taxed on their South African income on source-based rules. Withholding amounts from payments to non-resident sellers of immovable property are equal to 5 per cent of the amount so payable in the case where the seller is a natural person or, in the case where the seller is a company, 7.5 per cent of the amount so payable, and at 10 per cent in the case where the seller is a trust. This amount must be paid over to the South African Revenue Service within a prescribed time limit. No withholding tax is levied on interest and dividends. Visiting entertainers and sports people are liable for a final withholding tax of 15 per cent. Royalty payments are subject to a withholding tax of 12 per cent, but can be reduced depending on the double taxation agreement signed.

Taxes on income

Employment income in South Africa is subject to tax in South Africa in terms of a source-based rule on a progressive scale, with a maximum rate of 40 per cent.

Dividends from South African companies are tax-free. The tax-free portions for lump sums received from a pension, provident fund and retirement annuity are all calculated differently.

Deductions and allowances

Certain deductions are allowed against employment income, such as medical expenditure, travelling costs, donations to public benefit organizations, and contributions to pensions, retirement annuities and provident funds. All of the above are subject to certain limits, which might be deducted.

If employers grant various benefits to employees, such benefits are taxed in terms of fringe benefit legislation, which is contained in the Seventh Schedule. Such benefits include travelling allowances, company vehicles, low-interest loans, subsistence allowances, residential accommodation and entertainment.

Social security

Employers must contribute the equivalent of 1 per cent of gross income for each employee plus a 1 per cent deduction from the employee to the Unemployment Insurance Fund.

Capital gains

Capital gains tax was introduced to South Africa with effect from 1 October 2001. Non-residents are not subject to capital gains tax except on gains made on immovable property situated in South Africa and gains made on assets of a permanent establishment of such a non-resident. The current rate for residents is 25 per cent of the gain.

Inheritance/estate tax

Estate duty is payable at the rate of 20 per cent on the estate of an individual who dies while resident in South Africa, with a standard deduction of ZAR3.5 million per estate. Certain other deductions are allowed, particularly for property accruing to the surviving spouse.

Real property tax

Transfer duty is paid on the acquisition of immovable property where the transaction is not subject to VAT. Transfers to individuals are subject to duty at progressive rates up to 8 per cent.

The municipal authorities levy 'rates' on the occupation of real property.

Other taxes

There is no net wealth/net worth tax, capital acquisitions tax or capital duty. Stamp duty is charged at 0.25 per cent on the transfer of shares.

Double taxation agreements

Double taxation agreements are in place with 55 countries, including the United States and the UK.

Filing and payment

The tax year for individuals runs to the end of February. Tax returns must be filed by a date set by the Commissioner of the South African Revenue Service. Income not subject to PAYE is self-assessed. Individuals must make payments at six-monthly intervals during the tax year and a final payment six months after the end of the tax year. Penalties and interest apply for failure to comply.

To access a fuller range of country profiles, available to download as part of the Kogan Page title *Working Abroad*, please go to www.koganpage.com/workingabroad (password: WA50571).

Spain

WORKING CONDITIONS

Working conditions in Spain increasingly resemble those in other European countries, with city offices abandoning the siesta. The normal working week is 40 hours, and overtime (paid at the rate of at least 175 per cent of normal rates) cannot be forced. Annual leave is, on average, 30 days, plus 12 public holidays.

USEFUL INFORMATION

Banking hours: 9.00 am to 2.00 pm Monday–Friday, 9.00 am to 1.00pm Saturday (except in the summer).

Shopping hours: 10.00 am to 8.00 pm, closed between 1.00 and 4.00 pm, Monday–Friday.

Health care: Under the social security system, hospital and medical treatment is free, and 40 per cent of prescription charges are covered, but you will have to pay for dental work other than extractions. About 40 per cent of hospitals are private.

Education: State education, compulsory between ages 6 and 14, is free; private education (much of it run by the Catholic Church) is not as expensive as in other countries. There are estimated to be at least a quarter of a million British residents in Spain, and they have created a market for private English-speaking schools, which exist in most of the main cities – Madrid, Barcelona, along the east and south coasts and in the Balearic and Canary Islands. Up-to-date information on fees can be obtained from Mr A Muñoz, Legal Adviser, National Association of British Schools in Spain, Avenida Ciudad de Barcelona 110, Esc. 3a, 5oD, 28007 Madrid.

Useful contacts:

British Embassy, Callde de Fernando el Santo 16, 28010 Madrid (tel: 3491 700 8200)

Spanish Embassy, 39 Chesham Place, London SW1X 8SB (tel: 020 7235 5555)

Instituto Cervantes, 102 Eaton Square, London SW1W 9AN (tel: 020 7205 0750)

Labour Office of the Spanish Embassy, 20 Peel Street, London W8 7PD (tel: 020 7221 0098)

Spanish Tourist Office, 22–23 Manchester Square, London W1M 5AP (tel: 020 7486 8077, website: www.uk.tourspain.es)

PERSONAL TAXATION

Residence

An individual is resident if he or she spends more than 183 days of the tax year in Spain or if the main centre of the taxpayer's business, professional activities or economic interest is in Spain. Residents of Spain are subject to personal income tax on a worldwide basis. Non-residents are taxed under a separate regime on Spanish-source income.

Income tax

Taxable income of individuals includes earned income (eg salaries, wages and business or professional income) and passive income (eg interest, dividends and capital gains). Rates are progressive from 24 per cent to 43 per cent. However, savings income is subject to a flat rate of 18 per cent.

Deductions and allowances

A deduction for social security payments is permitted. Additionally, income earned irregularly over a period of more than two years is allowed a 40 per cent deduction.

Social security

Mandatory social security contributions are levied on an employee's wages at 28.3 per cent, with the employer contributing 23.6 per cent and the employee paying 4.7 per cent.

Capital gains

Short-term gains of individuals on assets held for less than one year are taxed as income. Long-term gains on assets held for more than one year are subject to a separate capital gains tax of 18 per cent.

Net wealth/net worth tax

Residents are subject to tax on their worldwide assets on 31 December each year. Non-residents are taxed on their property situated in Spain.

Inheritance/estate tax

Inheritance and gift taxes are imposed on Spanish-resident heirs, beneficiaries and recipients at rates ranging up to 34 per cent.

Capital acquisitions tax

A 7 per cent transfer tax is applicable.

Other taxes

Capital duty is levied at 1 per cent. Stamp duty is applicable at 0.5 per cent.

Tax treaties

Spain has concluded more than 60 tax treaties, including those with EU fellow members and the United States.

Filing and penalties

Married couples may choose to file jointly or separately. The tax year is the calendar year. Employment income is taxed by withholding. Individuals must file a self-assessment tax return within six months following the end of the tax year. The minimum work income threshold to file a tax return is €22,000. Where there is no loss to the tax authorities, the penalty for late filing is limited to a fixed amount of €200.

To access a fuller range of country profiles, available to download as part of the Kogan Page title *Working Abroad*, please go to www.koganpage.com/workingabroad (password: WA50571).

The United Kingdom

PERSONAL TAXATION

Residence

If an individual is present in the UK for 183 days or more in a tax year, or makes visits to the UK that average 91 days or more for four consecutive years (which also constitutes ordinary residence), he or she is deemed resident. An individual is ordinarily resident if resident for three tax years or if he or she has moved to the UK with the intention of staying for the following three years. An individual's domicile status is complex and may be either acquired or determined by his or her parents' domicile.

Basis

Individuals who are resident, ordinarily resident and domiciled in the UK are subject to tax on their worldwide income and gains. Different treatment may apply where a person, although resident, is not ordinarily resident or not domiciled in the UK. Residents who are not ordinarily resident and non-UK-domiciled individuals are subject to UK tax on UK-source income and offshore income on the basis of remittance.

Tax on income

Employment, trading and investment income (other than deductions) is taxable at 20 per cent on the first £34,800 and at 40 per cent thereafter (2008/09).

Investment income

Dividend income is taxable at 32.5 per cent, with dividends from UK companies (and up to £5,000 of foreign dividends from April 2008) subject to a 10 per cent credit, resulting in a 25 per cent effective tax rate.

Deductions and allowances

Individual taxpayers are entitled to a personal allowance deduction from gross income in calculating taxable income (£6,035 for 2008/09). Additional age allowances are available for individuals aged 65 and over.

Capital gains

From 6 April 2008 capital gains tax is payable on all disposals at 18 per cent. There is a special 'lifetime' rate of 10 per cent on the first £1 million of capital gains.

Inheritance/estate tax

Property passing on death, certain gifts made within seven years of death and some lifetime transfers (eg to certain trusts) are subject to inheritance tax. Tax at rates of 40 per cent for chargeable transfers and 20 per cent for chargeable lifetime transfers of assets in excess of £300,000 is payable.

Real property tax

There is a National Non-Domestic Rate (NNDR) that is payable by every occupier of business premises, collected by local authorities. Local council tax applies to the occupation of domestic property.

Other taxes

There is no net wealth/net worth tax, capital acquisitions tax or capital duty.

Social security

Employers, employees and self-employed individuals all pay National Insurance contributions (NICs). Employees pay NICs at 11 per cent on income between £105.01 and £770 per week and 1 per cent in addition on the excess. Employers pay 12.8 per cent NICs on employee earnings in excess of £105.01 per week and on most benefits in kind.

Self-employed individuals pay Class 2 NICs at a flat rate of £2.30 per week on profits in excess of £4,825 per annum and Class 4 NICs at 8.00 per cent on profits from £5,435 to £40,040, with a further 1 per cent on the excess.

Double taxation treaties

The UK has concluded more than 115 tax treaties.

Filing

Individuals file tax returns independently irrespective of marital status. The employer withholds tax on employment income under the PAYE system and remits it to the tax authorities. Income not subject to PAYE is self-assessed. As of 2008, an individual must file a tax return annually by 30 September and pay any outstanding tax by 31 January after the tax year. Payments on account of the following year's tax liability may be required on 31 January of that tax year and 31 July of the following tax year.

Penalties

Individuals are liable to a penalty of £100 for failure to file a tax return by the due date and an additional £100 if the return is not submitted within six months of the due date. Surcharges and interest are also applied if the payment of tax is late.

To access a fuller range of country profiles, available to download as part of the Kogan Page title *Working Abroad*, please go to www.koganpage.com/workingabroad (password: WA50571).

6.14

The United States

WORKING CONDITIONS

US salaries are generally higher than in the UK, but there is nothing like the range of benefits and degree of employment protection that you may receive in Europe. The Medicare health scheme is limited to the elderly, and medical treatment is very expensive. If insurance is not included in the remuneration package, this could make quite a hole in an imposing salary. US executive salaries are less perk-laden than those in some other countries; for example, very few US executives get cars unless their job necessitates it.

Job advertisements in the United States, certainly at executive level, tend to demand a lot from the applicant but to be rather coy about what he or she is going to receive. Salaries, for instance, are rarely stated. It is as well to get advice from someone who has worked in the United States before accepting any offer, unless it is from a multinational, where conditions are usually fairly standard.

Although the 35-hour week prevails, working conditions are a great deal more strenuous and exacting than in some firms in the UK. US employers expect results and are fairly ruthless about removing people who do not deliver them. Senior executives come and go, and it is not unusual for a shake-up at the top to work its way right down the ladder. In some firms, considerable conformity with the image of the company in relation to dress, lifestyle, etc is expected, even in the private lives of the employees. Holiday entitlement is relatively low in comparison to Europe.

There is no VAT in the United States, but there are sales taxes, which vary from state to state or town to town – rates are generally between 2 and 10 per cent. Since they are not shown as part of the price of the goods, as VAT usually is, this can mean a nasty shock when you receive a bill for an expensive item.

Work permits and visas

An essential part of moving abroad is to ensure that the individual travelling holds the requisite visa or work permit. Nowhere are immigration practices and procedures more complicated and arduous than in the United States. At the last count, there were almost 60 types of temporary visas for the United States, in addition to several routes to permanent residency, or 'the green card' as it is more commonly known. The greatest difficulty faced by individuals wanting to transfer to the United States is which visa they should apply for. US immigration law is very complex and can sometimes be very confusing. You will need to take expert advice.

USEFUL INFORMATION

Shopping hours: 10.00 am to 9.00 pm, with later shopping one or two evenings a week. All shops are open on Saturday and most on Sunday.

Driving: Driving is on the right. An international or UK licence is valid for one year, but it is advisable to get a US licence from the State Department of Motor Vehicles – after a test. Most highways and super-highways have several lanes, and lane discipline is very strict, as is the enforcement of speed limits. In 1995 the government repealed the national speed limits. Some states now have no restrictions. Many expatriates buy a new or used car locally and resell it when they leave. The American Automobile Association (AAA) is an extremely helpful organization for motorists.

Transport: Americans have taken to the air as naturally as our great-grandparents took to rail. Flying is the most efficient and quickest (and relatively cheap) way of getting round this vast country. All the main cities are connected by internal flights, and there are frequent shuttle services between some cities (eg New York to Washington, New York to Boston, and San Francisco to Los Angeles). Helicopter services are often available, as well as private plane hire.

There has recently been some revival of the railways. Long-distance coaches (usually air-conditioned) are the cheapest way of travelling, if you can stand the boredom. Americans are also used to travelling long distances by car.

There are underground trains or 'subways' in New York, Boston, Philadelphia and Washington. New York city bus services are regular and frequent – although you will need the exact fare.

Health care: Medical treatment is of a very high standard, but is extremely expensive. If possible, people are advised to get full medical insurance for themselves and their families before departure, even for a short stay. However, many European insurance companies no longer offer cover for expatriates and their families in the United States; instead, they advise that insurance should be arranged with a US company such as Blue Cross.

Education: Nursery school groups can be found in most centres. All children between 7 and 16 must attend school. The school year lasts from September to June. The system includes public schools – there are about 90,000 in the whole country, with over 50 million pupils – and there are 12 grades, 1–6 elementary, and 7–12 in secondary or high school. After the 12th grade the pupils will probably go to college. Schools are operated by boards of education and are free.

There are fee-paying private schools and a number of boarding schools, modelled on the UK pattern, where tuition and boarding fees are usually fairly high. There are international schools in New York (the United Nations) and Washington. The UN School takes children from kindergarten to high school age and sometimes can take in children whose parents are not UN officials. Instruction is in English and French.

Useful contacts:

British Embassy, 3100 Massachusetts Avenue, NW, Washington DC 20008 (tel: 1 202 588 7800, website: www.britainusa.com/embassy)

United States of America Embassy, 24 Grosvenor Square, London W1A 2LQ (tel: 020 7499 9000)

United States Information Service, 24 Grosvenor Square, London W1A 2LQ (tel: 020 7499 9000)

Expatriate contacts:
www.britishinamerica.com

PERSONAL TAXATION

Residence

In order to be resident in the United States for tax purposes, a foreign national must meet one of the two separate residency tests: the green card test or the 'substantial presence' test. Tax residents are taxable on their worldwide income in the same way as US citizens.

The green card test

A green card, or an alien registration card, is given to a foreign national who is granted lawful permanent resident status, according to US immigration laws. A foreign national is regarded as a US resident from the first day he or she is present in the United States, while in possession of a green card, and residency continues as long as the green card is held.

Substantial presence test

In order to be regarded a resident in the United States for tax purposes, a foreign national must meet the substantial presence test for all or part of the tax year. This test is based on the number of days a foreign national is present in the United States in three consecutive calendar years. To meet the substantial presence test, a foreign national must be physically present in the United States for at least 31 days during the current year, and 183 days during the three-year period that includes the current year and the two previous years, under the following formula:

current year = number of days × 1
first preceding year = number of days × 1/3
second preceding year = number of days × 1/6

If this test is satisfied, a person is resident from the first day present in the United States during the current year, subject to a certain *de minimis* presence.

Tax on income

US tax residents, including resident aliens and citizens who reside outside the United States, are taxable on their worldwide income, irrespective of where it is earned.

Non-resident aliens are taxable on all US-source income (and benefits in kind, unless they are specifically excluded under US tax law) and income effectively connected to US trade or business. Employment income is 'ordinary income', and taxed at regular graduated progressive tax rates up to 39.6 per cent.

Investment income

Generally, US residents' worldwide investment income is taxed as ordinary income, at graduated tax rates. Non-qualified dividends and long-term capital gains are considered separately.

Non-resident aliens are taxable only on investment income from US sources; however, portfolio interest income is not taxable for non-residents. Certain investment income that is not effectively connected to a US trade or business is taxed at 30 per cent (or a lower treaty rate, if applicable). This tax rate is applied to gross income, without taking into account deductions.

Deductions and allowances

Individual taxpayers are entitled to a standard deduction from gross income in calculating taxable income or they may 'itemize' deductions. Numerous credits are also available.

Local income taxes

The states impose income tax on persons residing in the territory of the state, using varying tax bases and rates, but the burden of state income tax is comparatively slight. Counties and municipalities may also levy an income tax.

Capital gains

Capital gains are distinguished as short-term or long-term (long-term being gains on assets held for more than 12 months). Generally, long-term gains are subject to a tax rate of 15 per cent (5 per cent for lower-income recipients), while short-term gains are included in ordinary income and taxable at regular graduated tax rates. The capital gain rate is also applicable to dividends from US corporations and from certain foreign corporations.

Capital gains and certain interest income of a non-resident alien are exempt from US taxation.

Inheritance/estate tax

Inheritance (estate) tax and gift tax are levied by the federal government. For US citizens and residents, the estate tax assessment is based on all assets of the deceased. For non-resident aliens, the tax is imposed on US-based property only. A separate gift tax applies only for aggregate gifts in excess of US $2,000 to any one person in a year.

Individual states also impose varying taxes on transfers by reason of death.

Real property tax

Real property tax is imposed by local governments at various rates.

Other taxes

There is no net wealth/net worth tax, capital acquisitions tax, capital duty or federal stamp duty. States may impose stamp duty on various instruments.

Double taxation treaties

The United States has a wide network of more than 60 comprehensive tax treaties. US and UK residents may utilize the protection granted by the UK–US double taxation treaty.

Filing and penalties

The categories for individuals filing are single, married filing jointly, married filing separately, head of household or qualifying widow(er). The tax year is the calendar year, unless another fiscal year ending on the last day of a month is selected. Tax is deducted at source from employment income. Individual self-assessment tax returns are due by the 15th day of the fourth month following the end of the tax year. An extension of four months is granted if the taxpayer makes an election before the due date for the return and pays the estimated final tax due. US tax rules include a comprehensive set of penalty and interest provisions for failure to pay and failure to file.

To access a fuller range of country profiles, available to download as part of the Kogan Page title *Working Abroad*, please go to www.koganpage.com/workingabroad (password: WA50571).

Contributor contact details

Abels Moving Services
Wimbledon Avenue
Brandon
Suffolk IP27 0NZ
Tel: +44 (0)1842 816600
Fax: +44 (0)1842 813613
Contact: Philip Pertoldi
e-mail: enquiries@abels.co.uk

DLA Piper UK LLP
3 Noble Street
London EC2V 7EE
Tel: +44 (0) 8700 111111
Fax: +44 (0)20 7796 6666
Contact: Jonathan Exten-Wright
e-mail: jonathan.exten-wright@dlapiper.com

Fragomen LLP
4th Floor
Holborn Gate
328–330 High Holborn
London WC1V 7QY
Tel: +44 (0)20 3077 5000
Fax: +44 (0)20 3077 5001
Contact: Alex Paterson
e-mail: apaterson@fragomen.com
DDI: +44 (0) 20 3077 5050
Contact: Owen Davies
e-mail: odavies@fragomen.com
DDI: +44 (0) 20 3077 5100

Frank Hirth plc
1st Floor
236 Gray's Inn Road
London WC1X 8HL
Tel: + 44 (0)20 7833 3500
Fax: +44 (0)20 7833 2550
Contact: Stephen Asher
e-mail: StephenA@frankhirth.com

Hessel Group
Croham House
Croham Road
Crowborough
East Sussex TN6 2RW
Tel: +44 (0)1892 669901
Fax: +44 (0)1892 669902
Contact: Geoff Davidson
e-mail: info@hessel.co.uk

Orgdesign Limited
8A Malden Park
New Malden KT3 6AS
Tel: +44 (0)20 8949 5755/780 278 2659
Contact: Natarajan Sundar
e-mail: nsundar@btinternet.com

Stephen Gill Associates
Stanton Lodge
Aston-on-Trent
Derby DE72 2AH
Tel: +44 (0)1332 793399
Contact: Stephen Gill
e-mail: steve@stephengill.eu

White & Case LLP
1155 Avenue of the Americas
New York
NY 10036–2787
USA
Tel: +01 212 819 8665
Fax: +01 212 354 8113
Contact: Donald C Dowling, Jr
e-mail: ddowling@whitecase.com

Index

Index of advertisers

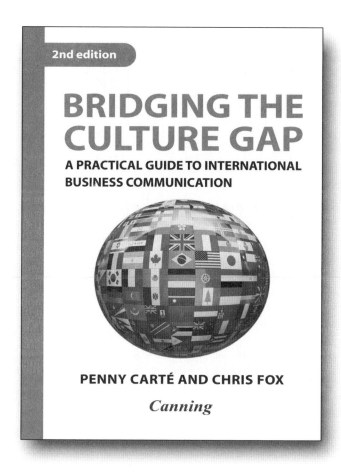

ALSO AVAILABLE FROM KOGAN PAGE

"A great resource that covers a wide range of issues vital to the British expatriate."
The Weekly Telegraph

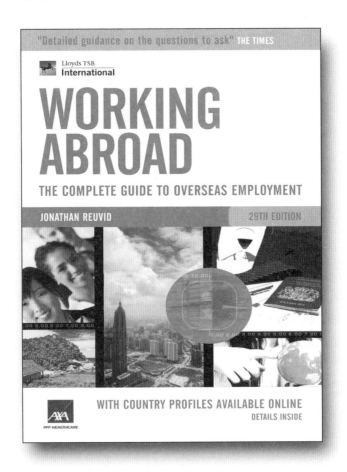

ISBN: 978 0 7494 5057 1   Paperback   2008

ALSO AVAILABLE FROM KOGAN PAGE

"For any business thinking of doing business in China, the information in this book will make it a 'must read'. The practical advice it contains, written and edited by experts, will be of enormous assistance – and I commend it to you."

Miles Templeman, Director General, Institute of Directors

ISBN: 978 0 7494 5060 1   Hardback   2008

Order online now at www.koganpage.com

Sign up for regular e-mail updates on new
Kogan Page books in your interest area

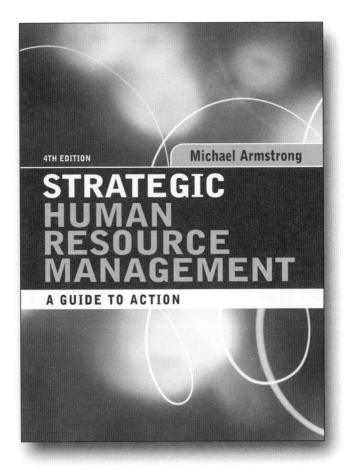

ALSO AVAILABLE FROM KOGAN PAGE

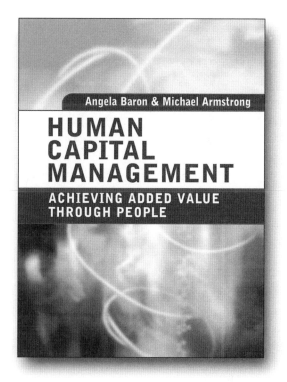

ISBN: 978 0 7494 5384 8   Paperback   2008

Order online now at www.koganpage.com

ALSO AVAILABLE FROM KOGAN PAGE

"Offers jargon-free advice on how to manage your personal and business-related finances and covers all aspects on wealth management in clear and comprehensible language."
Pensions World

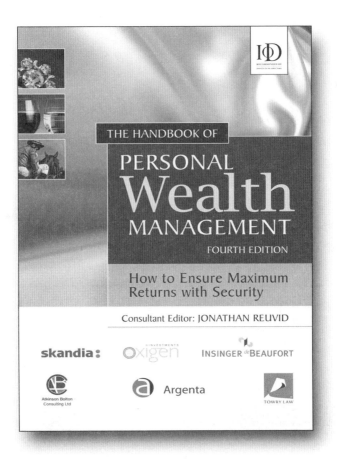

ISBN: 978 0 7494 5060 1   Hardback   2008

Order online now at www.koganpage.com

Sign up for regular e-mail updates on new
Kogan Page books in your interest area